The defining image of the gin craze:
William Hogarth's *Gin Lane,* 1751.

William Hogarth's *Beer Street*, 1751.
The companion piece to *Gin Lane*, less well-known
but just as loaded with moral meaning.

# THE
# BOOK OF GIN

RICHARD BARNETT

Grove Press
*New York*

First published in Great Britain in 2011 by Dedalus Books
as *The Dedalus Book of Gin*

*Printed in the United States of America*
*Published simultaneously in Canada*

ISBN-13: 978-0-8021-2043-4

Grove Press
an imprint of Grove/Atlantic, Inc.
841 Broadway
New York, NY 10003

Distributed by Publishers Group West

www.groveatlantic.com

12 13 14 15   10 9 8 7 6 5 4 3 2 1

To Matthew Barnett

London's Victorian gin palaces: gaily lit and full of bustling conviviality, but also the setting for violence, obscenity and despair. "Scene in a London Gin Palace," *The Working Man's Friend,* and *Family Instructor,* vol. 1 no 4, 25 Oct 1851, p 56.

Juniper—sacred herb, medicine, and one of the two crucial ingredients in gin. "Juniperus communis," from Franz Eugen Köhler, *Köhler's Medizinal-Pflanzen,* 3 vols, Berlin, 1897.

# Contents

# CONTENTS

## Prologue

## The Murder of Mrs. Atkinson

O N THE MORNING of Wednesday 23rd February 1732 a prisoner was brought up from the dank, cramped cells of Newgate Prison into the open-fronted courthouse of London's Old Bailey. Robert Atkinson—a leather-worker from the parish of St. Martin-in-the-Fields—was on trial for his life, and he knew that, if found guilty, he would be hanged before the crowd at Tyburn. Atkinson stood accused, in the eighteenth century's vivid, precise legal language, of murdering his mother:

> by throwing her down a pair of Stairs, upon a Pavement of Tiles below, and by which fall her Skull was broke, and she receiv'd one mortal Bruise, of which she instantly dy'd, the 15th of this Instant February.

The case against Atkinson seems, at first glance, to have been unanswerable. He lived with his mother, Ann, and her maidservant, Mary, in rooms above his shop. Mary testified that on the night of the crime, she had gone to bed just after midnight, but her mistress had stayed up to let her son in when he returned. Woken in the small hours by Atkinson battering on the front door, she heard him bellow "Damn ye, ye old bitch, do ye think I'll be lock'd up in my own House?" Ann let him in, entreating him to go quietly to bed, but he had other things on his mind. He burst into Mary's room:

I

I was very much frighted, for he was stark naked without his Shirt. Sir, says I, you had much better go to Bed: No, says he, I will have a Buss first. He came to my Bed-side, and as he did not offer any Rudeness, I suffer'd him to kiss me once or twice, in hopes that he would then go away. But instead of that, he got upon the Bed (outside the Bed-Clothes) and lay upon me very hard, and endeavour'd to put his Hands into the Bed, but with much difficulty I kept them out.

At this moment his mother entered the room, catching her son on the cusp of a bodice-ripping violation: "You Dog, said she, what business have you upon the Maid's Bed?" Atkinson turned on her, and she tried to slip past him into a cupboard, but he seized her and threw her out of the room. Mary did not see the rest of the incident: she heard "a great Scuffle, and a Struggling in the Passage at the Stairs Head as if he was running after her, and she was endeavouring to get away from him." In the next moment Ann tumbled down the stairs with such violence "as if Part of the House had fall'n with her." After this she made no sound, not even a groan.

How could Atkinson possibly justify his actions? A coroner's inquest had indicted him for murder, and he did not dispute that his mother had died after a brutal quarrel. Indeed, in the heat of the moment he appeared to have admitted his guilt. Seeing his mother lying at the foot of the stairs, he cried out "Damn the old Bitch, I have murder'd her, and I shall hang for it." Atkinson's defence hinged upon intoxication, and no ordinary intoxication—the vicious, malevolent haze induced by gin. Cross-examining Mary, he forced her to admit that her mistress was a regular and heavy drinker, who had rounded off her last evening on earth with "half a Pint of Gin and Bitter (I think they call it)." Mary fought back—"I know she would drink a great deal; but she was so much used to it, that it would hardly disorder her"—but she acknowledged that Ann was almost dead drunk by the time he had returned. And Atkinson himself had spent the night in a circuit of local taverns and gin-shops, enjoying a binge which had, he admitted, inflamed his "great Passion."

Gin, it seems, enabled Atkinson to get away with murder. The jury found him not guilty, concluding that his mother's death was not even manslaughter but a mere accident, and he left the dock a free man. And this episode of gin-fuelled violence was far from unique. Leaf through the *Newgate Calendar,* the *Ordinary of Newgate's Accounts* or the *Proceedings of the Old Bailey* for any year in the second quarter of the eighteenth century, and you will find dozens of similar examples. To many of Atkinson's contemporaries, these cases proved that English law and society were dissolving in a flood of cheap gin. This episode—the "gin craze"—has had a profound effect on our historical perceptions of gin, but it also captures a truth central to the story of this book. Gin is not (like absinthe) the drink of velvet-trousered aesthetes, nor is it (like port) the toast of respectable merchants and scholars, nor (like ale) the refreshment of peasants in the meadows of "Merry England." It is urban, and it possesses—or has been said to possess—all the vices and virtues of urban life.

What is gin, this liquid fire both pleasurable and deadly? One place to start is with Atkinson's and Hogarth's contemporary, Samuel Johnson. In his mighty *Dictionary of the English Language,* published in 1755, Johnson defined "gin (contracted from GENEVA)" as "the spirit drawn by distillation from juniper berries." As any modern master distiller will tell you, Johnson slightly missed his mark here: gin is not distilled from juniper berries, but is rather a neutral spirit flavored principally (though not exclusively) with juniper. The best base spirit is produced from grain or maize, though it can be (and has been) made from almost anything that contains enough carbohydrate to produce alcohol when it ferments. It is rectified, or, in other words, distilled at least twice—once or more to produce the base spirit, and once or more with juniper berries and other botanicals to develop the flavor. And it is un-aged—no years or decades in sherry casks, but as near as possible straight from the still into the bottle.

Even this straightforward definition, however, conceals a rich and diverse history. Modern premium gins are flavored with up to a dozen botanicals (of which much more later), but for Arthur Hassall, a Victorian physician obsessed with food adulteration, almost anything apart from juniper counted as a potentially hazardous impurity. In much eighteenth- and nineteenth-century gin the juniper was replaced entirely by a zingy combination of turpentine and sulphuric acid. And in what we might recognize as its very earliest incarnation—a fortifying cordial made at monastic medical schools in eleventh-century Italy—an *aqua vita* distilled from wine was combined with juniper oil to make gin at its most potent and most basic.

But definitions are, in a sense, a distraction. The point is that gin's proverbial clarity, like a prism of clear glass, refracts a rainbow of historical color. To tell the story of gin is to follow the fortunes of alchemical secrets and scientific treatises, royal houses and poor migrants, armies and navies, fashions and diseases, as they have moved around Europe and across the globe. It is a tale with ethical and philosophical overtones, an anatomy of pleasure and pain, revealing how we have got to grips with outcasts, drunks and criminals, how we have comforted ourselves when times were tough, and how we have aspired to elegance and modernity when life was good.

Gin is the grandchild of the alchemists' elixir of life, and it came of age in a series of world-changing collisions. It first achieved popularity in two Protestant powers with connections around the (known) world—England and Holland—and the contours of its consumption reflected the cultural and geographical watershed separating the cold, Protestant, grain-fed north from the warm, Catholic, vinous south. In the aftermath of the Glorious Revolution gin, like tea, was a modish and exotic commodity, but by the mid-eighteenth century William Hogarth was portraying "Gin Lane" as the corrosive, subversive antithesis of "Beer Street." Nineteenth-century writers like Dickens saw gin as the handmaiden of squalor, melodramatic poverty and the workhouse. And in the early-twentieth century it gained powerful new enemies, in the shape of the Prohibition movement: for a few turbulent years of U.S. history, "bathtub gin" was the order of the day.

But gin has always enjoyed multiple lives, and its mystique—the enigma of secret recipes and the alluring tang of botanical flavorings—has helped to carry its influence around the world. Eighteenth- and nineteenth-century traders and explorers carried gin with them to Africa, Asia and South America. As a way of making the daily dose of bitter quinine more palatable, gin and tonic became the tipple of choice for colonial soldiers, planters and bureaucrats. They and their descendents carried the habit back to the mother country, where it chimed with a new fashion for drinking mixed cocktails rather than straight shots of spirit. Shipwrights and factory hands swigged beer; Europhiles sipped wine; but the (sub)urban smart set drank gin with tonic, vermouth, bitters or a whole happy hour of mixers.

In the early-twenty-first century gin has come full circle: once a drink of the rich, then a drink of the poor, it is again in vogue, having experienced a striking renaissance with the growth of small-batch distilling and the revival of Thirties and Fifties couture, décor and drinks. But this dissolute tale of consumption and excess begins with the alchemical laboratories of Dark Age Europe, the precepts of Classical medicine, and the sacred rituals of pre-Christian Europe.

For nineteenth-century temperance campaigners, gin and other spirits were the last step on a long journey into degradation and squalor. Nathaniel Currier, *The Drunkard's Progress, from the First Glass to the Grave,* c. 1846.

# I

# Living Water

SOME TIME BEFORE 1310 Arnaud de Ville-Neuve, a physician and alchemist at the University of Paris, poured wine into a glass alembic and heated it in a sand bath over a charcoal brazier. Ville-Neuve was not the first person in the world, or even in Europe, to do this: he was well aware of the long and distinguished tradition of Arabic alchemical distillation, and from his reading he must have had some inkling of the principles he was playing with. Others had already named the fluid which condensed in the neck of his alembic: some called it *aqua ardens*, "fiery water," or *aqua vine*, "water of the grape," but to Ville-Neuve it was *aqua vita*, "living water":

> This name is remarkably suitable, since it is really a water of immortality. Its virtues are beginning to be recognized, it prolongs life, clears away ill-humors, revives the heart, and maintains youth.

Ville-Neuve wondered whether this liquid might be the essence of sunshine, distilled by vines into their grapes. And his "living water" captured the imaginations of all kinds of Europeans: gentlemen pursuing natural philosophy in their private closets, physicians seeking new medicines and restoratives, alchemists searching for the elixir of life, and (not least) tradesmen looking to make money from the basic, visceral human drive for intoxication. It was instrumental in forging new connections between alchemy and medicine, politics and religion, trade and empire, East and West. These factors all came together in the Dutch Republic in the late-sixteenth and early-seventeenth centuries, and one result of this fruitful collision was "genever"—a rectified liquor named after its principal flavoring, juniper. It was once argued that this rich, rough drink was the creation of one man, Sylvius de la Boë—a deeply contentious point, as we'll see. But the early history of gin (the subject of this chapter) is much more than a flash of inspiration in the laboratory of an Amsterdam physician. It is the gradual coming together of two heady, symbolically-charged substances—juniper and spirit—both of which had many adventures before they were united in a glass of genever.

But why was genever—the first incarnation of gin, born in an age of global trade and exchange—flavored with the berries of a plant well-known throughout the West for millennia? The solution to this puzzle takes us back through the depths of European prehistory to the end of the last ice age. Around twelve thousand years ago, as the glaciers and tundra began to retreat, juniper and other conifers began to spread north alongside bands of Neolithic farmers. This double migration established the earliest rhythms of a relationship: juniper thrived in the open heaths and moorlands created by farmers, as they began to clear the primeval forests of northern Europe and the British archipelago. Archaeological evidence suggests that juniper quickly found its way into the diets of these pastoralists, and traces of this ancient taste can be discerned in the traditional cuisines of Scandinavia, Germany and the Low Countries. The berries (actually tiny, fleshy cones) balance a resinous, balsamic warmth with a fresh, citrus clarity, which cuts through the richness of dark meats and game.

A handful of berries might be thrown into a prehistoric communal cooking-pot, but juniper also added a refreshing tang to the drinks of early Europeans. Finnish *sahti*—a beer flavored with juniper berries instead of hops, and filtered through juniper twigs—has been brewed since the sixteenth century (and possibly much earlier), making it the only medieval-style beer still widely drunk in

Europe. Slovak *borovička,* a juniper brandy, has been drunk throughout the former states of the Habsburg empire for at least seven
hundred years. And there are reports, though little firm evidence,
that some Scottish Highland clans drank juniper-flavored whisky,
and used fires kindled with juniper sticks to heat their pot-stills.

But its culinary use was only one aspect of juniper's significance,
and evidence from the earliest literate cultures reveals a parallel
strand of sacred symbolism and healing power. For the Syrian Ca-
naanites juniper was associated with the fertility goddess Ashera,
and it makes many appearances in the Old Testament, typically
as a sign of protection and fruitfulness. King Solomon built the
first Temple from juniper and cedar wood, and in the Apocrypha
a juniper tree was said to have sheltered the Holy Family as they
fled from Herod's troops. In other Middle Eastern cultures juniper's religious and medical virtues were seen to be intertwined:
the crushed berries were one ingredient in the salves used for em-
balming in ancient Egyptian funerary rites, and Egyptian medical
papyri recommended the berries and needles as a treatment for
tapeworm infestation.

In AD 50 the Roman physician Pedanius Dioscorides brought
together the various Mediterranean medical traditions involving
juniper in his *De Materia Medica.* Unlike so many other Classical
texts, this remained in continuous circulation and use throughout
the West for more than a thousand years, and served as the standard pharmacopoeia for European physicians until the sixteenth
century. Dioscorides recommended the application of crushed
juniper berries to the genitals as an effective form of contracep-
tion, and also lauded the fumigant virtues of its needles and twigs.
Producing an aromatic smoke when burned, they might drive out
the miasmas thought to be responsible for many epidemics. This
view led some medieval physicians to include juniper berries and
twigs in the long, beaklike masks they wore when attending the
victims of the Black Death.

Almost fifteen hundred years after *De Materia Medica,* a self-
proclaimed successor to Dioscorides—the seventeenth-century

English apothecary Thomas Culpeper—continued to insist upon the therapeutic value of juniper. Culpeper inherited the Classical tradition of Hippocrates, Galen and Dioscorides, but he also brought a radical twist to their thinking. His experiences serving as a surgeon with the Parliamentary forces during the English Civil War convinced him that the secrets of effective medicines should not be concealed within the pages of expensive Latin tomes, but should be available to all—a dangerously extreme position even at a time when, in Christopher Hill's phrase, the world had been turned upside down by the execution of Charles I. Culpeper described his *English Physitian,* published in 1652 after the end of the war, as:

> a Compleat Method of Physick, whereby a man may preserve his Body in Health; or cure himself, being sick, for three pence charge, with such things as only grow in England, they being most fit for English bodies.

Culpeper made Classical thought, astrological reasoning and the folk medicines of unlettered wise-women march together in the service of a common aim—to help the poor maintain their rude English heath. The *English Physitian* was a self-help book for those who could not afford the expensive, and not always satisfactory, attentions of apothecaries. Culpeper argued that anyone could treat themselves far more effectively with what was to hand, and juniper—growing wild in hedgerows, and on moors and chases—could cure a multitude of English diseases:

> [Juniper berries] are admirably good for a cough, shortness of breath, and consumption, pains in the belly, ruptures, cramps, and convulsions. They give safe and speedy delivery to women with child, they strengthen the brain exceedingly, help the memory, and fortify the sight by strengthening the optic nerves; are excellently good in all sorts of agues; help the gout and sciatica, and strengthen the limbs of the body.

In Culpeper's cosmology, juniper also tapped into the powers of the divine macrocosm, and his full entry is reproduced in

Appendix 1.The *English Physitian* was not only a practical herbal, but also an "Astrologico-Physical Discourse": each herb, and each malady, was associated with a heavenly body, and (in good Classical fashion) treatment was a matter of balancing one influence with its opposing partner. Juniper, a "solar herb," was naturally efficacious against diseases associated with the moon.

Though mainstream belief in astrology and the power of the macrocosm faded, juniper's reputation as a medicine did not. A new generation of practitioners came to value juniper oil for its antiseptic and insect-repellent powers (hence its use in flea collars), and it is still used occasionally in dressing wounds and in the treatment of urinary tract infections. It continues to play an important part in the traditional medical systems of Eastern Europe, frequently in the form of *brinjevec,* a Slovenian spirit produced by fermenting and then distilling juniper berries.Valued for its digestive properties, *brinjevec* is also said to relieve stomach ache and menstrual pain, and is variously consumed, inhaled or rubbed into the skin.

Folkloric uses of juniper have likewise continued, particularly in northern Europe, and tend to reflect its medical function as a fumigant. Juniper branches were thrown on to the Beltane fires, and a faggot of smoldering juniper twigs was used to purify farmsteads and stables on the first morning of the New Year. With a darker purpose, the wise-women of Lothian prescribed a tea made of juniper berries and needles as an abortifacient, and farmers included it in their hedges, where it was believed to guard against the depredations of wolves and wildcats.These usages and meanings have been carried over into modern magical and neo-pagan practices: juniper twigs, or juniper-laced incense, provide fragrant smoke for manifestations and rituals of purification, and pouches of berries are hung around the necks of infants to ensure a lifetime of good health.

But juniper also provided a setting and title for that most chillingly Sophoclean of folk-tales—"The JuniperTree," a Low German story collected by Jacob and Wilhelm Grimm at the beginning of the nineteenth century and published in their *Children's and*

*Household Tales* in 1812. Driven by the primal jealousy between a
stepmother and her stepson, this deliciously pre-Freudian allegory
features cannibalism and metamorphosis, filicide countered with
matricide. (It has since inspired an eponymous novel by Barbara
Comyns Carr, a 1985 opera with music by Philip Glass, and a 1990
Icelandic film starring Björk.)

"The Juniper Tree" begins with a moment of innocence, tinged
with shades of the Fall. A pregnant wife, walking in the garden of
her house, eats a handful of berries from her juniper tree. She falls
ill—the reasons for which are unexplained, as juniper berries are
not notably poisonous—and dies during birth, though her new son
survives. She is buried beneath the roots of the tree, and her widower takes another wife, who gives him a daughter. The daughter
and her half-brother get on well, but the stepmother resents her
stepson who will one day inherit his father's estate, leaving her
daughter with nothing. So she asks him to choose an apple from
a wooden chest; as he bends down, she brings the lid down on his
exposed neck and strikes his head from his shoulders.

In a hideous parody of the conscientious housewife, she does not
waste the carcass: she turns her stepson into a stew and black pud-
dings, and feeds them to her husband, who—unaware—pronounces
his child delicious. But the daughter appreciates the horror of
what has happened, and when her mother is occupied she col-
lects the bones of her half-brother from the cauldron, and buries
them beneath the juniper tree. In a flash of fire his soul rises from
the bones in the form of a bird, singing of his murder. The bird
grows more powerful, until he can carry a millstone high enough
to bludgeon his stepmother to death. As she dies, he returns to
human form, and lives happily with his father and his half-sister.

So it seems that by the sixteenth century, when it was taken up
as the distinctive flavoring for genever, juniper already had a long
history of gastronomic, sacred and medicinal meaning. What of
spirit—that playful, ambiguous word, which can signify a demon,

a ghost, a principle of life, the essence of human character, or an extract of wine or beer?

Evidence for the origins of distillation is fragmentary to say the least, and what we have is a fairly speculative story elaborated from hints in ancient texts and traditions. The Sanskrit *Vedas,* thought to have been written around 2500 BC, mention a process which sounds like distillation, and which was used to produce the entheogenic *somasara* consumed during festivals. Stronger evidence comes from Chinese philosophical treatises of the eighth century BC, describing fragrances and tonics distilled from herbs. This raises the tantalizing possibility that knowledge of the technique may have passed along the Silk Road to the Middle East.

In the centuries around the birth of Christ various scholars and artisans in trading ports around the eastern Mediterranean began to write about distillation. In Alexandria the alchemist and Gnostic Zosimos of Panopolis recorded the exploits of the semi-legendary Maria the Jewess, a female alchemist said to have invented distillation. In Athens Aristotle noted the paradox of wine: soup became stronger as it was reduced, but wine lost its power to intoxicate. This idea was taken up by Dioscorides, and *De Materia Medica* includes a recipe for a fortified *vinum hippocraticum,* made by heating wine in a clay pot and collecting the distillate in wool or a sponge laid over the mouth of the vessel. Ancient Greek sailors appear to have used a similar method to make drinking water from seawater on long voyages.

Wherever the technique originated, historians agree that distillation came of age in the intellectual and cultural ferment of the Muslim empire in the seventh and eighth centuries AD. At the Persian medical school of Jundishapur in the sixth century apothecaries were distilling rose-water, juniper oil and other herbal medicines, but the full flowering of Arabic "philosophical chemistry" came with the establishment of the new Abbasid capital at Baghdad in 763 AD. The caliphate established a large library, known as the "House of Wisdom," along with schools teaching all the learned and humane arts. The result was an original and diverse research community, a torrent of translations from Latin and Greek texts, and the emergence of a distinctively Arabic alchemical tradition.

The leading figure in Baghdad alchemy was Abu Musa Jabir ibn Hayyan, known to his medieval Western successors as "Geber." In the course of his work Geber created the "alembic"—the swan-necked alchemical still made of glass, ceramic or copper. He experimented rapaciously, distilling just about any liquid he could get his hands on, and his writings describe the clear, flammable liquid obtained from the distillation of wine. His colleague at the House of Wisdom—Abu-Yusuf Ya'qoub ibn 'Ishaq ibn al-Sabbah ibn 'Omran ibn Isma'il al-Kindi, known, mercifully, as "al-Kindi"—used the alembic to make cordials and perfumes, but it was the ninth-century physician Muhammad ibn Zakariyā Rāzī, "Rhazes," who collected and codified the secrets of wine-distillation. Rhazes became fascinated with the properties of this volatile, ephemeral liquid, and gave it an Arabic name—*al-koh'l*. Already we can see the doubleness, the playfulness, wrought by this substance on the minds that contemplated its nature. In Arabic, *al-koh'l* signified both a psychoactive substance and a *djinn,* prefiguring the double meaning of "spirit" in English. And it recalled and transformed the central image in "Aladdin's Wonderful Lamp" from *The Thousand and One Nights,* compiled in Persia around the time Rhazes was writing: the *djinn* rising from the spout of Aladdin's lamp, just as *al-koh'l* rose from the neck of the alembic.

But this magical substance, and the technique that produced it, did not make a single grand leap across the Mediterranean. Rather, it took a more gradual route from the libraries of Baghdad to the monasteries and universities of Europe. A ninth-century monastic treatise nicknamed the *Mappae Clavicula* ("The Little Key to the Map")—a practical handbook for blacksmithing and copying manuscripts—also contains the first known European instructions for distillation. By the eleventh century, the secrets of Arabic philosophical chemistry had reached the most important center of medical education in post-Roman Europe, and the place where juniper and spirit first came together: the Benedictine monastery at Salerno in southern Italy.

Juniper grows abundantly in the hills around Salerno, and both monks and apothecaries worked with alembics in the workshops and kitchens of the monastery. A textbook written in 1050, the *Regimen Sanitatis Salernitatum,* recommended bandages impregnated with juniper, and the *Compendium Salernita,* a collection of treatments compiled around 1055, includes a recipe for a tonic distilled from wine infused with juniper berries. Was this the first gin, or perhaps an archetypal "proto-gin"? Perhaps: it is certainly the earliest recipe we have for anything that looks (to modern eyes) like gin. But this Salernitan proto-gin was created in a very different context from later genevers and gins. It was a medicine, one of many herbal tonics produced by hand in monastic kitchens, prescribed in small quantities and according to strict rules derived from the canon of Greco-Roman medicine. And it was a simple and unsweetened distillation of wine and juniper berries—and hence fiery and mouth–puckeringly sharp.

This proto-gin—a fusion of Arabic alchemy and Classical medicine—signalled a new European interest in what had been lost with the fall of Rome, and what might be gained from a thorough study of the new Islamic corpus. Geber was translated into Latin in 1144, and Rhazes in 1279, as new universities and medical schools (particularly Montpellier, and the Sorbonne in Paris) began to incorporate Arabic learning into their curricula. Knowledge of distillation, and the medical possibilities of distilled herbal spirits, spread rapidly across Europe, and were taken up by the highest echelons of the leading political and spiritual power—the Catholic church. In his mid–thirteenth–century *Liber de Oculis* ("Book of the Eyes"), Pedro Julião, later Pope John XXI, described another proto-gin in the shape of his celebrated "eye water." Intended as a restorative rinse for weary or inflamed eyes, this did not feature juniper, but it did prefigure another aspect of later gin manufacture by including a mix of "botanicals," including fennel, endive and rue. Following his example, many monasteries began to produce their own distinctive cordials, rectified with local herbs. Probably the most famous survivor of this tradition is Bénédictine, produced at the abbey of Fécamp in Normandy from 1510.

Medieval Catholic scholars owed far more than they were usually prepared to admit to the works of the "Islamic Renaissance," and it is telling that the two great physician-alchemists of the thirteenth and fourteenth centuries were born in what had once been Muslim Spain. Arnaud de Ville-Neuve, Latinised as Arnaldus Villanovus, was born in Catalonia, but spent most of his life in Paris and Montpellier, where he studied and improved the existing translations of Geber and Rhazes. In his own writings he described the processes of distilling wine to make spirit, and then re-distilling with herbs or botanicals to make tonics. As we saw at the beginning of this chapter, Ville-Neuve also coined the name *aqua vita,* which when translated provided many European languages with their word for spirit: *eau de vie* in French, *akvavit* in Swedish, *usquebaugh* in Gaelic. Ville-Neuve's pupil, the aristocratic Catalan monk Ramon Llull, went further. In his *Secunda Magia Naturalis* he argued that the distillation of wine was a way of concentrating its "quintessence," and that seven re-distillations would produce the most pure form of quintessence available on this fallen planet. For Llull, the transformative power of this discovery seemed unlimited, and the spirit of wine was:

> An emanation of the divinity, an element newly revealed to man, but hid from antiquity, because the human race was then too young to need this beverage, [which is] destined to revive the energies of modern decrepitude.

What did Europeans make of this mysterious, ephemeral substance —a water which burned, a spirit which intoxicated, a hidden essence which could dissolve into the air, leaving no trace behind? For some, the stigma of pagan alchemy was too much to bear: in 1288 the Dominican friars at Rimini abjured their stills, and denounced distillation as a black art. But for an elite coterie of European scholars, this black art held out the promise of eternal life and unlimited power over the world around them. By the sixteenth century most European gentlemen and aristocrats might be expected to possess some knowledge of the learned art of alchemy—far from a kind of "failed chemistry," but a profound and esoteric body of scholarship which held that the true meaning of the Book of Scripture and the Book of Nature was occult, and could be discerned only through deep allegorical reading and reflection.

For these would-be magi, the great work of alchemy was transformation. Just as nature turned seeds into flowers, and bakers turned flour into bread, so the physical and chemical transformations in retorts and alembics were mirrored by transfigurations in the soul of the alchemist. The end—in both senses, the purpose and the conclusion—of transformation was the extraction and contemplation of quintessence, the occult substance permeating and underlying the visible world. Alchemists used various techniques to pursue quintessences—sublimation, calcination, corrosion—all of which aimed to separate what was impure, earthly and mutable from what was pure, heavenly and eternal. But lines in the *Emerald Tablet,* a short, cryptic text attributed to Hermes Trismegistus, the legendary founder of alchemy, seemed to suggest that only distillation would reveal the full glory of the quintessence:

8. Separate the earth from the fire, the subtle and thin from the crude and coarse, prudently, with modesty and wisdom.

9. This ascends from the earth into the sky and again descends from the sky to the earth, and receives the power and efficacy of things above and of things below.

10. By this means you will acquire the glory of the whole world, and so you will drive away all shadows and blindness.

11. For this by its fortitude snatches the palm from all other fortitude and power. For it is able to penetrate and subdue everything subtle and everything crude and hard.

There is much truth in the image of the Renaissance alchemist as a solitary magus, working for decades in a secluded laboratory to discover the secrets of transformation. But alchemists also saw their work as transforming the world around them—not least in the pursuit of long life and good health—and the "quintessences" produced via distillation were taken up by some physicians as an effective new therapeutic. The leading figure in linking alchemy with medicine was the Swiss physician and occultist Philippus Aureolus Theophrastus Bombastus von Hohenheim, better known as "Paracelsus." Transformation was, Paracelsus thought, all around, and (literally) within: the human body was a living alembic, in which food was transformed into the "spirit of Man" through fermentation and distillation. So the quintessence of Llull and the alchemists was not merely an elixir of health and life, but also the living flame within each soul. In the *Archidoxa,* written around 1520 but not published until after his death, Paracelsus summarized the virtues of the quintessence:

> A nature, a force, a virtue, and a medicine, once, indeed, shut up within things, but now free from any domicile and from all outward incorporation ... It is a spirit like the spirit of life, but with this difference, that the life-spirit of a thing is permanent, but that of man is mortal.

In the Paracelsian cosmology disease was a disharmony between the human microcosm and the heavenly macrocosm, and the role of the physician-alchemist was to restore health by readjusting the proportions of the three "cardinal principles": salt, representing solidity; mercury, representing fluidity; and sulphur, representing flammability. This could be done with the aid of "spagyric" therapies—medicines combining Salernitan proto-gins with the principles of alchemical transformation. From the Greek *spao ageiro,* meaning "to break open and pull out," spagyric tonics mixed spirit and the distilled extract of a plant with the ash of its leaves, a technique which extracted the quintessence just as one might prise a nut from its shell. It seems that Paracelsus acquired a taste for his own medicines: one rumor, circulating after his death, had it that he died after drinking himself into a stupor with one of his spagyric proto-gins.

Paracelsus was an iconoclast, a figure who divided as he sought to unify. Even his name was a boast, proclaiming his equality with the illustrious Roman physician Celsus. But by the time of his death in 1541 variants of his spagyric medicines were finding their way into the mainstream of Renaissance medicine alongside Salernitan proto-gins. Here, too, health was a matter of balance. The four humors of Classical Greco-Roman medicine—blood, black bile, yellow bile, and phlegm—had to be kept in their correct proportions, determined by interactions between the microcosm of individual constitution and lifestyle, and the macrocosm of the natural world and the heavens. Within this tradition, wine had high status as a medicine. For the Roman physician Galen, wine embodied the heat and moisture characteristic of living things, and those melancholy individuals in whom black bile predominated could cheer their outlook by consuming blood-like red wine. But wine, like any medicine, affected different people in different ways, and was only beneficial in the correct proportions. In excess it could dry the body by provoking urination, and its cloudy vapors could rise to the head and fog the faculty of reason.

These ancient ideas shaped the attitudes of medieval and Renaissance physicians to the new proto-gins. The friar and philosopher Roger Bacon, writing in the thirteenth century, suggested that *aqua vita* was an exact counterpart of the human life force, and could also be produced by the ghoulish expedient of heating fresh human blood in an alembic. But for most physicians, spirits offered the powers of wine in a concentrated form. Following the Salernitan tradition, they could be used as a carrier for the healing powers of botanical medicines like juniper, and by the fifteenth century apothecaries were using them to preserve seasonal herbs, making them available all year round. But spirit itself was celebrated as a general tonic, reflected in the name given to spirit-based medicines:

"cordial," from the Latin *cordis,* "heart." A shot of spirit could warm the cockles of the heart, and stimulate a flagging intellect. After 1348, with the Black Death ravaging the population of Western Europe, juniper cordials were in high demand to fumigate the body and strengthen the constitution against infection.

Following the invention of printing with movable type in the fifteenth century, treatises revealing the secrets of distillation quickly began to move beyond elite medical and alchemical circles. One of the most successful was the *Liber de Arte Destillandi* (*The Book of the Art of Distillation*), published by Hieronymus Braunschweig, an Alsatian physician, in 1500. Braunschweig praised distilled spirits as "the mistress of all medicine," and (in the words of a 1651 translation by the English physician John French) enumerated their virtues:

> [Spirit] eases diseases coming of cold. It comforts the heart. It heals all old and new sores on the head. It causes a good color in a person ... it eases the pain in the teeth and causes sweet breath ... it heals the short-winded. It causes good digestion and appetite ... and takes away belching. It eases the yellow jaundice, the dropsy, the gout, the pain in the breasts when they be swollen, and heals all diseases in the bladder ... it heals the bites of a mad dog ... It gives courage in a young person and causes him to have a good memory.

Endorsements like this made proto-gins seem to be truly an elixir of life, a medical miracle fulfilling the stale promises of quack nostrums. But medical interest was balanced with concern, and as spirits became part of European physicians' armamentaria, some writers began to warn of the dangers of excess consumption. The Austrian physician Michael Puff von Schrick gave one of the first caveats in his *Hienach volget ein nüczliche Materi von manigerley ausgepranten Wasser* (*Useful Material on Distilled Waters*), published in 1478. Puff von Schrick reassured his readers that small quantities of spirit could keep one in near-perfect health, but warned that apothecaries, quacks and *wasserbrennerinnen*—village wise-women who "burnt waters" as a sideline—were encouraging dangerous overindulgence. The Nuremberg surgeon and poet Hanz Folz was more concerned about keeping up appearances: in a pamphlet published in 1493, he argued that excessive consumption of *aqua vita* would lead to embarrassing and un-gentlemanly conduct in public.

But it was midwives, rather than physicians, who were seen to embody the double face of distilled spirits. They used cordials and *aqua vita* as part of their practice, both to blur the pain of childbirth and to help "ungrease" the child. Wet-nurses, meanwhile, might consume botanical cordials as an indirect way of administering them to the child. According to the Dutch-English distiller and alchemist William Y-Worth, to whom we'll return, proto-gins were especially popular for this purpose:

> It is a general Custom in *Holland,* when the Child is troubled with Oppressions of Wind, for the Mother whilst the Child is sucking, to drink of the Powers or Spirits of Juniper, by which the Child is Relieved.

Therapeutic dispensation sometimes shaded into pleasurable carousing, and midwives and wet-nurses acquired a reputation as secret tipplers if not outright sots. In *Romeo and Juliet* Juliet's nurse drinks *aqua vita* to calm herself after hearing that Romeo has killed Tybalt, and in *Twelfth Night* a forged letter works with Malvolio "like aqua vita with a midwife." Stories of wet-nurses so drunk that they smothered their charges, or failed to notice when they fell into the fire, were common currency in this period, and (as we'll see in the next two chapters) went on to become one of the principal tropes of anti-gin literature in the eighteenth and nineteenth centuries. And some midwives took their passion for cordials to an extreme: in 1447 one Giovanna of San Ambroglio in Florence was censured by the church authorities for distilling a love-potion from wine mixed with powdered skulls dug up in her parish graveyard.

Increasingly public disapproval of genteel drunkards and tipsy midwives reveals that the place of distilled spirits in early modern culture was beginning to shift. By the sixteenth century distillation was no longer the exclusive province of alchemists, apothecaries and physicians. More and more people across Europe were producing proto-gins, flavored with a range of botanicals—some for medicine, but many more for pleasure and profit.

As with so many aspects of English history, Henry VIII had a hand in this. Monastic kitchens and workshops disappeared with the Dissolution of the Monasteries in the 1530s, and well-to-do women began to take up the role of producing cordials and other medicines. The "stillatory"—a descendent of the alchemists alembic, typically made of copper—was a fairly standard piece of equipment in the kitchens of medieval manor houses, and some larger mansions had a separate still-room overseen by the lady of the house. Lady Margaret Hoby kept a diary throughout her life, and often noted that she "went about my stilling." And in *Delightes for Ladies,* published in 1602, Hugh Platt gave a recipe for a proto-gin flavored with juniper and other herbs, though he suggested it should not be used to clean the teeth before retiring to bed:

> Distil with a gentle heat either in balneo [a water bath], or ashes, the strong and sweet water wherewith you have drawn oil of cloves, mace, nutmegs, juniper, rosemarie, &c after it hath stood one moneth close stopt, and so you shall purchase a delicate spirit of each of the said aromaticall bodies.

But distillation was never an exclusively female pursuit, and it continued to play a central part in the repertoire of aristocratic natural philosophers. Sir Walter Raleigh, confined to the Tower of London after the death of Elizabeth I, turned his polymathic attention to distillation, devising a *spiritus dulcis* ("sweet spirit") and a "Great Cordial" requiring forty botanicals plus amber, pearls and coral. Because of the cost and complexity this was made only when members of the royal family were already on their deathbeds. Raleigh began production when Prince Henry, son of James I, fell desperately ill in 1612, but Henry expired long before the "Great Cordial" was ready to pass his lips.

By the mid-sixteenth century the manor houses and mansions of Europe were witness to a thriving culture of private distillation—so much so that writers began to warn ladies of the fine line separating occasional doses of medicinal cordials from regular nips of potent spirituous "treats." It was becoming abundantly clear that many Europeans liked to drink proto-gins and other cordials for pleasure, in the same way as sack or ale, and that there was money to be made from the manufacture of spirits on a commercial scale. In the early fifteenth century northern Italian city-states had small commercial producers of spirits and fruit-flavored cordials, and German towns along the Rhein were making *gebrant wein* ("burnt wine" or brandy) from nearby Riesling vineyards. Most spirits, however, were distilled in a small-scale, dispersed way, with apothecaries, tavern-keepers and private householders selling "hot waters" by the glass or the flask.

This cottage industry underwent a revolution in the mid-sixteenth century, thanks to two factors. One was the burgeoning print culture mentioned earlier, which enabled techniques to be learned from the page rather than via word of mouth. A new generation of handbooks, written in the vernacular rather than in Latin, concentrated on the practicalities of producing spirit on a large scale rather than the metaphorical mysteries of alchemical transformation. The other was the realization that intoxicating spirits did not have to be distilled from wine, but could be made from anything that would ferment: fruit, potatoes, and above all grain. For farmers, commercial distillation offered a way of preserving and concentrating the value of their surplus grain after a good harvest. A barrel of spirit was far easier to store, transport and sell than a dozen bushels of grain. For tavern-keepers, merchants and drinkers, spirits kept better than even the best wines or ales. They could be exported over long distances, even overseas, and distillers found it easier to make a consistent product than did brewers or wine-makers.

The first major centers of grain spirit distillation were the coastal cities of the Low Countries, building on their existing expertise in brewing and their trade with the fertile bread-basket plains of northern and central Europe. After 1618 the Thirty Years' War stimulated demand for their product by interrupting supplies of French and German brandy, and from the mid-seventeenth century new connections with the grain markets of the Baltic states enabled Dutch distillers to import truly enormous volumes of grain. Many critics voiced concerns over grain spirits: some saw them as a dangerous drain on food supply, and it was agreed that they were stronger and rougher than liquors distilled from wine. But the voice of the market was clear and distinct, as a large, new public appetite demanded grain spirit for pleasurable consumption. By 1621 London had more than two hundred distillers making "Aqua Vitae, Aqua Composita and other strong and hott waters." Some were rumored to be deeply unscrupulous, using spoiled cider, wine dregs and turnip tops (or worse) to pad out their grain. And the industry was acrimoniously split, between a few larger, more influential companies turning grain into neutral spirit (known as "low wines"), and many smaller, poorer distillers carrying out rectification or "compounding" with botanicals to produce the finished, flavored drinks.

In 1638, after a struggle with the Society of Apothecaries (who had a lucrative sideline in distillation), a group of wealthy London distillers acquired a royal charter for their new alliance—the Worshipful Company of Distillers. The Company's eminence reflected its regal connections: amongst its founders were Sir Thomas Cademan, physician to Queen Henrietta Maria, and Sir Theodore de Mayerne, physician to Henrietta's husband, Charles I. It was given practical power, in the shape of a monopoly over distilling within twenty-one miles of London, but it also acquired symbolic authority in the shape of a coat of arms. This captured, beautifully and succinctly, the fusion of alchemical symbolism and hard-headed commerce characterizing the commercial production of proto-gins.

The principal image, mounted on a shield, speaks to Classical and Renaissance thought about the connections between the macrocosm and the microcosm. On the upper half of the shield the sun shines on clouds, which drop rain on a rolling landscape. On the lower half is a stylized copper still. As above, so below: the whole world is a still driven by the heat of the sun, and (reciprocally) grain spirit is as natural and as nourishing as God's rain. This sentiment is made manifest in the Company's motto: "Drop as raine, Distil as dew." The shield is crowned with a hop-vine twining around a sheaf of wheat, and is flanked by two figures: a "Russe" merchant in a heavy fur cape, symbolising Baltic grain, and an "Indian Savage"—a seventeenth-century interpretation of a central American warrior, symbolising the exotic botanicals which were becoming increasingly important as flavors. Mayerne's personal recipe for a heavily botanical *aqua vita* reveals this new, cosmopolitan dimension to proto-gins:

> Rue, sage, lavender, marjoram, wormwood, rosemary, red roses, thistle, pimpernel, valerian, juniper berries, bay berries, angelica, citrus bark, coriander, sandalwood, basil, grain of paradise, pepper, ginger, cinnamon, saffron, mace, nutmeg, cubeb, cardamom, galingall.

These proto-gins, and other distilled "hot waters," were part of a revolution in European drinking habits across the seventeenth century, in which a combination of commercial nous and popular appeal had turned an alchemical medicine into a pleasurable drink. But what were the contours of this drinking culture? What was being drunk, and by whom? And how did existing attitudes to drink and drunkenness shape European attitudes to the first botanical spirits?

Early modern drinking culture can be broadly and crudely summarized as ale in the country, hopped beer in the towns and cities, and wine (plain or fortified) for the ruling classes. By the seventeenth century this convivial consumption might also include "drinking" or "dry-drinking" tobacco—another commodity with both medical and pleasurable faces. In one sense, spirits slipped easily into this culture. They were sold alongside ale and sack in taverns, and certainly did not supplant traditional drinks, as stereotypical Englishmen continued to gorge themselves on roast beef and ale or beer. In John Fletcher's play *The Pilgrim,* written in 1621, a band of Spanish bravadoes demand an "aquavite" binge, but the constant cry of the English madman is "Fill me a thousand pots, and froth 'em, froth 'em!"

But spirits were seen to be different from existing drinks, in two ways. First, they seemed to cause a new kind of drunkenness, wilder and more socially destructive than the rolling English stupor engendered by beer—a concern which predated the eighteenth-century "gin craze" by at least a hundred and fifty years. Second, spirits were seen to mark a broader revolution in European life, with the beginnings of a distinctively urban culture and identity. Ale was a cornerstone of medieval village life, based around the rhythms of the seasons and the stations of the Christian ritual year. It was made in the parish, from parish grain, and was drunk by parishioners at festivals, marriages and wakes. Spirits were completely different, the product of a new age of trade and empire, industry and social upheaval, an age both exhilarating and anxiety-provoking. Proto-gins embodied, in other words, all the things that gave early modern Europeans the feeling that the world was shifting beneath their feet.

And the growing popularity of proto-gins and other spirits also began to change the relationship between individuals and governments, raising urgent political questions about intervention and personal responsibility that would run through the next five centuries of Western history. The rising European taste for spirits ran in parallel with stronger and more frequent forms of state regulation and control—licensing laws, punishments for public drunkenness or violence, and most of all duties and excises. When rulers were first confronted with outbreaks of spirit-fed unrest, their typical response had been prohibition: in the fifteenth and sixteenth centuries France and various German states experimented with banning brandy. But the heads of exchequers began to realize that, if taxed or even turned into a state monopoly, spirits could be a lucrative source of revenue. By the seventeenth century almost all European nations were caught up in political, commercial and ethical arguments over whether the social evils of excessive spirit consumption outweighed the benefits of trade and the hefty income from duty.

Some, in search of moral clarity on this issue, turned to the Church, but traditional Christian attitudes to drinking were (to say the least) ambivalent. On one hand, Christ turned water into wine; he used vines, grapes and wine continually in his parables; at the Last Supper he instituted the commemorative meal of bread and wine; and—if one followed the orthodox Catholic line—in the miracle of the Mass his blood took on the outward form of red wine. Following his example, most monks and priests were happy to consume wine and beer, and monasteries grew rich on the proceeds of their vineyards and breweries. On the other hand, however, the Bible specifically condemned drunkenness as a sin, and preachers—particularly Calvinist preachers—accused drunkards of a kind of treason, like guards who fell asleep on duty and allowed the forces of Satan into the citadel of the soul. During the Reformation almost all factions calumnized their opponents as sots, and almost all went on drinking—a practical acknowledgement, perhaps, of the popularity of wine, beer, and spirits, the money made from their production, and their importance in the daily lives of most people.

By the early seventeenth century, however, English preachers, politicians and pamphleteers were pointing towards a rupture in the traditional pattern of drinking. A rash of books like Thomas Young's *England's Bane: or, the Description of Drunkennesse,* published in 1617, and Richard Rawlidge's *A Monster Late Found Out and Discovered,* published in 1628, claimed that Britons were the most drunken people in the world, and that intoxicating drinks were sapping the nation's vigor. Some writers blamed the mushrooming numbers of alehouses, but most pointed towards two habits brought back by mercenaries fighting in the Low Countries during the Dutch wars of independence and the Thirty Years' War.

RICHARD BARNETT

One was the German habit of drinking healths or toasts, in which groups of hot-blooded English soldiers might egg each other on to violence and oblivion. The other was a new, juniper-flavored grain spirit—Dutch genever.

Late in 1653, at the height of the first Anglo-Dutch war, the poet and MP Andrew Marvell was moved (or perhaps paid) to write a piece of propaganda on the impudence of the youthful Dutch Republic. Marvell vaulted into his task, beginning with a denunciation of the very Dutch soil:

HOLLAND, that scarce deserves the name of land,
As but the off-scouring of the British sand . . .
This indigested vomit of the sea
Fell to the Dutch by just propriety . . .

In Marvell's estimation the Dutch were little more than duplicitous amphibians, inhabiting a bleak and undesirable corner of northern Europe and subsisting on herring and rancid butter. Moreover, they were suspiciously cosmopolitan, tolerant of "sect" and "schism," and happy to do business with any "Turk-Christian-Pagan-Jew" who might help them to turn a profit:

Sure when religion did itself embark,
And from the East would Westward steer its ark,
It struck, and splitting on this unknown ground,
Each one thence pillaged the first piece he found:
Hence Amsterdam, Turk-Christian-Pagan-Jew,
Staple of sects and mint of schism grew,
That bank of conscience, where not one so strange
Opinion but finds credit, and exchange . . .

What actually seems to have troubled Marvell, and many English propagandists, was not that the Dutch were desperately immoral or indecently industrious. Rather, it was that they were too much like the English: an ambitious, mercantile, Protestant state with pretensions to worldwide power and prestige, which was ominously close to challenging English naval supremacy. Though he did not know it, Marvell was writing at the apogee of what has been called the Dutch Golden Age. Usually dated to the century after 1570, this was a period of immense political, cultural and even physical transformation in the Netherlands, and it was in precisely this period that genever emerged as both a global commodity and the Dutch national spirit. As we'll see, the particular circumstances of Dutch commerce and culture shaped both the content and the meaning of genever—and, reciprocally, genever embodied much of what it meant to be Dutch.

By the seventeenth century the Netherlands were one of the most densely populated regions in the world, deeply connected to the rest of Europe and the world. Europe's first stock exchange opened in Rotterdam in 1602, and Amsterdam became known as the Protestant Venice. The architecture and atmosphere of Dutch cities expressed the lineaments of the Dutch *burgerlijk* character: republican, capitalist, urbane, tolerant, but also Calvinist and hence not excessively tolerant. The Dutch were known across Europe as hearty folk, tall and fat, grave but not sober. They were renowned as eager consumers of bread, cheese, beer, fish (particularly herring) and an early incarnation of the sandwich in the form of *belegde broodje*—a classic tavern snack consisting of slivers of air-dried beef between thick slices of buttered bread.

But less than a century before Marvell wrote his satire, none of this existed. The Low Countries were under the repressive rule of the Spanish Habsburg monarchy, and there was no Dutch republic, no empire, no vast wealth. In a series of bloody wars from 1568, armies under William I of Orange expelled the Spanish forces and established a federal republic of seven "United Provinces," which finally concluded peace with Spain in 1648. This struggle laid down the bones of a new Dutch sense of self: an imposed Catholic tyranny overthrown by Protestant righteousness, demanding constant watchfulness on the part of every Dutch citizen (just as the polders and dykes required unceasing maintenance to keep out the North Sea). But flesh was put on the bones of this nascent national identity by the creation of the *Vereenigde Oost-indisch Compagnie* (VOC)—the United East India Company.

In November 1665, during the second Anglo-Dutch war, the diarist and civil servant Samuel Pepys took a carriage to Erith in Kent. As Surveyor-Victualler to the Royal Navy, he was required to supervise the distribution of a prize cargo from two captured ships of the VOC fleet. Pepys—an obsessive chronicler of novelty and news—was beside himself, finding it:

> As noble a sight as ever I saw in my life, the greatest wealth in con-
> fusion that a man can see in the world. Pepper scattered through
> every chink. You trod upon it and in cloves and nutmegs I walked
> above the knees, whole rooms full. And silk in bales and boxes of
> copper plate, one of which I opened.

Pepys' bewildered astonishment captures the sense of excite-ment felt by Dutch merchants, sailors and statesmen. The VOC opened a window on the world for the young republic, and the acquisition of a maritime empire in what was then called the "East Indies" (now south-east Asia) brought new wealth, new power and—most importantly for our purposes—a plethora of new, sumptuous *things*. The Dutch Golden Age was the first consumer revolution, bringing spices, silks, ceramics, tobacco, coffee, tea, sugar and many other commodities into the heart of Europe. And genever was a prime example of what happened when these exotic imports collided with increasingly cosmo-politan Dutch tastes.

Historically, the European spice trade had been dominated by Islamic traders until the tenth century, and then by new monopo-lies in the hands of northern Italian city-states. In this sense, the European "Age of Exploration" was driven as much by a desire to break these mercantile monopolies as it was by missionary fervor or royal imperialism. The first substantial post-Roman European empires were the Spanish and Portuguese territories in South and Central America, but from the 1570s both the Dutch and the English began to muscle in on Iberian trade. The VOC received its charter on 20th March 1602: in the mood which characterized northern European mercantile Protestantism, it was neither an empire nor an army, but a private company formed by investors looking to turn a profit. Granted a twenty-one-year monopoly over Dutch trade with Asia, the VOC established a new capital at Batavia—now Jakarta in Indonesia—in 1619. It is difficult to exaggerate the scale of the VOC's operation: five thousand ships, fifty thousand employees, more than two and a half million tons of goods imported over the course of the seventeenth century (compared with a measly half-million tons brought home by the English East India Company). It is also difficult to exaggerate the cruelty involved, as native populations were killed, driven out, or enslaved and made to work on nutmeg plantations.

VOC ships returning to Amsterdam and Rotterdam brought two things. First, these vessels generated a munificent 18% dividend for investors, and this in turn gave Dutch *burghers* the capital to purchase the second thing they carried—goods. The account-books of Amsterdam apothecaries in the early seventeenth century reveal a very high demand for all manner of imported spices: English saffron, Chinese ginger, Maltese anise, Polish cumin, ambergris, petroleum, senna, sarsaparilla, cassia, galangal, cubeb, opium, cassia wood, sugar, and possibly cannabis. Some of these were used to flavor tobacco—the Dutch are known to have relished pipe-smoke scented with (amongst other things) lavender, prunes, vinegar and coriander—but many were also used to flavor genever.

The circumstances in which genever was first distilled are semi-mythical—myths which are, as we'll see, just as revealing as the truth—but one thing is clear. By the late sixteenth century Dutch distillers, drinkers and doctors were already intimately familiar with distilled grain spirit, juniper cordials and botanical flavorings. The poet Jacob Maerlant te Damme discussed juniper oil as a thera-peutic in 1269, in his *Der Naturen Bloeme* (*On the Nature of Flowers*), and in the *Constelyc Distilleerboec,* the first Dutch handbook on distillation, published in 1552, Philippus Hermanni gave a recipe for juniper eau-de-vie. Much spirit was initially imported from France, but the Dutch had a strong native brewing industry, and by the mid-sixteenth century Dutch brewers and apothecaries were moving into the distillation of grain spirit. This made sound agricultural sense—the leavings from stills were used to feed pigs, often on large farms adjacent to distilleries—and likewise juniper made good economic sense as a basic flavoring. It grew wild across the Low Countries, and its flavor helped to mask the roughness of grain spirit.

At this point, we encounter the man most often cited as the creator of genever—one "Sylvius de la Boë," usually described as a professor of medicine at the University of Leiden in the years around 1572. But these historical waters have been muddied by two points of confusion. First, "Sylvius" was not a single character: he appears to be a conflation of Sylvius de Bouve, an apothecary to the University of Leiden at the end of the sixteenth century, and François dele Boë Sylvius, Professor of Medicine at Leiden from 1658 to 1672. Both men were deeply interested in the medical potential of distillation and fermentation, and it seems likely that both experimented with juniper cordials. Some sources suggest that by 1595 de Bouve was marketing a juniper-based grain spirit called "Genova" as a treatment for lumbago. But—secondly—there is no evidence to show that either man "invented" genever. As we have seen, the idea of a juniper-flavored grain spirit was well-known in the Dutch Republic in the late sixteenth century, suggesting that genever—like the alchemists' quintessence—was the product of a tradition in flux rather than a single moment of inspiration.

Rather than dismissing this story out of hand, however, we can see it as capturing a metaphorical truth about the origins and nature of genever—a union of two substances reputed to have great medicinal, sacred and alchemical virtues. Distillation was a distinctive tool of Dutch medicine and natural philosophy: indeed, the Dutch word for chemistry, *scheikunde,* means "separation." Trained in universities across northern Europe, dele Boë Sylvius was deeply familiar with the principles of Paracelsian medicine. He used distillation to extract the quintessences of herbs and spices, and to make long-lasting cordials which preserved the therapeutic powers of peppermint, licorice or juniper. One of his close friends—Louis de Bils, son of a wealthy Dutch merchant—aided dele Boë Sylvius in his dissections, and developed a process for "balsaming" or preserving bodies. According to this method, corpses were immersed for sixty days in a tin bath filled with a mixture of spirit, alum, pepper, myrrh and juniper.

Whatever the truth behind the mysterious "Sylvius de la Boë," it is certainly true that the Dutch appetite for genever rocketed in the first half of the seventeenth century. Distilleries initially clustered around Rotterdam, the leading entrepôt for Baltic grain merchants, but within a few decades Schiedam, a small town only a few miles from Rotterdam, had become the center of genever production. This industry dominated the local economy, with not only dozens of distillers but also windmills grinding grain, malthouses, glass-blowers, coopers and porters. As in English distilling, genever production was split into two stages. In the first, neutral grain spirit—known as *moutwijn,* "malt wine," or "liquid bread" after its rich, yeasty aroma—was made from a variable mixture of malted barley, wheat flour and rye. In the second stage, *moutwijn* was rectified with juniper and other botanicals, before being casked or bottled for distribution.

Two of the most famous names in Dutch distilling—Bols and De Kuypers—were founded during this first Dutch infatuation with genever. By 1575 the Bulsius family had moved from Cologne to open a distillery in Amsterdam, and had changed their name to the more agreeably Dutch Bols. The family cultivated a close relationship with the VOC: by 1602 they had arranged to supply their spirits to leading members of the Company, and in return they were given preferential access to the VOC spice warehouses. This close, reciprocal association came out in their products: by 1664 Bols were manufacturing genevers flavored with both Dutch juniper and more exotic, imported botanicals. De Kuypers came a little later, and began as a family-run cooperage, but by the early eighteenth century they had moved from barrel-making to distilling their own genevers.

As in other parts of Europe, the emerging Dutch taste for genever went along with a rising sense of unease about the consequences of strong spirits for society. These concerns had a distinctively Dutch flavor, drawing on apprehension about the new prosperity and new perspectives brought by the VOC. For the leaders of Calvinist thought in Amsterdam, wealth and glamorous merchandise might distract Dutch merchants and sailors from the narrow path of salvation. Genevers laced with the alluring, pagan tang of cubeb or galangal might leave the drinker dissatisfied with good, plain Dutch bread and cheese (and, perhaps, with good, plain Calvinist religion). In a 1634 sermon Gisbertus Voetius, a theologian at Utrecht, fulminated against tobacco and strong drink. The former offered merely a foretaste of the sulphurous fires of hell, but the latter verged on sacrilege, a kind of anti-mass in which "liquid bread" and spirits of wine were guzzled for base, physical pleasure. For Voetius, genever was nothing less than Protestant wheat corrupted by an alchemical transformation, and spiked with pagan spices and sugar—an emblem of the sinister side of Dutch imperial might.


But the novel pleasures of genever were not limited to the citizens of the Dutch Republic. An appreciation for the new drink was quick to spread, first and foremost through the voyages of the VOC. Just as Royal Navy tars received their daily rum ration, so VOC officers and men were issued with half-pints of genever, and by the end of the seventeenth century Schiedam genever was on sale in Batavia and other Dutch outposts in the East Indies. It also achieved enduring popularity amongst Dutch soldiers, and this seems to have been the route along which a taste for genever reached Britain. In 1585 Elizabeth I sent troops to support the Dutch army in their struggle for independence. These soldiers, along with English mercenaries who fought in the Thirty Years'

War, brought back both a sneaking admiration for "Dutch courage" (a Victorian phrase, though the idea is much older) and a raging thirst for genever.

The most striking upsurge in English appetites for gin (the subject of the next chapter) is usually dated to the aftermath of the Glorious Revolution in 1688, but it was foreshadowed by the return of another monarch from the Low Countries—Charles II. After the end of the English Civil War and the execution of his father, Charles and his comrades lived for a decade in exile at the courts of Europe. Though he spent most of his time in France, he passed a few months in The Hague, and witnessed the contrast between the rich, cosmopolitan Dutch Republic and poor, war-torn England. Writing in 1726, with the hindsight of two generations, Daniel Defoe saw Charles' return in 1660 as the turning point in English spirit consumption:

> Our drunkenness as a national vice takes its epoch at the Restoration . . . Very merry, and very mad, and very drunken the people were, and grew more and more so every day.

Genever—"gin" or "Hollands" to English tongues—did not take off immediately. In his diary for October 1663 Samuel Pepys recorded that "Sir W. Batten did advise me to take some . . . strong water made of juniper," but this was a medical prescription for a nasty colic. Pepys, who made a point of recording every new food and drink that he encountered, does not mention gin, genever or Hollands elsewhere in his writings. The great alteration in English tastes came in the 1670s, and was driven by two developments. First, a run of good harvests and a consequent fall in grain prices enabled distillers to make grain spirit in larger volumes. Second, the end of the third Anglo-Dutch war in 1674 removed one major bar to the importation of Dutch genever. By the end of the century a cask of Schiedam Hollands cost thirty-six florins, compared with seventy florins for a barrel of French brandy. Defoe noted that London "suddenly . . . began to abound in strong Water-shops," and genever was also sold by the glass in many taverns, particularly in ports. New distilleries were founded to meet this demand, and by 1697 a former monastery and debtors' prison in Plymouth was working as a malt-house and distillery—the beginnings of the first distinctively English gin.

But even at the end of the seventeenth century there was still a creative interfusion between alchemy and the commercial gin trade. Consider, for example, the career of William Y-Worth. Little is known about Y-Worth's origins: he seems to have been born in Rotterdam, and his name is apparently anglicised from the Dutch. Most likely he came over shortly after the Glorious Revolution, capitalizing on the budding English taste for genever and the ban on imports of French brandy. By the early 1690s he owned a distillery in London, and later wrote a series of practical guides to distilling and brewing. Y-Worth's *Compleat Distiller,* published in 1705, includes some of the earliest published recipes in English for gin as a drink rather than a medicine, and these are reproduced in Appendix 1. The end of his career is as mysterious as its beginning: for reasons lost to history, he had left London by 1710, and was practicing surgery at Woodbridge in Suffolk.

Wider reading, however, reveals that Y-Worth's stills produced much more than gin. As "Cleidophorus Mystagogus, Professor of Spagyric Medicine" and member of the "Accademia Spagyrica Nova," he published on alchemy and Paracelsian medicine, in books like the *Pharmacopoeia Spagyrica Nova* and *Trifertes Sagani, or Immortal Dissolvent.* But alchemical thought and imagery suffused all his writings: he saw brewing, distilling and alchemical work as aspects of a "chymical" tradition reaching back through Paracelsus to the philosopher-chemists of ancient Egypt. In *Cerevisiarii Comes, or, The New and True Art of Brewing,* published in 1692, he described—in appropriately metaphorical language—how distillation might yield cordials and elixirs beyond the imagination of the average genever-swilling Londoner:

> Distillation is a converting of Bodies into Water, Oyl and Spirit; Rectification is a reiterated Elevation, by which the before mentioned are separated from their more hidden and internal impurities; and the Spiritual, Essential humidity, from the more Phlegmatick and Aqueous.

Y-Worth, like the medieval alchemists, saw his work as drawing on the grand transformations of the cosmos. And like Paracelsus, he saw the human body as an alchemical still:

> Nature makes various Degrees of Concoction, by each of which the Nourishing Vertues are bettered: You have an Example of this in Man; for by the first Concoction the Food is made Chyle, by a higher one, Blood, and as it is inspired with the Vital Flame so doth the pure and truly Sublime Spirits rarefy themselves for the Vital Nourishment, which indeed is the highest degree of Separation and Concoction, whereby the seed is spiritualized and made the *Quintessence* of all, to remain in its proper Vessels for another Generation.

Distillation could concentrate this quintessence and, in the same gesture, expel "the Wild and Unruly *Gass,* which is the grand Enemy and fatal Destroyer of the Life of Man." Further transformations might yield the mighty "Liquor Alkahest of Helmont, the great Hilech of Paracelsus, the Sal Circulatum Minus of Ludovicus de Comit"—the highest form of quintessence that could be made on Earth:

> An Universal Fire, [it] dissolves and opens the Textures of all Beings, in the Vegetable, Animal and Mineral Kingdoms, into their next nearest Matter, which is Saline, Sulphureous, Aqueous and Potable, diffusive in any *Liquor,* and so comes immediately to Nature's Relief, and by the Specifick Virtue manifested from Power into Act, Diseases, tho' never so deplorable, may be overcome and cut down, as Grass or Weeds with a Scythe in the hand of a Mower.

Even the greatest human alchemist, however, could not hope to replicate God's achievement in distilling his own quintessence into his son: "that *Grand Tincture and Divine Essence,* I mean the Magisterial Blood of Christ, which is the *Quintessence* of Heaven and Earth, and the Fulness of all the Glories thereof."

Y-Worth's alchemical *credo* may well have chimed with the views of his most famous collaborator—Isaac Newton. The quantity of Newton's work on optics and gravity pales in comparison with his vast corpus of unpublished writings on alchemy and theology. In his private library at Trinity College, Cambridge, he had well-thumbed copies of most of Y-Worth's alchemical works, and he wrote to Y-Worth several times to compare notes on the "Indefatigable Search" for alchemical wisdom. Indeed, Y-Worth seems to have been his final correspondent on this subject, as the locus of Newton's career moved from the cloisters of Trinity to the more public, less forgiving setting of the House of Commons and the Royal Society. If Newton was (in John Maynard Keynes' lapidary phrase) the last of the magicians, this Dutch-born gin-distiller was Newton's last alchemist.


Y-Worth embodies the transformations—metaphorical and literal —through which gin had passed by the end of the seventeenth century. Over the course of five hundred years a medicinal tonic distilled by Italian monks had become, through a series of global encounters, an all-too-worldly and highly lucrative pleasure. And his work makes quite clear that, through all these mutations, the fusion of juniper and spirit continued to carry ancient meanings and resonances. This was not simply an intoxicating beverage, but a cordial that carried overtones of therapeutic power, Oriental mystique, and alchemical awe. But the political revolution that brought Y-Worth to England also wrought a revolution in the status and meaning of gin. In the next chapter we'll walk the streets of eighteenth-century London, and witness what happened when this highly-charged liquid became an agent of oblivion.

James Gillray, *The Dissolution, or, the Alchymist Producing
an Aetherial Representation,* 1796. Satirists from Hogarth
to Gillray seized upon distillation as a symbol for transience
and ephemerality—here, William Pitt's dubious ambitions
in the House of Commons.

# 2

# Rough Spirits

THE CONSOLATIONS OF poverty in eighteenth-century London were few and far between. But in *Geneva: A Poem in Blank Verse,* published in 1734, the poetaster Stephen Buck proposed that one thing might take away the manifold cares of destitution, cutting across rank and status, and making each man the equal (though not the superior) of his fellows:

> What can impart such Solace to Mankind,
> As this most powerful Dram, which levels All
> The different Ranks in this unequal World?
> The poor Plebeian, elevate by Gin,
> Fancies himself a King . . .

Faced with the torrent of invective unleashed by his peers against gin and gin drinkers, however, Buck's stumbling verses were nothing more than a few ineffective trickles. In their eyes, gin was "Scorch-gut," "Strip-me-naked," "Kill-me-quick," "Cuckold's Comfort"—a moral, medical and mercantile disaster played out on the streets of the capital. It consumed vast quantities of good English grain, to produce nothing more than a street drug cut with industrial by-products. Fathers drank away their wages, leaving their families destitute. Mothers abandoned or even murdered their children, turning to prostitution to get a few pennies for gin. Infants were quieted and stunted with gin-laced possets, and some met violent ends through the drunken neglect of their nurses. All trades, all commerce, all relationships were thrown aside in the pursuit of this rough, potent liquor. What would become of the nation, its economy, its navy, its church, its hearty Anglo-Saxon stock, if a tide of gin continued to erode the very foundations of English life?

The gin craze has become one of the set-piece scenes of eighteenth-century English history. Tobias Smollett, Thomas Babington Macaulay, G.M. Trevelyan, and a small army of more recent scholars have taken their turn at re-imagining the scenes of drunkenness and destitution portrayed by Buck's contemporaries. And the gin craze is no hazy historiographical construction. Contemporary statistics show a dramatic rise in gin consumption from the first years of the eighteenth century, peaking in 1743. Public fears were expressed in pamphlets, plays, and news-sheets between the early 1720s and the early 1750s. And political concern was reflected in eight Acts of Parliament, known collectively as the "Gin Acts," passed between 1729 and 1751.

But the closer one looks, the more one begins to realize that the story of the gin craze is not so straightforward. All of the anxieties expressed by eighteenth-century writers about the effects of gin—from the negligence of inebriated midwives to the destruction of the English character—had, as we saw in the last chapter, been common currency for a century or more. Likewise the notion that spirits caused a new and peculiarly aggressive kind of drunkenness, and that commercial distillation threatened the nation's supply of bread. And the gin craze was not, in truth, a national phenomenon. Gin did not run freely through the streets of Polperro, nor did it threaten scholarly pursuits in Oxford, nor did it distract Highland clansmen from their Jacobite discontent. It was confined to a handful of large, wealthy, port cities: Bristol, Norwich, Portsmouth, and most of all London. Even in London, the worst excesses took place in two districts—the slums of the East End, and the fleshpots of the West End. And drinking to wild excess was not limited to poor Londoners and their gin: gentlemen's clubs around the country, like the Select Society in Edinburgh (whose members included Joseph Black, Adam Smith and David

Hume), became famous for their wild antics and inebriated routs. But these men favored more respectable tipples—sherry, brandy, claret, port—and their drunkenness seemed to have a very different meaning. As Jessica Warner, the most incisive historian of the gin craze, has observed, there were in reality two gin crazes. One was conducted in print and in Parliament, and was couched in the language of righteous indignation and moral hysteria. The other took place in taverns and gin-shops, courtrooms and prisons, and most of all in the lives of London's poorest citizens.

How can we untangle these two intertwined threads, mythopoeic hyperbole and quotidian reality? What went into eighteenth-century gin, and who made it? What did it mean to drinkers, and to those who denounced them? Strangest of all, how did juniper-flavored spirit—once a mysterious quintessence, a medicine, a symbol of Dutch independence—become the object of such vilification? Just as the creation of genever was the result of world-changing cultural collisions, so the gin craze offers a microcosm of the fault-lines within English society at the beginning of the Enlightenment. The dominant and the disenfranchised, the rich and the poor, John Barleycorn and Madame Geneva, the city and the countryside, agriculture and industry, Whig and Tory, private life and the public sphere—all these divisions influenced the course of the gin craze. But its roots lie in one deeply symbolic encounter, between the English people and the Dutch prince who came to rule them.

On Guy Fawkes' Day 1688 a slight, asthmatic, Protestant man stepped from a ship's boat on to the shingle at Torbay in Devon. William, Prince of Orange, Stadtholder of the Dutch Republic, expected to face heavy resistance from the forces of James II, the reigning king, and brought with him twenty-one thousand troops. But William's forces saw very little action on the march to London, though they were later party to bloody fighting in Ireland and Scotland. After a week or two of uncertainty, army commanders and most of the population welcomed the Dutch prince, and on 23rd December James fled to France—the beginning of a long and bitter exile.

Was this, as Dutch historians have long insisted, an invasion, or a "Glorious Revolution"—the term preferred by generations of English scholars? James' authority was hopelessly compromised by his Catholicism, and for many of his subjects the final straw came with the birth of his son, Prince James (later the Jacobite "Old Pretender") in June 1688. Neither Whigs nor Tories—the leading factions in the English court and Parliament—could bear the prospect of a Catholic dynasty on the English throne, and on 18th June the "Immortal Seven," a cabal of six noblemen and a bishop, wrote to William, inviting him to take the throne. After protracted negotiations William and his wife Mary, James' daughter, were crowned in Westminster Abbey on 11th April 1689.

Both the old divisions and the new unities of the Glorious Revolution found expression in drink. Tories quaffed claret, and Whigs toasted one another in port or beer, but gin was the *boisson du jour* of the new settlement. We have no concrete evidence that William drank gin, though he certainly enjoyed other spirits, and on many occasions his courtiers noted, with a touch of weariness, that their master and his boon companions had once more drunk themselves into unconsciousness. For satirists and propagandists, however, the connection between the Dutch liberator and the Dutch national spirit was a gift. During the debates over the first Gin Act in 1729 one "Alexander Blunt"—pen-name of Elias Bocker, a prominent distiller—tried to give gin a royal touch:

Martial WILLIAM drank
GENEVA, yet no Age could ever boast
A braver Prince than He.

And in an anonymous pamphlet, *The Life of Mother Gin,* published in 1736, another hack parodied William's journey to the English throne and gin's route to the English palate:

Mother Gin was of Dutch parentage, but her father, who was a substantial trader in the city of Rotterdam ... came to settle in London, where ... he married an English woman, and obtained an Act of Parliament for his naturalization.

But the association between the new regime and gin was more than merely symbolic, and at the turn of the eighteenth century a number of factors came together to enlarge the English appetite for gin. English naval power grew as the VOC declined: by the 1720s, the English were the largest trading nation in Europe, and could back up their ambitions with the largest and most feared navy of any Western power. The first stirrings of an English consumer revolution transformed the nation's outlook, as the old, rural, agrarian order began to give way to an urban economy based on commerce and manufacture. For the aristocrats whose plotting had brought William to power, this was bad news: their fortunes were built on land rents, and they needed to maintain the value of grain grown on their estates. One of the first major pieces of legislation passed under William—an "Act for encouraging the distilling of brandy and spirits from corn" in 1690—did exactly this, lowering the duties on low wines distilled from English malted corn, but raising the duties on beer and spirits made from any other materials, and allowing anyone to begin distilling gin if they bought an inexpensive license and gave ten days' notice to the local excise-man.

Brandy was another target of the 1690 Act, and this points towards another consequence of the Glorious Revolution: more than a century of European wars, mostly against France. By placing punitive duties on French wines and spirits, the government hoped to accomplish two things. First, to bankrupt their enemy by reducing their income. Second, to prop up the market for native spirits, and in doing so both protect the price of grain and raise government revenue from duties on English gin. In one sense, these measures were staggeringly effective. According to Exchequer statistics, the quantities of spirits consumed in England and Wales rose from 572,000 gallons in 1684 to 1,223,000 gallons in 1700, with a corresponding jump in government income. Land rents, however, continued to fall, as a series of bumper harvests flooded the nation's corn exchanges, and aristocrats put pressure on the government to transfer even more of the tax burden to excisable commodities. There were good precedents for this—after the Great Fire of London, St. Paul's Cathedral had been rebuilt with the proceeds of a tax on sea-coal—and public appetites for tobacco and spirits seemed limitless.

English enthusiasm for gin survived the death of William in 1702, the reign of Mary's sister Anne (during which the 1707 Act of Union created the kingdom of Great Britain), and the accession of another European house—Hanover—in 1714. To all these governments, the idea of raising duties on a lucrative and popular drink, one that did so much to keep the wheels of commerce turning, was a far more tempting prospect than yet another raid on the coffers of powerful and vociferous noblemen. Whig landowners made common cause with commercial distillers: in a pamphlet printed in 1710, the Company of Distillers warned the government against taking any action to depress sales of gin:

> The Making of [spirits] from Malted Corn and other Materials, hath greatly increased, and been of service to the Publick, in regard to her Majesty's Revenue, and the Landed Interest . . . There is nothing that ever more required the Care of the Legislature, than the preserving and improving of the British Distillery. It is by the Consumption of Grain that Rents are raised, Tillage kept up, Labor and Industry of the common People rewarded, the Revenue improved . . .

This logic found its most controversial expression in the writings of Bernard de Mandeville. Mandeville, like "Mother Gin," was Dutch by extraction, and after studying medicine at Leiden he came to London as the dust of the Glorious Revolution was settling. Setting up as a philosopher and economist, he made a niche for himself as the first serious analyst of the British consumer revolution. In *The Fable of the Bees, or Private Vices, Public Benefits*, published in 1714, Mandeville used a poem—"The Grumbling Hive, or Knaves turn'd Honest"—as a springboard for a scathing allegory of British hypocrisy:

> A Spacious Hive well stock'd with Bees,
> That lived in Luxury and Ease;
> And yet as fam'd for Laws and Arms,
> As yielding large and early Swarms;
> Was counted the great Nursery
> Of Sciences and Industry.
> No Bees had better Government,
> More Fickleness, or less Content.

But Mandeville's bees are also corrupt, greedy fraudsters, and this is—of course—the secret of their success. Lacking virtue themselves, they generate, through their tireless industry, a state of prosperity and happiness. Poverty and failure come only when Jove, tired of hearing the bees lament their depravity, makes them all unfailingly honest. In a masterstroke of unsentimental, Machiavellian *realpolitik,* Mandeville pointed out that the consequences of vice actually contributed to the sum of collective happiness, and he demonstrated the truth of this argument with the example of gin. Mandeville was no friend of gin, and gave a withering critique of its effects on poor drinkers:

> Nothing is more destructive, either in regard to the Health or the Vigilance and Industry of the Poor, than the infamous Liquor ... Gin, that charms the unactive, the desperate and crazy of either Sex, and makes the starving Sot behold his Rags and Nakedness with stupid Indolence ... It is a fiery Lake that sets the Brain in Flame.

But he also recognized that these ills, however painful to behold, were countered with the many social and economic benefits of gin distillation:

The rents that are received, the ground that is tilled, the tools that are made, the cattle that are employed, and, above all, the multitude of poor that are maintained, by the variety of labor, required in husbandry, in malting, in carriage, and distillation.

Mandeville's argument touched a raw nerve in an England coming to terms with the new cultural landscape of the consumer revolution. He was dubbed "Man-Devil," and accused of cynicism, amorality and atheism, though Samuel Johnson later said that reading *The Fable of the Bees* at Oxford had "opened his eyes into real life very much." Johnson's tipple was tea—he knew from bitter experience that once he started drinking anything harder, he could not stop—and in this sense he was part of another consumer craze, one which took place in the drawing-rooms of the fashionable *demi-monde* rather than the slums. Tea was expensive and exotic, its consumption ritualized and fraught with *faux-pas,* and to some it was as deadly in its effects as were spirits. The philanthropist Jonas Hanway yoked them together in his *Essay on Tea,* published in 1757: "What an army has gin and tea destroyed." Hanway's histrionics remind us that mounting fears over gin were only one aspect of a broader sense of apprehension about the impact of exotic new stimulants on the lower orders, as a desire for expensive consumables trickled down through the social hierarchy. Tea, coffee, chocolate and spirits could over-excite the body and the brain, but they might also provoke aspirations for a life of leisured elegance and spendthrift consumption—a perilous prospect in an age obsessed with the promise of progress and the threat of *déclassement.*

The upheavals of the Glorious Revolution and the consumer revolution were followed by further financial and political turmoil. In 1713 the Treaty of Utrecht concluded the War of the Spanish Succession, and the return of thousands of demobbed soldiers heightened public fears of beggars, muggers and highwaymen. Quarrels between Whigs and Tories were at their most rancorous in the years of Queen Anne's reign, and outbreaks of sustained political violence were met with a repressive Riot Act in 1715. The South Sea Company—a glorified pyramid scheme—collapsed in September 1720, suicides, recriminations and bankruptcies trailing in its wake, and in the autumn of 1721 the bubonic plague reached Marseilles, terrifying those who could still recall the Great Plague of 1665. Londoners were frightened, anxious, and obsessed with the kind of street crime and social breakdown fast becoming associated with cheap gin.

But why did England alone experience a gin craze? Dutch soldiers and traders had brought a taste for genever to the New World—it was produced, briefly, in the Dutch port of Nieuw-Amsterdam, later New York, on Long Island—but it remained a minority taste, and American pioneer farmers and plantation-owners preferred brandy, rum or raw moonshine whisky. Though Parisian cafés and street-vendors sold flavored *eaux-de-vie* and brandies, the guilds of the French *ancien régime* held strong monopolies over distillation, and the pervasive presence of government spies made tight-lipped sobriety a safer bet than inebriated verbal incontinence. When poor Parisians drank to excess and into the night, they preferred the watered wine sold in *guinguettes*—taverns and dance-halls set up outside the walls of Paris, and hence beyond the reach of its laws. Some Scottish drinkers, particularly in the lowland cities, favored gin, and James Boswell gulped shots of it to enliven bacchanals with his Edinburgh cronies. Most Scots, however, continued to favor claret or whisky, drinks which came to stand for the exiled Stuart "King o'er the Water."

Only in London were the raw materials of the gin craze—deregulated distilling, low grain prices, urban poverty, a taste for cheap consumables—all present. And it was here, in this roiling, bubbling human alembic, that they were distilled into the very quintessence of a scandal.

London in the second quarter of the eighteenth century was a city of superlatives. By 1716 it was the largest conurbation in Europe, a grand experiment in metropolitan living, teeming with more than half a million people. It was rich in theaters and bookshops, opera-houses and art galleries, and for the time its population was positively literate. Current estimates suggest that around 45% of male and 48% of female Londoners could read, and they were not short of reading matter: pornography and sermons, journals and pamphlets, many by Daniel Defoe, Jonathan Swift or Alexander Pope, all at the height of their powers. London was the principal trading station of the British East India Company, and anything bought and sold anywhere in the known world was available in the warehouses of the city's merchants. The only commodities wanting were peace and privacy, and these could hardly be had at any price. The city was groaning with food and awash with drink, available to all ranks and qualities, in taverns and pubs, markets and coffee-houses, sold by Cockney eel-girls and Devonshire pie-men. And drink was everywhere, filling the interstices of life and culture, the all-purpose lubricant of London's social and commercial wheels.

The dazzling growth of the capital changed the face of the nation, and around eight thousand people migrated to London every year. They came to make fortunes, but also to remake themselves. New arrivals quickly realized that London offered a matchless opportunity to cast off their old identities, and to become whatever they could talk themselves into. But fortunes could vary as quickly as the skies over the Thames valley, and one might, if one lacked luck, see both faces of the city: a vibrant paradigm of progress and prosperity, but also a *tableau vivant* of miserable, drunken poverty. In 1743 Henry Lowther, Viscount Lonsdale, left the fastness of his Cumbrian estate to take up his seat in the House of Lords, but found the streets around Whitehall so sordid that he quickly returned to the Lake District:

> Whoever shall pass among the Streets, will find Wretches stretched upon the Pavement, insensible and motionless, and only removed by the Charity of Passengers from the Danger of being crushed by

Carriages or trampled by Horses, or strangled with Filth in the common Sewers; and others less helpless perhaps, but more dangerous, who have drunk too much to fear Punishment, but not enough to hinder them from provoking it, who think themselves in the Elevation of Drunkenness intitled to treat all those with Contempt whom their Dress distinguishes from them, and to resent every Injury which in the Heat of their Imagination they suppose themselves to suffer, with the utmost Rage of Resentment, Violence of Rudeness, and Scurrility of Tongue.

England's capital was in reality two cities—the Roman City of London and the Saxon seat of Westminster—and the two great city churches, St. Paul's Cathedral and Westminster Abbey, connected by the bustling thoroughfares of Fleet Street and the Strand, became the twin poles around which London life revolved. But it was the hinterland between these two cities that became the most notorious public forum for the iniquities of the gin craze. Hanoverian London's pleasure district was concentrated in a triangle, defined by the crossroads of Seven Dials to the north, Charing Cross to the west, and the church of St. Clement Danes to the east. Here one could find gambling dens, cock-pits, brothels, taverns, theaters—and the highest concentration of gin-shops in London.

Johnson's entry on "geneva" in his *Dictionary* casts some light on the nature of the gin sold within the bounds of this unholy trinity. Johnson illustrated his definition with a quotation from John Hill's *History of the Materia Medica,* a pharmacopoeia published in 1751:

> At present only a better kind is distilled from the juniper-berry: what is commonly sold is made with no better an ingredient than oil of turpentine, put into the still, with a little common salt and the coarsest spirit.

Other eighteenth-century gin recipes, reproduced in Appendix 1, drive Hill's point home. One of the immediate consequences of the gin craze was a fundamental shift in the character of the drink itself. Juniper—the defining ingredient of proto-gins and Dutch genever—was supplanted by a veritable chemistry set of additives, which could mimic juniper's flavor for a fraction of the effort involved in harvesting, drying and preparing juniper berries. And sugar, grown on slave plantations in the West Indies, could be used to smooth the rough edges of poor-quality spirit. This made gin more appealing to women consumers with a taste for traditional sweet cordials. Some distillers, reaching for the higher end of the market, continued to follow the Dutch example. In his *Complete Distiller,* published in 1757, Ambrose Cooper blamed the "the Vulgar" for driving up demand for gin, and forcing distillers and apothecaries to adulterate their wares. His own recipe for "Royal Geneva" was straight out of Schiedam:

> For making 10 gallons of Geneva—take of juniper berries three pounds, proof spirit 10 gallons, water 4 gallons. Draw off by a gentle fire until the feints begin to rise and make up your goods to the strength required with clean water.

Even Cooper, however, included a recipe for "what is generally sold at the common Ale-houses," based on "ordinary Malt Spirits," oil of turpentine and salt. "It is surprising," he noted dryly, "that People should accustom themselves to drink it for pleasure." Other manufacturers went even further. In the 1740s Beaufoy, James & Co, a distillery based in Vauxhall, produced a gin which included not only oil of turpentine, but also oil of almonds as a substitute for coriander, and "oil of vitriol"—sulphuric acid. This, plus pepper or ginger, gave cheap gins an attention-grabbing fieriness, while allowing distillers to water down their products—a move aided by the latest developments in natural philosophy.

Well into the eighteenth century, the standard method for assessing the strength of spirit was to mix a sample with gunpowder and then apply a flame. If the powder caught, the spirit was at least "100° proof"—in today's terms, roughly 57% alcohol by volume. In 1729 John Clarke published a short description of his new "hydrometer" in the *Philosophical Transactions of the Royal Society*—a calibrated and weighted glass tube designed "to shew the different Specifick Gravity of all Wines or Waters, by sinking deeper in the lighter, and emerging more out of the heavier Liquors." Clarke's hydrometer was difficult to use, and was not taken up by the Excise until 1787, but it reflected a new mood amongst London's deregulated gin-distillers. How could innovative techniques and instruments, alongside more traditional scams like adulteration and watering, be used to maximize profit and minimize the duties they had to pay? And their profits kept rising, alongside the British appetite for gin. National consumption of excisable spirits reached two million gallons in 1710, three million in 1730, six million in 1735, and peaked in 1743 at more than eight million gallons—roughly a gallon a year for every man, woman and child in the country, though perhaps as high as ten gallons a year in gin hotspots like London.

Even at the height of the gin craze, however, gin was never the only game in town. Daniel Defoe noted some of the different kinds of "hot waters" on sale in Hanoverian London:

> Aqua Vitae, Aqua Mirabilis, Aqua Solis, Aqua Dulcis, Aniseed Water, Cinnamon Water, Clove Water, Plague Water, Colic Water, which in short was Geneva.

And with nicknames ranging from "Tow Row" and "Royal Poverty" to "South Sea Mountain" and "King Theodore of Corsica," who could be certain exactly what had gone into the sweet, fiery liquid being doled out by the cupful? In this sense, the drink at the heart of the gin craze was not a particular brand or recipe, but rather an idea—the heady idea of hot, cheap spirit consumed to excess. But where was this idea on sale, and who bought into it?

> Gin-shops are undoubtedly the Nurseries of all manner of Vice and Wickedness. There it is that the old Practitioners in Roguery assemble, where meeting with young idle Fellows, who elope from

their Parents, Friends or Masters, they instruct them in all the Arts and Tricks of their own Profession, which is, of robbing on the Highway, picking Pockets, forging Hands, breaking open Houses, Clipping and Coining, and all other Crimes.

Thus Henry Fielding, magistrate and novelist, writing towards the end of the gin craze in 1751. And here is Thomas Wilson, Bishop of Sodor and Man, at the height of public concern in 1736:

In one place not far from East Smithfield a trader has a large empty room backwards, where as his wretched guests get intoxicated, they are laid together in heaps promiscuously, men, women, and children, till they recover their senses, when they proceed to drink on, or, having spent all they had, go out to find the wherewithal to return to the same dreadful pursuit; and how they acquire more money the session papers too often acquaint us.

Fielding's and Wilson's fulminations underline the biggest challenge we face in understanding the gin craze. The enemies of gin wrote vividly and at length about the iniquities of gin-shops and gin-sellers, but surviving sources rarely preserve the voices of traders and consumers themselves. What evidence we do have suggests that gin was made in all manners of places, from large, licensed, commercial distilleries to small, illicit stills concealed in the cupboards and outhouses of slum tenements. And it seems to have been sold at almost every conceivable opportunity: in church crypts and prison yards, private clubs and public executions, river-boats and horse-drawn carts, and most of all in gin-shops.

Some scholars—notably the German sociologist Jürgen Habermas —have contrasted gin-shops with that other eighteenth-century institution, the coffee-house. Habermas sees coffee-houses as outposts of rational debate and civil conversation, one of the places in which a free and fairly democratic "public sphere," so central to the European Enlightenment, was conceived. Gin-shops, on the other hand, were little more than bear-pits of invective and drunken violence. Habermas is right on the money when it comes to idealized portrayals of coffee-houses in eighteenth-century literature, but in reality the line between high talk and low brutality was rather less distinct. Many coffee-houses also sold brandy and gin on the side, and a number of gin-shops brewed coffee for their regulars. Both were spaces for convivial gatherings and occasional brawls, and both witnessed all kinds of deals and encounters, from bank loans to dog-fights, from share issues to cross-dressing show-marriages.

Moralists and satirists execrated the gin-shops, but itinerant gin-vendors were the most calumnized of all. Often women, scraping a living in the months when seasonal employment dried up, they were dismissed as "the very Rubbish of the Creation":

> The worst of both Sexes, but most of them weather-beaten Fellows, that have misspent their Youth. Here stands an old sloven in a Wig actually putrify'd, squeez'd up in a Corner, recommending a Dram of it to the Goers-by: There another in Rags, as rusty as a Nonjuring Clergyman's Cassock, with several Bottles in a Basket, stirs about with it, where the Throng is the thinnest, and tears his Throat like a Flounder Fellow, with crying his Commodity: And further off you may see the Head of a third, who has ventur'd into the middle of the Current, and minds his Business as he is fluctuating in the irregular Stream: Whilst higher up, an old decrepit Woman sits dreaming within on a Bulk, and over-against her, in a Soldier's Coat, her termagant Daughter sells the Sots Comfort with great Dispatch.

If London's gin-sellers were denigrated so aggressively, what of those who bought and consumed their wares? Once again, we have many descriptions by those who sought to take the moral high ground. Take, for example, the account of "Saynought Slyboots" in *The Tavern Scuffle, or the Club in an Uproar,* a satire published by the city's brewers in 1726, attacking the "Scorch-Gut" distillers:

> Go along the streets and you shall see every brandy shop swarming with scandalous wretches, swearing and drinking as if they had no notion of a future state. There they get drunk by daylight, and

after that run up and down the streets swearing, cursing and talking beastliness like so many devils; setting ill examples and debauching our youth in general. Nay, to such a height are they arrived in their wickedness, that in a manner, they commit lewdness in the open streets.Young creatures, girls of 12 and 13 years of age, drink Geneva like fishes, and make themselves unfit to live in sober families; this damn'd bewitching liquor makes them shameless, and they talk enough to make a man shudder again; there is no passing the streets for 'em, so shameless are they grown . . .

But in order to encounter these folk on their own terms, we have to look elsewhere, in the theaters and the courts and on the steps of the gallows. The characters in John Gay's *Beggar's Opera,* first performed in January 1728 and one of the biggest successes of the Hanoverian stage, are intimately familiar with all three, and ease their passage through life with lashings of gin. In this scene, set in the gloomy precincts of Newgate Prison, Peachum, the leader of a criminal gang, flirts with Mrs. Trapes, a fence:

PEACHUM: One may know by your kiss, that your Ginn is excellent.
MRS. TRAPES: I was always very curious in my Liquors.
PEACHUM: There is no perfum'd Breath like it—I have been long acquainted with the Flavor of those Lips . . .
MRS. TRAPES (*holding out cup*): Fill it up—I take as large Draughts of Liquor, as I did of Love.—I hate a Flincher in either.

Real-life criminal encounters might be equally theatrical. On 4th December 1724 Eleanor Lock, a pie-seller in Clerkenwell, appeared before the Old Bailey, charged with stealing "a Silver Watch and Chain, value 3l. 10s." from one Thomas Miller. According to Miller, they had met as he walked home to Islington on a night in late November:

Tis a long way, (says she) and you had better drink before you go any further, for fear you should faint upon the Road.—Come, my

Dear, treat me with a Pint. With all my Heart (says he), but what House shall we go to?—Why, I'll tell you Child, I don't much Care for drinking Beer; but if you'll go to my Landlady's in Butcher's Alley, we'll have a Quartern of Gin.

Finding himself susceptible to her charms, Miller took her to the gin-shop, and left after half an hour or so of carousing. He did not get far, however, before "he mist his Watch, but could not imagine which way it could be gone without his perceiving it." A constable was called; Eleanor at first denied all knowledge, but when she was taken before a magistrate "she confest [sic] that she had hid it in a Hole in the Chimney; and being brought back, she shew'd them the Place, and took it out." Found guilty, she was sentenced to transportation. Others, though, were treated less leniently.

Amongst the mob at any public execution would be hawkers crying copies of the last confession and dying speech of the condemned—one of the most enduringly popular genres in Enlightenment publishing. Londoners, then as now, loved a good murder, and their city was, according to Henry Fielding, "a vast Wood or Forest, in which a thief may harbor with as great Security as wild Beasts do in the Desarts of Africa or Arabia." A provoking combination of confessional piety and tabloid prurience, last confessions were the perfect medium for the ghost-writers and printers of Grub Street and Paternoster Square. This meant, ironically, that the speeches printed and distributed to the crowd at Newgate or Tyburn had, as often as not, been put into the mouth of the prisoner by a hack; their real last words were slurred or rendered inaudible by the effects of a final mouthful of gin.

The most infamous criminal celebrity of the gin craze was Jack Sheppard—house-breaker, highwayman, and loudmouth. Born in Stepney in 1702, Sheppard was apprenticed to a carpenter, but quickly turned to crime. He was caught and sentenced to hang, but in the space of one year he escaped four times from the condemned cell at Newgate. He ran rings around his bumbling captors, even Jonathan Wild, the legendary "Thief-Taker General," but his bravado was his downfall: rather than fleeing the city, he returned ostentatiously to his old haunts "like a Dog to his Vomit," drinking gin and eating oysters in the taverns of Drury Lane and Bishopsgate. Sheppard's fondness for gin is recounted here in his own words, in a letter he wrote to a friend during his last escape in 1724 (which also demonstrates his relish for dubious puns on London street-names). After "Fileing, Defileing, Sawing, Climbing" his way out of the condemned cell at Newgate, he:

> went on to *Shoe-lane* end but there meeting with a *Bully Hack* of the Town, he would have shov'd me down, which my Spirit resenting, though a *brawny Dog,* I soon *Coller'd* him, fell *Souse* at him, then with his own Cane I *strapp'd* till he was forced to *Buckle* too, and hold his *Tongue,* in so much he durst not say his *Soul* was his own, and was glad to pack off at *Last,* and turn his *Heels* upon me: I was glad he was gone you may be sure, and *dextrously* made a *Hand* of my *Feet* under the *Leg-Tavern* . . . By this time being Fainty and nigh Spent, I put forward, and seeing a *Light* near the *Savoy-Gate,* I was resolved not to make *Light* of the Opportunity, but call'd for an hearty Dram of *Luther* and *Calvin, that is, Mum* [beer] and *Geneva* mix'd; but having Fasted so long before, it soon got into my Noddle, and e'er I had gone twenty steps, it had so intirely *Stranded* my Reason, that by the time I came to *Half-Moon-street* end, it gave a *New-Exchange* to my Senses, and made me quite *Lunatick.*

Other convicts lacked Sheppard's flamboyance, but made up for it by keeping their wits about them. In the mid-1720s the street robber James Dalton was convicted of the theft of thirty-nine shillings' worth of unspecified articles, and sentenced to transportation to "his Majesty's plantations in *America.*" Dalton, however, had other plans:

> One *Hescot,* a Prisoner, who had about fifty Pound of Bisket, two Caggs of Geneva, a Cheese and some Butter on board, went up one Day upon Deck for the Air, and in the mean while we ransacked

all his Stores; but upon his Return, he finding out what had been done, went and made Complaint to the Captain, who threaten'd to whip us all round to find out the right Man, whereupon sixteen of us agreed to secure the whole Ship's Crew (being but twelve in Number, Captain and Boy included) before the *Whipping Gale blew harder,* which we accomplished.

Taking control of the ship, the prisoners shared out Hescot's genever, but made an agreement that "every one that was drunk upon his Watch, so as his Arms could be taken from him, or was caught in the Hold with the Women Prisoners, should receive twelve Lashes." Dalton and his fellow mutineers put themselves ashore at Cape Finisterre—drinking a final toast in genever with the captain and the mate—and made their way across the Pyrenees to Amsterdam, where he made himself a good living as a pickpocket. But London called, and he returned—a mistake, as he was twice more convicted and transported, before being sent to the gallows.

Men like Sheppard and Dalton achieved fame for their bluster and boldness, but the figure most closely identified with the gin craze was not a gin-hawker or a highwayman (though in many stories she did meet her maker at the end of a rope). No portraits survive of "Madame Geneva" or "Mother Gin"—perhaps the closest thing we have is the female figure in the foreground of William Hogarth's "Gin Lane"—and depictions of her in ballads and satires are far from complimentary: one writer had her family "springing from the Dunghill." A feminine counterpart to the much more venerable John Barleycorn, Madam Geneva embodied another social taboo broken in the gin craze. For the first time, women were drinking publicly, even brazenly, and to monstrous excess—a prerogative previously reserved for men.

Madam Geneva first appears in a satire published in 1713, at a time when distillers feared that peace with France would flood their market with second-rate brandy. Having staked their livelihoods on gin, some—like the anonymous author of *The Whole Tryal,*

*Indictment, Arraignment, Examination and Condemnation of Madam Geneva, Taken in Shorthand by Dorothy Addle-Brains, Fore-woman of the Jury*—were all too keen to bring Madam Geneva to book. She had, they claimed, ruined the lives of many ordinary Londoners:

> Journeymen taylors and shoemakers, tinkers and porters, doxies, butchers' wives, young strumpets, rotten bawds, tarpaulins and soldiers ... old basketwomen, and other honest and well-meaning people.

At the scaffold, Madam Geneva followed the conventions of the penitent prisoner to the letter:

> She bewail'd her faults, and made open confession of her manifold crimes, with floods of tears, acknowledging herself guilty of death was turn'd off, and her body conveyed in a hurdle to Mumpers Hall, where her ... friends caus'd her to be embalmed, and laid ten days in state.

But reports of this old lady's death were, as we'll see, greatly exaggerated.

What we might call the "street-level" gin craze was engendered by the policies of William III, and nursed by the particular circumstances of British life in the early eighteenth century. But what sparked the other gin craze—that sustained outpouring of moral indignation in pulpits, print and Parliament? If we wanted to identify one movement that set the agenda for the revolt against gin, we might look no further than the Society for the Reformation of Manners. Initially established in east London in 1691, the Society had chapters in most major cities by 1700, including more than twenty in the capital. Its members were the shock troops of the respectable "middling sort," aiming to sweep away the hedonistic liberality of Restoration England and replace it with a plainer, narrower, more pious vision of public morality. Dominated by clergymen, magistrates and MPs, they paid a network of constables and informers to collect evidence against drunkards, pimps, prostitutes, sodomites and Sabbath-breakers. They raided brothels and molly-houses; they brought the golden age of Restoration comedy to an end; they published blacklists of offenders and hundreds of sermons and pamphlets; and, where possible, they took their enemies to court and pressed for the harshest penalties.

These societies flourished in the first quarter of the eighteenth century, and under their influence the terms of the debate over gin began to change, moving away from capitalist economics and towards the more disputatious terrain of public morality. Their attacks on gin were part of a campaign against what they saw as the indolence, indecency and indiscipline of the lower orders. Gin was socially subversive, loosening the morals of the poor and leading them on to idleness and crime. It encouraged prostitution and black-marketeering, and weakened the constitutions of a generation of laborers, sailors and artisans. Through inebriated carelessness it led to gruesome death, as in the case of a housewife who was:

> so much intoxicated with Geneva that she fell on the fire, and was burned in so miserable a Manner, that she immediately died and her bowels came out.

Equally, it might cause the demise of more vulnerable individuals. Mary Eastwick, a nursemaid, was reported to have come home one night, drunk on gin, and:

> sate down before the fire, and it is supposed, had [her] child in her lap. Which fell out of it on the hearth, and the fire catched hold of the child's clothes and burned it to death.

More than this, gin was itself a poison—or, at least, many of the leading medical men of the day were prepared to testify that it was. Bishop Thomas Wilson reported the views of an eminent surgeon, who found that when gin and other spirits were:

> not drunk in such large Quantities as to kill immediately, but are daily used; then, besides many other Diseases, they are apt to breed *Polypuses* or Fleshy Substances in the Heart ...

Others argued that gin-drinking was the common factor connecting a series of spontaneous combustions, but the most lurid fears were over its effect on pregnant women. Stephen Hales, a respected physician and clergyman, published *A Friendly Admonition to the Drinkers of Brandy, and Other Distilled Spirituous Liquors* in 1734. Here he warned that spirits would "coagulate and thicken the Blood, [and] also contract and narrow the Blood Vessels [causing] Obstructions and stoppages in the Liver; whence the Jaundice, Dropsy, and many other fatal Diseases." Even this, however, paled before the consequences for infants:

> We have too frequent Instances where the unhappy Mothers habituate themselves to these distill'd Liquors, whose Children, when first born, are often either of a diminutive, pygmy Size, or look wither'd and old, as if they had number'd many Years, when they have not, as yet, alas! attained to the evening of the first Day. How many more instances are there of children who, tho' born with good Constitutions, have unhappily suck'd in the deadly spirituous Poison with their Nurse's Milk?

For the middling sort, this last sentence was the most frightening prospect. Even if a mother abstained from spirits, who could tell what her wet-nurse might do when she was left alone with the child? In the words of the anonymous *Elegy on the Much-Lamented Death of the Most Excellent, the Most Truly-beloved, and Universally-admired Lady, Madame Gineva,* published in 1736:

> The sucking Brat declines her shrivil'd Pap,
> The cordial Bev'rage sips, and takes a Nap.

Hush'd with few Drops he holds his Infant cries,
And spares the maudlin Nurse her Lullabies.

The earliest stirrings of government action on this deeply emotive issue came in 1729, with the passage of the first Gin Act. Intended to damp down public appetites for gin, the Act more than doubled the duty on spirits (from 2s to 5s per gallon), and required spirit retailers to purchase a £20 license. Like all the Gin Acts, this was a messy political compromise between distillers, landowners and reformers. Its immediate consequence was not a reduction in gin sales—only 453 licenses were issued—but a sudden spike in illicit distilling and bootlegging. Caught on the hop, the government hurriedly repealed the first Gin Act, and in 1733 replaced it with more liberal provisions. Unlicensed street-vendors, however, were now liable to be fined, and—a touch inspired by the methods of the Society for the Reformation of Manners—informers could be paid from the proceeds of these fines. But gin consumption continued to rise, and horror stories continued to captivate the public. In 1734 one Judith Defour confessed to the murder of her son—a crime motivated by nothing more than the wish for a quarter-pint of gin:

> On Sunday night we took the child into the fields and stripp'd it, and ty'd a linen handkerchief hard about its neck to keep it from crying, and then laid it in a ditch. And after that, we went together, and sold the coat and stay for a shilling, and the petticoat and stockings for a groat. We parted the money, and join'd for a quartern of Gin."

By the mid-1730s the Society for the Reformation of Manners had achieved most of its founding aims, and its membership was in decline. But the Society's campaign against gin was taken up by a new faction of reform-minded Whigs, many of them members of another aggressively evangelical body: the Society for Promoting Christian Knowledge. Bishop Thomas Wilson was a member, as was Sir Joseph Jekyll, MP and Master of the Rolls. In *The Trial of the Spirits,* published in 1736, Jekyll painted a grim picture of the way in which poor Londoners were being ensnared by the demon drink:

> Why, the miserable creatures, in such a situation, rather than pur-
> chase the coarser Joynts of Meat, which the Butchers used to sell at
> a very easy rate . . . repair to the Gin-Shops, upon whose destructive
> commodities they will freely lay out all they can rap or rend, till
> the Parish Work-Houses are filled with their poor, starv'd families,
> Trade and Country depriv'd of their Manufactures and Labors, while
> the Butchers cannot so much as give these Joynts to the common
> People . . . but are forc'd, either to bury 'em, or give 'em to the dogs.

Jekyll became the patron of the next attempt to overthrow the tyranny of Madam Geneva—the 1736 Gin Act. He persuaded Wilson to write *Distilled Spirituous Liquors the Bane of the Nation,* and had copies of the pamphlet, with an endorsement from Stephen Hales, sent to all members of the Society for Promoting Christian Knowledge. He also had the ear of Queen Caroline, wife of George II, *de facto* head of state when George was in Hanover, and a staunch opponent of gin herself. Jekyll's bill faced strong opposition in Parliament—not only the usual grumblings from the distillers' lobby, but also a concerted stand from Sir Robert Walpole, First Lord of the Treasury. Walpole, who led a significant but shrinking Whig majority in the House of Commons, was reluctant to do anything that might upset his allies in the House of Lords, and insisted on several redraftings of the bill to make it more palatable to the landed interest. As Walpole and Jekyll began their horse-trading over the bill in February 1736, a Whig newspaper printed a short paragraph that came to symbolize the moral and economic dilemmas of the gin craze:

> We hear that a strong-water shop was lately opened in Southwark,
> with the inscription on the sign:
> "Drunk for 1d.
> Dead drunk for 2d.
> Clean straw for nothing."

After three months of bitter debate, the new Gin Act was passed in early May, and despite Walpole's hostility Jekyll got most of what he wanted. The cost of a license for selling spirits was raised to £50, and the duty was increased fourfold, to 20s per gallon. Jekyll's aim was clear: he wanted to make gin prohibitively expensive both for manufacturers and drinkers, and in doing so he hoped to drive the lower orders into abstinence. Though the Act would not come into force until the last day of September, the drinking public's response was swift and unambiguous. By order of Parliament, their celebrated Madam Geneva was to be exiled, or executed, or starved to death, and their grief and outrage was captured in a slew of satires, engravings and plays. The most famous of these—*To the Mortal Memory of Madam Geneva*—is reproduced in Appendix 1, but Henry Fielding also capitalized on public anger with a "Heroic Tragi-comical Farce," *The Deposing and Death of Queen Gin, with the Ruin of the Duke of Rum, Marquee de Nantz and the Lord Sugarcane,* which ended with a general cry of "Liberty, Property and Gin forever!"

As the date of the Act's enforcement drew nearer, a nervous Walpole made preparations for what he feared would be a major outbreak of civil unrest. Troops were deployed in the major ports, but in the event they were required to do nothing more than watch as hundreds of protesters, dressed in black, staged funerals for Madam Geneva. A government-sponsored news-sheet in Bristol, reproduced in Appendix 1, played down their escapades, but in London taverns swathed their signs in black crepe, and the traffic on Piccadilly was held up by the solemn progress of a gin-laden hearse. A small mob outside Newgate Prison baited the soldiers with cries of "No Gin, No King," but most made their point more subtly, by drinking what they believed might be the very last legal mouthfuls of gin.

Contrary to appearances, this outburst of public sorrow did not set an epitaph on Mother Gin's tomb—far from it. Like its predecessors, the 1736 Act was deeply flawed, and in practice it did little more than drive the gin trade further underground. Only twenty licenses were ever issued under the Act, while sales of juniper cordials by apothecaries and surgeons—an area of trade untouched by gin legislation—mysteriously rose. Unlicensed vendors, meanwhile, became more and more ingenious in exploiting the loopholes in the Act: witness, for example, "Bradstreet's Cat."

*The Life and Uncommon Adventures of Captain Dudley Bradstreet,* published in 1755, was not the work of a shy or modest man. In his subtitle, Bradstreet described his autobiography as "the most genuine and extraordinary perhaps ever published." Born in Tipperary in 1711, this hot-blooded Anglo-Irishman began his career as a trooper, but found military discipline intolerable. He tried his hand at brewing and linen-selling, but with little success, and drifted between Ireland and England, always, it seems, with some money-making ruse at hand. After the outbreak of the second Jacobite rebellion in 1745 Bradstreet was taken on as a government spy and sent into the Scottish Highlands, with orders to get as close as possible to the "Young Pretender," Prince Charles Edward Stuart. Bradstreet did this—in the process acquiring, not quite legitimately, his rank of captain—and for his pains received £120 from George II. Back in London he made a name for himself as a prestidigitator, and wrote a five-act play—*The Magician, or the Bottle Conjurer*—which was suppressed by the Westminster magistrates, for reasons he chose not to explain.

Bradstreet's posthumous fame, however, rests on none of these "uncommon adventures," but on one of his smaller enterprises—an ingenious scheme for selling gin. In 1736 he found himself in London with a near-empty purse. In the aftermath of the Gin Act he realized that demand was stronger than ever, and that the public might pay a premium for a reliable and discreet source of liquor. Bradstreet rented a house on Blue Anchor Alley, and on the front wall erected a painted sign of a cat—"Old Tom"—with its paw outstretched. Beneath this paw was a lead pipe, which ran through the wall and into the front room, and a wooden drawer. Customers would slip their coins into the drawer, and whisper, "Puss, give me two penny-worth of gin." Bradstreet would then pour the gin through the pipe and into their cup. Because the ownership of the house was in dispute and *sub judice,* informers could not find out whose name was on the lease. This "Scheme of Puss," also known as "Puss and Mew," was a runaway success, and soon he was making twenty pounds a week—though he complained that a plague of imitators "greatly diminished my Business and made me drop it, and turn my Head to something else."

Bradstreet's guile was a response to the importance of informers in enforcing licensing laws, and this, perhaps, was the most devastating unintended consequence of the Gin Acts. As Jessica Warner has pointed out, what started out as a high-minded moral crusade against the social effects of cheap gin quickly degenerated into a scrum of state-sponsored espionage and racketeering. Neighbors denounced one another; informers demanded protection money from near-destitute street vendors; magistrates took bribes to drop cases; and poor Londoners began to view their political masters with something like outright derision. The leading anti-gin magistrate—Sir Thomas de Veil, doyen of the Bow Street court—was stabbed in 1734, and on many other occasions was almost lynched by angry crowds. His stable of informers were even less popular: one was tarred and feathered, another torn from her grave and staked through the heart, and many were simply beaten or subjected to the traditional "rough music." In January 1737 one Pullin, an informer in Westminster, was:

> carry'd in Effigy about the several Streets, Squares, &c. in the Parish of St. George Hanover Square, for informing against a Victualler in Princess Street . . . and after the Procession was over he was fix'd upon a Chair-Pole in Hanover Square, with a Halter about his Neck, and then a Load of Faggots placed round him, in which Manner he was burnt in the Sight of a vast Concourse of People.

Further Gin Acts in 1737 and 1738 strengthened the penalties for unlicensed trading—street vendors could expect to be "whipped until bloody"—and also made assaults on informers a felony punishable by transportation. And prosecutions for unlicensed gin-selling did increase, reaching 12,000 by 1738. But spirit production also continued to rise, and the statistics reveal the extent to which the Gin Acts had failed. In 1743 British spirit production peaked at more than eight million gallons, but in the previous year only forty gallons of gin had been declared for duty. Street vendors sold much of the illicit excess, but even licensed retailers sidestepped the law by mixing gin with wine or bitters and selling it as "Parliamentary Brandy" or "Sangaree."

The political climate, too, was changing. Walpole fell in 1742, and the new administration was far more concerned with the *realpolitik* of raising funds to fight Continental wars than the high-minded sermonizing of Jekyll and the Society for the Reformation of Manners. In 1743 Parliament debated a new Gin Act, intended not to suppress consumption but to make licenses more affordable and duties more easily collected. For John Hervey, former Lord Privy Seal under Walpole, this strategy was a deeply unsavory prospect:

> We have now mortgaged almost every fund that can decently be thought of; and now, in order to raise a new fund, we are to establish the worst sort of drunkenness by a law, and to mortgage it for defraying an expense which, in my opinion, is both unnecessary and ridiculous. This is really like a tradesman's mortgaging the prostitution of his daughter, for the sake of raising money to supply his luxury or extravagance ... The Bill, my lords, is an experiment of a very daring kind, which none would hazard but empirical politicians. It is an experiment to discover how far the vices of the population may be made useful to the government, what taxes may be raised upon a poison, and how much the court may be enriched by the destruction of the subjects.

During these debates John Wesley, the founder of Methodism, continued to insist upon the absolute evil of spirit-drinking in his mission to London's outcast poor:

We may not sell any thing which tends to impair health. Such is eminently all that liquid fire, commonly called drams, or spirituous liquors. It is true these may have a place in medicine ... Therefore such as prepare and sell them only for this end, may keep their conscience clear.... But all who sell them in the common way, to any that buy, are *poisoners-general*. They murder His Majesty's subjects by wholesale, neither does their eye pity or spare. *They drive them to hell like sheep.*

But the bill was passed, and on its own terms the Gin Act 1743 was a major success. More than twenty thousand licenses were taken out, and within a year it had raised £90,000 in duty. It also had a subtler and more profound effect on the patterns of British gin-drinking. Larger numbers of licensed premises meant a smaller share of the market for unlicensed street-vendors, while a rise in duty made the drink itself more expensive for consumers. Gradually, less gin was produced, and less consumed. Bernard de Mandeville, had he looked down from his celestial bee-hive, would surely have smiled: the regulation of vice was proving far more profitable and beneficial than its suppression. But as it turned out, the most devastating salvos in the war on gin were yet to be fired.

Readers of the *London Evening-Post* on Valentine's Day 1751 might have found their eyes drawn to a large advertisement, trumpeting the latest productions of the painter and engraver William Hogarth:

This Day are publish'd, Price 1 s. each.
Two large Prints, design'd and etch'd by Mr. Hogarth called
BEER-STREET and GIN-LANE
A Number will be printed in a better Manner for the Curious, at
1s. 6d. each.
And on Thursday following will be publish'd four Prints on the
Subject of Cruelty, Price and Size the same.

N.B. As the Subjects of these Prints are calculated to reform some
reigning Vices peculiar to the lower Class of People, in hopes
to render them of more extensive use, the Author has published
them in the cheapest Manner possible.
To be had at the Golden Head in Leicester-Fields, Where may be
had all his other Works.

In one inexpensive print Hogarth created the defining image
of the gin craze—an allegory of social breakdown and suffering
which has transcended its original historical setting, and which
continues to inspire satirists more than two and a half centuries
later. "Gin Lane" deserves, and has received, some searching and
sustained attention, but its story begins with a paradox. Why did
the most scathing and emotionally wrenching attack on gin come
at a time when both production and consumption were falling,
and when its social effects were far less apparent than they had
been two decades earlier? The answer lay, once again, in international politics. In October 1748, after eight years of bloody
conflict, the War of the Austrian Succession was concluded with
the Peace of Aix-la-Chapelle. This had two consequences for
British attitudes to gin. First, by ending a major drain on the nation's resources, it eliminated the principal justification for a more
relaxed attitude to gin-drinking. Second, within a few months
almost eighty thousand demobbed soldiers and sailors were back
on the streets of the nation's cities, looking for lodgings, livelihoods, and pleasurable distractions.

For London's increasingly influential middling sort, this invasion
threatened to let loose a new wave of drunken, violent crime—a
fear not without grounds, as more than half of those hanged at
Tyburn in the year after Aix-la-Chapelle were former soldiers.
Some also began to question the basic economics underlying the
liberalization of gin licensing. In a prescient piece of political arith-
metic Josiah Tucker, a West Country rector, attempted to quantify
the social and commercial costs of gin-drinking. He concluded
that, while annual excise returns on spirits came to an impressive

69

£676,125, the ill-health, indolence and squalor caused by gin lost the nation almost four million pounds per year. Likewise, the Board of Governors of St. George's Hospital, one of the largest hospitals in London, estimated that admissions had risen more than three-fold over the previous two decades "from the melancholy conse-quences of gin-drinking, principally." As another piece published in the *London Evening-Post* shows, gin was back on the moral and political agenda:

This *wicked* GIN, of all *Defence* bereft,
And *guilty* found of *Whoredom, Murder, Theft,*
Of rank *Sedition, Treason, Blasphemy,*
Should *suffer death,* the *Judges* all agree.

Hogarth's blistering attack on gin found its origins in his friend-ship with the writer Henry Fielding. In many ways Fielding was a most unlikely figurehead for any kind of moral crusade. An Old Etonian and a rake in his youth, by the late 1740s he was an aging roué, his literary career at a near-standstill. His wife, Charlotte, had died in 1744, and as a widower he lived in genteel poverty, but in 1748 his friends in Parliament managed to secure for him a position as a magistrate in Westminster. Though he looked more at home in the dock than on the bench, this appointment seems to have revivified Fielding's mind. In the last half-decade of his life he not only established London's first semi-official police force, the "Bow Street Runners," but also produced his masterpiece —the novel *Tom Jones,* published in 1749.

Fielding took up his new position just in time to witness the post-war crime wave, and in the intervals between court sessions he began to marshal his thoughts on the matter. Like Joseph Jekyll in the 1730s, Fielding had close friends in the Society for Promoting Christian Knowledge, including Bishop Thomas Wilson and the new Bishop of Worcester, Isaac Maddox. In a sermon preached at St. Bride's Church in January 1751 Maddox adopted Wilson's line against gin, claiming that it was:

destroying in the Course of a few Years more Lives than Sword, or Plague, or Famine; lessening the Number of our People by daily Slaughter; diminishing and enfeebling Posterity; and in every respect both as to Number, Health, and Vigour, keeping down the Offspring and Breed of the Nation.

Fielding, too, found this line of argument utterly convincing. In *An Inquiry into the Causes of the Late Increase in Robbers,* published in 1751, he concluded that one factor was responsible: drunkenness, and a particular kind of drunkenness at that:

> The Drunkenness I here intend is that acquired by the strongest intoxicating Liquors, and particularly by that Poison called *Gin;* which, I have great reason to think, is the principal Sustenance (if it may be so called) of more than an hundred thousand People in this Metropolis. Many of these Wretches there are, who swallow Pints of this Poison within the Twenty-four Hours; the dreadful Effects of which I have the Misfortune to see every Day, and to smell too.

This "Poison" was so strong that its consumers could hardly be held responsible for their actions, and Fielding's response to those "wretches" who came up before him at Bow Street was pity rather than hatred:

> Wretches are often brought before me, charged with Theft and Robbery, whom I am forced to confine before they are in a Condition to be examined; and when they have afterwards become sober, I have plainly perceived, from the State of the Case, that the *Gin* alone was the Cause of the Transgression, and have been sometimes sorry that I was obliged to commit them to Prison.

But his greatest fear was one we have encountered many times before—the effect that gin consumption might have on the future of the nation:

> What must become of the Infant who is conceived in *Gin?* with the poisonous Distillations of which it is nourished both in the Womb

and at the Breast. Are these wretched Infants (if such can be supposed capable of arriving at the Age of Maturity) to become our future Sailors, and our future Grenadiers? Is it by the Labor of such as these, that all the Emoluments of Peace are to be procured us, and all the Dangers of War averted from us? What could an *Edward* or a *Henry,* a *Marlborough* or a *Cumberland,* effect with an Army of such Wretches? Doth not this polluted Source, instead of producing Servants for the Husbandman or Artificer; instead of providing Recruits for the Sea or the Field, promise only to fill Alms-houses and Hospitals, and to infect the Streets with Stench and Disease?

Whoever came up with this misbegotten liquor was, Fielding thought, nothing more than "the Poisoner of a Fountain, whence a large City was to derive its Waters." His recommendation was stark: instead of tolerating gin in the name of raising revenue, all right-thinking men should press for complete Prohibition.

Fielding circulated his pamphlet to his friends in Parliament and the Society for Promoting Christian Knowledge, but he also passed a copy to Hogarth. Born in 1697, Hogarth was the son of a debt-ridden Cockney schoolmaster, and began his career apprenticed to an engraver with a shop in Leicester Fields. He began to sketch the lives and the faces he saw around him, inspired by the conventions of Dutch genre paintings and the low, bawdy wit of British print culture. His first satirical print, produced in 1721, lampooned the South Sea Bubble, and by the late 1740s he was not only the city's leading satirist, with works like "The Rake's Progress" and "Marriage à-la-Mode" under his belt, but also a noted portraitist who could do for London faces what John Constable later did for London skies.

Less than a month after Fielding's *Inquiry* was published, Hogarth had completed "Gin Lane" and "Beer Street." Speed and accessibility seem to have been uppermost in his mind, as he worked straight from his preliminary drawings, rather than his usual practice of painting in oils and then engraving the result. The low price of 1s, while still too much for the very poorest, made the prints cheap enough to be tacked up in shops, ale-houses and windows.

This was a work expressly intended to make a splash in London's public sphere.

If we want to understand the many meanings of "Gin Lane," the best place to start is with Hogarth's own interpretation of his work, written towards the end of his life:

> In Gin Lane, every circumstance of its horrid effects is brought into view *in terrorem*. Idleness, poverty, misery, and distress, which drives even to madness and death, are the only objects that are to be seen; and not a house in tolerable condition but the pawnbroker's and Gin-shop ... In Beer Street, all is joyous and thriving. Industry and jollity go hand in hand. In this happy place, the pawnbroker's is the only house going to ruin; and even the small quantity of porter that he can procure is taken in at the wicket, for fear of further distress.

"Gin Lane" is set in the parish of St. Giles, close to the center of London's pleasure district, and renowned for its "rookeries" or criminal slums. The street and its buildings are near-derelict, and one house is tumbling into the street. There is a church—St. George, Bloomsbury, with its distinctive ziggurat spire—but it is set in the distance, and the figure of George II atop the spire has averted its face. Gin Lane itself is alive with activity, and the pawnbroker, the "Kilman" distillery, the gin-shop, and the undertaker are thriving, but all else is squalor and destitution. The street's inhabitants are pawning anything they can get their hands on, everything that is most essential to life, in order to buy gin. In an upper attic a barber has hanged himself: no one has the money for a shave or a haircut. A lame man beats a blind man with his crutch, and two orphaned wards of the parish are drinking gin. Another child cries while the parish beadle lumbers his dead mother into a pauper's grave, and—most horrible—a drunkard has, in his frenzy, impaled a baby on a fire-iron.

But the eye is drawn again and again to two figures in the foreground of the picture. On the right a demobbed soldier, clad in rags and skeletal with hunger, has starved to death, a gin-glass in his hand and a basket of anti-gin sermons by his side. This figure seems to have been based on a well-known street vendor in St. Giles, whose cry was "Buy my ballads, and I'll give you a glass of gin for nothing!" And in the center, a sottish, pox-raddled woman takes a pinch of snuff, not noticing that her child has slipped from her lap. It falls, arms outstretched, towards the unforgiving stone floor of a cellar which is also a gin-shop. Cut into the stone over the archway is a stark and familiar refrain: "Drunk for a penny . . ."

If the message of "Gin Lane" was not clear enough, Hogarth drove the point home with verses by the dramatist and clergyman James Townley, engraved below the picture:

Gin, cursed Fiend, with Fury fraught,
Makes human Race a Prey.
It enters by a deadly Draught
And steals our Life away.

Virtue and Truth, driv'n to Despair
Its Rage compells to fly,
But cherishes with hellish Care
Theft, Murder, Perjury.

Damned Cup! that on the Vitals preys
That liquid Fire contains,
Which Madness to the heart conveys,
And rolls it thro' the Veins.

After this quagmire of hopelessness and anguish, the flourishing jollity of "Beer Street" comes as a breath of fresh air. Commerce and prosperity are present in abundance, and only the pawnbroker has been forced out of business. Drink—in the form of good English beer—is everywhere, quaffed by blacksmiths, draymen, butchers, builders and housemaids, but it is being consumed as refreshment after the rigors of honest labor. A news-sheet on a table reports the King's speech on the "Advancement of Our Commerce and Cultivating the Art of Peace." This is a patriotic

celebration of English virtues over foreign vices, and once again
Townley's verses make the point abundantly plain:

Beer, happy Produce of our Isle
Can sinewy Strength impart,
And wearied with Fatigue and Toil
Can cheer each manly Heart.

Labor and Art upheld by Thee
Successfully advance,
We quaff Thy balmy Juice with Glee
And Water leave to France.

Genius of Health, thy grateful Taste
Rivals the Cup of Jove,
And warms each English generous Breast
With Liberty and Love!

In his other works, Hogarth was clear about the dangers of
distilled spirits. Both "The Rake's Progress" and "Marriage à-
la-Mode" feature stills and alembics as symbols of false hope,
instruments for making only what is fleeting and ephemeral. But
there is a broader ethical point at work here. Hogarth was at heart
a moralist, fascinated by original sin and the redemptive powers
of civil society. Like Tom Nero, anti-hero of "The Four Stages
of Cruelty," the denizens of "Gin Lane" are not inherently good
people perverted by gin or by a repressive government. Rather,
they are a terrible warning of what happens when a society fails
to teach its citizens a sense of morality and a concern for the
wellbeing of others. In this sense, the message of "Gin Lane" and
"Beer Street" is that (to misquote W.H. Auden) we must converse
and trade with one another, or die.

"Gin Lane" was an immediate hit with London's reading public,
and the central figure of the drunken mother prompted particular
revulsion. Only a few weeks after the print appeared, the journalist
Edward Cave published a poem written in her voice:

I must, I will have Gin!—that skillet take:—
Pawn it:—No more I'll roast, or boil, or bake.
This juice immortal will each want supply,
Starve on, ye brats! so I but bung my eye.
Starve? No!—This Gin ev'n mother's milk excels;
Paints the pale cheeks, and hunger's dart repels.
The skillet's pawn'd aready.—Take this cap;
Round my bare head I'll yon brown paper wrap.
Ha! half my petticoat was torn away
By dogs (I fancy) as I maudlin lay.

Later Romantic critics, too, loved "Gin Lane." William Hazlitt thought the buildings "reeled as if drunk and tumbling about the ears of the infatuated victims below," and Charles Lamb called it "sublime . . . terrible as anything Michelangelo ever drew." Pressure on Parliament, already increasing after Fielding's intervention, became heavier still. Though the new session had much important business (not least the introduction of the Gregorian calendar) it also found time to establish a new committee on licensing law, which was deluged with petitions to do something about gin. MPs and ministers had little appetite for another grand ideological struggle over spirits, and the legislation they put together was pragmatic and moderate. The 1751 Gin Act raised the duty on gin and the cost of licenses, but not to a point where black-market gin would become a more appealing option, and it also cracked down on the sale of gin in prisons. It faced no serious public opposition, and within a year the quantity of gin submitted for duty had fallen, quietly, by a third. The gin craze was over.

What was the legacy of this extraordinary episode, the first time in history that strong, cheap spirits were available in unlimited quantities to anyone with the means to purchase them? One result of this extended encounter with gin was a transformation in the way that people thought about drunkenness. For medieval and early modern writers, drunkenness was a kind of gluttony or overindulgence, punished in due course by sickness and shame, but not fundamentally different from a surfeit of roast beef. But as we'll see in the next chapter, drunkenness seemed very different for British drinkers at the end of the gin craze—an intense and violent intoxication, almost a poisoning, less Falstaffian and more Hogarthian.

And this change in attitudes to intoxication was paralleled by a change in the status and meaning of gin itself. In the slums and brothels of Hanoverian London gin lost its mystique and its innocence. Once a medicinal cordial flavored with the spices of the world, it emerged from the gin craze as *déclassé* and destructive, implicated in the decline and fall of an entire generation. For the middling sort and their representatives in Parliament, gin was like gambling or bull-baiting—a pleasure which marked its participants out as irremediably *low,* something to be avoided at all costs, and stamped out wherever it was found.

Ironically, it was at exactly this moment that many of the most well-known and long-lived gin distilleries were established. At the end of the 1760s a run of poor harvests led to a three-year ban on distillation throughout England. This forced many small distilleries to close, creating a gap in the market for entrepreneurs who, over a generation or two, established themselves as major powers in British gin-making: Thomas Dakin (later Greenall's) in Warrington in 1761, Alexander Gordon in Southwark in 1769, and Sir Robert Burdett in London around the same time.

But perhaps the most remarkable thing about the gin craze was the speed with which it entered British history and folklore. Less than a decade after the 1751 Gin Act, the novelist and historian Tobias Smollett published a vivid account, reproduced in Appendix 1, which still dominates modern historical writing about the gin craze. The gin craze haunted Victorian writers like Dickens and Thomas Carlyle, as they got to grips with the challenges of individual and collective morality in an age of industry and mass democracy. For the High Victorian historian W.H. Lecky, its importance could hardly be overstated. The gin craze, he concluded, had set the moral and political agenda for nineteenth-century England:

If we consider all the consequences that have flowed from [the gin craze,] it was the most momentous [event] of the eighteenth century, incomparably more so than any event in the purely political or military annals of the country.

Was Lecky right? We'll find out in the next chapter, as gin became caught up in another world-shaking event—the Industrial Revolution.

Coupe et plan d'un plateau rectificateur d'une colonne
de distillation continue.

Continuous distillation and rectification, pioneered in Britain by
Aeneas Coffey in 1830, produced a smoother base spirit which
required less sweetening—ideal for the "London Dry" style of
gin. "Distillation plateau," from Albert Seigneurie, Dictionnaire
encyclopédique de l'épicerie et des industries
annexes, Paris, 1904, p 40.

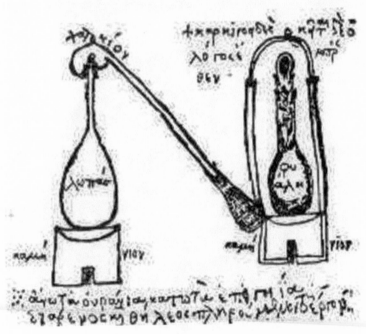

Ambix, cucurbit and retort of Zosimos of Panopolis, a
fourth-century Gnostic alchemist and one of the earliest writers
to describe distillation. From Marcelin Berthelot, Collection des
anciens alchimistes grecs, 3 vols, Paris, 1887-1888.

# 3

## The Infernal Principle

"WHAT'S THE QUICKEST way out of Manchester? Gin."
This is an old joke, but one more revealing than you
might think. It is not a quip William Hogarth would have got.
Even at the height of the gin craze there was very little gin in
Manchester, and also very little of Manchester. In the middle of
the eighteenth century this thriving little township was a hub for
the British cotton trade, connected to the world via the docks of
Liverpool, but the dizzying commercial expansion that turned
Manchester into a Victorian byword for industrial apocalypse
was still decades away. By 1836, however, when Charles Dickens
published his seminal account of a visit to a gin palace in *Sketches
by Boz,* the kind of grinding, hopeless poverty which had driven
Hanoverian Londoners to gin could be found in Manchester,
Birmingham, Liverpool, and scores of smaller towns. Writing in
1839, Thomas Carlyle—living up to his reputation as the gloomy,
irascible "Sage of Chelsea"—thundered over the plight of Glaswegian factory-hands:

> ...too surely they do in verity find the time all out of joint; this
> world for them no home, but a dingy prison-house, of reckless un-
> thrift, rebellion, rancour, indignation against themselves and against
> all men. Is it a green flowery world, with azure everlasting sky
> stretched over it, the work and government of a God; or a murky-
> simmering Tophet, of copperas-fumes, cotton-fuzz, gin-riot, wrath
> and toil, created by a Demon, governed by a Demon? The sum of
> their wretchedness merited and unmerited welters, huge, dark and
> baleful, like a Dantean Hell ...

And were these workers being driven deeper into this sulphurous pit by a "liquid Madness sold at ten-pence the quartern"?

> Gin justly named the most authentic incarnation of the Infernal Principle in our times, too indisputable an incarnation; Gin the black throat into which wretchedness of every sort, consummating itself by calling on delirium to help it, whirls down; abdication of the power to think or resolve, as too painful now, on the part of men whose lot of all others would require thought and resolution; liquid Madness sold at ten-pence the quartern, all the products of which are and must be, like its origin, mad, miserable, ruinous, and that only!

Encountered so soon after the moral and political tumult of the gin craze, Carlyle's dyspeptic fulminations seem wearily familiar. We have heard this before, from the pens of Henry Fielding, Bishop Thomas Wilson, and a host of anonymous Cockney satirists. So were nineteenth-century British attitudes to gin merely a re-tread of their eighteenth-century predecessors? At first glance, the parallels are manifold. By the early nineteenth century gin was once again relatively cheap. In London at least, a quarter-pint of gin cost threepence-halfpenny, compared with twopence for a pint of beer. The streets of the nation's cities were thronged with a new kind of gin-shop—known, with a certain Dickensian irony, as the "gin palace"—and gin was once more at the center of a collision between *laissez-faire* economics and Christian moral reform. Again, it provoked moral panics, questions in Parliament, and sparkling, savage satires by the leading writers and artists of the day. It is almost tempting to invoke another big beast of nineteenth-century political prose—Karl Marx, in the famous opening sentences of "The Eighteenth Brumaire of Louis Napoleon," published in 1852:

> Hegel remarks somewhere that all great world-historic facts and personages appear, so to speak, twice. He forgot to add: the first time as tragedy, the second time as farce.

Both the Hanoverian gin craze and its nineteenth-century counterpart had their tragic and their comic aspects, but (to extend
the theatrical metaphor) the setting and the characters were very
different. In the near-century separating Hogarth and Dickens, the
Industrial Revolution had remade British life. A new urban working class, concentrated in the north, was driven into penury and
radicalism by long, biting economic depressions and famines after
the end of the Napoleonic Wars in 1815. In the same generation, the
arrival of cholera—often referred to as a "filth disease"—and the
creation of a national network of workhouses under the 1834 New
Poor Law Act threw the hardships of working-class existence into
sharp relief. Deprived of the rich web of families and friendships
that characterized rural life, and subject to the enormous physical
and emotional pressures of factory life, working-class men and
women turned to new sources of solace and conviviality. Some
found it in Non-Conformist self-improvement, in the Wesleyan
chapels and free libraries and "Literary and Philosophical Societies" which sprang up all over the industrial north. Many more
preferred to pass their evenings in public houses, gin-palaces and
music-halls, where cheap beers and spirits, manufactured on an
industrial scale—another sign of the times—flowed liberally.

At the same time, the respectable working class and the reforming
middle class, which was coming to see itself as the true repository
of British moral fiber, established a new alliance against gin. Drawing on the (typically Victorian) resources of medicine and religion,
they took up the position expressed so luridly by Carlyle—that
gin was the epitome of everything dangerous about spirits. For
these advocates of temperance or abstinence, as for Hogarth and
his contemporaries a century before, it was a debilitating poison
which destroyed the body, the mind and the soul. It was leading
the working classes, and even some of the less vigilant members
of the middle classes, away from the strait gate of righteousness
and into a downward spiral of crime, violence, immorality, disease,
death and—horror of horrors—damnation.

But strong drink, and particularly spirits, had never been so central to British culture as they were to the Victorians, and not just as a mere intoxicant. For some, gin was a vile and degrading venom, but for many others it was a thirst-quencher, a proof of virility, an aphrodisiac, a rite of passage, a tonic, a nourishment, a pacifier for children, a fount of confidence and inspiration for the preacher or the soapbox ranter. And political attitudes to gin reflected this tension. The lure of revenue generated by duties on spirits was too much to resist, and the free trade ideology of the Manchester School—led by the Radical MPs Richard Cobden and John Bright—proclaimed the virtue of unregulated capitalism, arguing that any kind of state intervention in the gin trade, however well-meant, would work against the beneficent "hidden hand" of the market. For Liberals like William Ewart Gladstone, this was putting the cart before the horse: one duty of a responsible government was to bring cleanliness, godliness and sobriety to even the poorest members of society, and the social problems caused by heavy drinking were to be tackled in the High Victorian manner, by raising duties and strengthening the licensing laws.

From this widescreen perspective, we can see attitudes to gin as one of the fulcrums around which the whole of nineteenth-century British culture began to turn. Arguments over economic freedom and social responsibility helped to shift the center ground of politics away from the cut-throat free trade of the early nineteenth century and towards the more paternalistic, socially conscious ideology of the early twentieth century—a movement which, amongst other things, sowed the seeds of the welfare state and, in the U.S., prepared the ground for Prohibition. But the story of this revolution begins in a rather narrower frame, in the pages of a handful of medical treatises.

In the medical marketplace of eighteenth-century England, potency was all. If wealthy patients were going to pay through the nose for diagnosis and treatment, they wanted to feel some immediate effect. Despite their years of education and their weighty pharmacopoeias, physicians had few therapies which produced a gratifyingly instantaneous result: bloodletting, purges like senna and ipecacuanha, opium, and most of all spirits. These could be used in the medieval manner, as solvents for bitter medicines like opium, but they also did sterling work as all-purpose painkillers and restoratives. And changing medical ideas about the body meant that Hanoverian doctors had new reasons to recommend these trusted tonics.

Classical Greco-Roman theories of the body as a tidal estuary of humors did not disappear in this period, but they were increasingly challenged by a new interest in the nervous system. At the universities of Glasgow and Edinburgh William Cullen taught that "irritability"—the capacity of nerve fibers to detect and transmit sensations—was the basis of life, and a new language of sensibility and nervous exhaustion began to spread through fashionable society. John Brown, Cullen's pupil, took his master's ideas one step further by arguing that all diseases were at root a matter of nervous overstimulation ("sthenia") or understimulation ("asthenia"). Under this doctrine of "Brunonianism," the role of the physician was to position the patient on this spectrum of irritability, and then prescribe appropriate stimulants or calmatives—generally opium or spirits or, better still, both in the form of laudanum. Brown took enthusiastically to his own medicine, and by the end of his career was punctuating his lectures with draughts from a large tumbler of laudanum with whisky.

After the gin craze, however, some began to question the cozy confraternity of medicine and spirits. The benefits and evils of strong drink were no longer so easy to separate, and a growing number of physicians saw spirits as a cause of disease rather than a cure. In his *Essay on Regimen,* published in 1740, the Scottish physician George Cheyne claimed that "fermented and distilled liquors" were responsible for:

... all or most of the painful and excruciating Distempers that afflict Mankind; it is to it alone that our Gouts, Stones, Cancers, Fevers, high Hystericks, Lunacy and Madness are principally owing.

And when John Wesley came to compile *Primitive Physick,* a Culperesque collection of home remedies for the very poorest, in 1747, he refused to include any drink stronger than small beer. But it was in the decades of revolution at the end of the eighteenth century that mainstream medical opinion began to turn against intoxicating liquor in its most potent forms.

Benjamin Rush was something of an all-American hero: not only a leading figure in Philadelphia society, but also physician-general to the Revolutionary Army and a signatory of the Declaration of Independence. And in 1794, just as the Terror was reaching its bloody conclusion in revolutionary France, he published *An Inquiry Into the Effects of Ardent Spirits Upon the Body and Mind,* a scathing attack on the prescribing habits of his colleagues. Rush was uninterested in the social causes of spirit-drinking, but he gave a graphic description of its effects:

In folly [spirit-drinking] causes [the drinker] to resemble a calf—in stupidity, an ass,—in roaring, a mad bull,—in quarrelling, and fighting, a dog,—in cruelty, a tyger,—in fetor, a skunk,—in filthiness, a hog,—and in obscenity, a he-goat.

"Ardent spirits" were the last thing that any responsible physician should think of recommending to his patients:

As well we might throw oil into a house, the roof of which was on fire, in order to prevent the flames from extending to its inside, as pour ardent spirits into the stomach ...

Far from treating disease, gin and brandy were inflaming it, and their consumption could all too easily become a disease in itself. Rush was not the first physician to describe what would now be called chronic alcoholism—his ideas drew heavily on those of George

Cheyne and Stephen Hales—but his *Inquiry* exercised a profound influence over nineteenth-century temperance campaigners looking for medical evidence to back up their position. One of Rush's most convincing pieces of rhetoric was his "Moral and Physical Thermometer," a chart showing, in vivid terms, "the progress of temperance and intemperance." His leading British disciple, the Quaker physician and philanthropist John Coakley Lettsom, paid Rush the compliment of reprinting the "Thermometer" in his own treatise—*Hints to Beneficence*, published in 1797. At the top of Rush's thermometer were the healthiest and purest of beverages:

WATER; Milk and Water; Small Beer [produce] Health, Wealth, Serenity of Mind, Reputation, long Life, and Happiness.

Cyder and Perry; Wine; Porter; Strong Beer [produce] Cheerfulness, Strength and Nourishment, when taken only at meals, and in moderate Quantities.

But at the very bottom were stronger drinks like "Usquebaugh," "Hysteric Water," brandy, and gin. These, particularly if drunk throughout "the *Day* and *Night*," would lead only to vice, disease and punishment:

VICES. Idleness; Peevishness; Quarreling; Fighting; Lying; Swearing; Obscenity; Swindling; Perjury; Burglary; Murder; Suicide.

DISEASES. Sickness; Puking, and Tremors of the Hands in the Morning; Bloatedness; Inflamed Eyes; Red Nose and Face; Sore and Swelled Legs; Jaundice; Pains in the Limbs, and burning in the Palms of the Hands, and Soles of the Feet; Dropsy; Epilepsy; Melancholy; Madness; Palsy; Apoplexy; DEATH.

PUNISHMENTS. Debt; Black Eyes; Rags; Hunger; Hospital; Poor-House; Jail; Whipping; The Hulks; Botany Bay; GALLOWS.

Thomas Trotter, another alumnus of the Scottish medical schools, provided a less doom-laden portrayal of the problem in his *Essay on*

*Drunkenness,* published in 1804. Trotter argued that the metropolitan consumer culture of the eighteenth century had turned the British into neurotic and irresolute decadents, "wallowing in wealth and rioting in indulgence." The gin craze was, he thought, a case in point:

> A few years ago, the crops of grain were so deficient over this island, that the distillation of spirits from malt were prohibited: and thus scarcity, bordering on famine, became a blessing to the human race. But no sooner had fruitful seasons, and the bounty of Providence, covered the earth with plenty, than the first gift of Heaven, abundance of corn, was again, for the sake of taxation, converted into poisonous spirits, by opening the stillories.

For Trotter, gin was a terrible poison, acting swiftly and on the most vital of organs:

> Highly rectified spirit . . . could scarcely be admitted into the human stomach, even in very moderate quantity, without proving immediately fatal. The coats of the stomach would be unable to resist so concentrated a stimulus; they would be instantly decompounded, as is done by nitric or sulphuric acids.

To revive their own constitutions and the fortunes of the nation, Britons should foreswear gin and tea, sugar and spices, expensive silks and city smoke. Good health was to be found in the countryside, through hard work and fresh air, plain bread and English beer. Trotter, during his time as a naval surgeon, had played his own part in this campaign:

> During my residence at Plymouth Dock, towards the conclusion of the late war, I had the satisfaction of getting 200 gin-shops shut up. They were destroying the very vitals of our naval service.

By the early years of the nineteenth century, both medical attitudes to spirits and the meaning of drunkenness were changing rapidly. For members of the eighteenth-century Society for the Reformation of Manners, the decision to drink oneself into oblivion with gin was a free choice, one for which the drinker could be held entirely responsible. But for Rush, Lettsom and Trotter, the issue was more ambiguous. Gin itself had acquired some agency: it was, to use a word that acquired its modern meaning at the time they were writing, addictive. And we can see the consequences of this transformation mapped out in the works of one of Hogarth's most ardent admirers—the Regency satirist Thomas Rowlandson.

In "Death in the Nursery," part of a series titled *The Dance of Death,* published in 1815–16, Rowlandson portrayed the horror of a genteel family who return from a country walk to find their nursemaid stuporous with gin, and their infant rocked in its cradle by the bony, shrouded figure of Death. The moral of the story was driven home by a verse beneath the engraving:

Drown'd in inebriated sleep
No vigils can the Drunkard keep.
—Death rocks the Cradle, as you see,
And sings his mortal Lullaby.
No shrieks, no cries will not its slumbers break;
The infant sleeps,—ah, never to awake!

Depictions of gin-soaked nurses abandoning their charges to starvation, injury or death were, as we have seen, old hat by Hogarth's time, let alone Rowlandson's. But he seems to have been fond of the stereotype, and in "A Midwife Going to a Labor," published in 1811, he depicted a fat, ugly old woman clutching a lantern, a bindle and a bottle of gin as she struggled through a stormy evening to reach her client. "The Dram Shop," published in 1815, presented a more contemporary picture, with rowdy and voluptuous drinkers queuing at a counter for their gin. But they cannot see what we can see: in the back room of the dram shop a grinning skeleton pours jugs of "aqua fortis" and "oil of vitriol" (nitric and sulphuric acid) into a vat, to make "Brady's Best Cordial" and "Old Tom."

Rowlandson's magnificent skeletons stalked through his art as they are said to have clattered through his dreams, and were often, appropriately enough, the liveliest thing in them. One of his successors—George Cruikshank, the most popular cartoonist of the nineteenth century and later the illustrator of Dickens' works—borrowed them for his own spectral take on gin-drinking. In "The Gin Shop," published in 1829, Cruikshank portrayed a family of poor, dirty Londoners in a sparse and run-down bar. A mother feeds gin to her baby; an older child drinks from a glass; and the (presumed) father is snatching his own cup from the barmaid. But they stand in the jaws of an enormous man-trap, and their gin is poured from great rivet-studded coffins. In the cellar an alembic containing ghostly forms is surrounded by a horde of dancing demons, and the figure of Death, dressed as a nightwatchman, looks on, muttering, "I shall have them all dead drunk presently! They have had nearly their last glass."

By the time Cruikshank produced his study of seedy, down-at-heel gin-drinkers, the British public's attention had been captured by an altogether flashier kind of establishment—the gin palace. In the late 1820s gin palaces sprang up like strange and gilded fungi in almost every industrial town and city, from Glasgow to London, Hull to Portsmouth. We can get a sense of their appearance, and the tactics they used to drum up trade, from a report in the proceedings of the 1834 Select Committee on Drunkenness:

> [The gin palace] was converted into the very opposite of what it had been, [from] a low dirty public house with only one doorway, into a splendid edifice, the front ornamental with pilasters, supporting a handsome cornice and entablature and balustrades, and the whole elevation remarkably striking and handsome ... the doors and windows glazed with very large squares of plate glass, and the gas fittings of the most costly description ... When this edifice was completed, notice was given by placards taken round the parish; a

band of music was stationed in front ... the street became almost impassable from the number of people collected; and when the doors were opened the rush was tremendous; it was instantly filled with customers and continued so till midnight.

Like London's gin-shops a century before, the gin palaces were an unintended consequence of legislation. By the early nineteenth century the price of beer and porter was comparatively high, and Regency taverns began to court middle-class drinkers who could afford an evening of pricy pints and improving conversation. Seeing a gap in the market, gin-shops sought out a poorer clientele, and when in 1825 duty on spirits was cut by almost forty percent, to absorb the impact of a rare grain surplus, they took their chance. Within a year gin consumption in England and Wales had more than doubled, from 3.7 million gallons in 1825 to 7.4 million gallons in 1826.

As they jockeyed for position with tied pubs built by wealthy brewing firms, the owners of gin palaces looked to a new and innovative example of mass-market appeal—department stores. Borrowing the basic idea of a cheap product sold in high volume, they also adopted the principle of window-dressing. Gin palaces were bright, gaudily decorated, and welcoming, an oasis of warmth and light in the inhospitable nightscape of industrial towns. Inside, there were few tables or chairs—why distract from the business at hand?—and attention was focused on a long bar, behind which were barrel-heads marked "Old Tom," "Cream of the Valley," and "Celebrated Butter Gin." One can easily understand the appeal of such a place, a refuge from cold, damp slums, a setting in which men and women could forget money worries, or the demands of children and partners, or the boredom and exhaustion of long hours working in a factory. Foreign visitors thought that the success of the gin palaces also reflected the vagaries of the English climate: the French writer Hippolyte Taine believed that they provided an opportunity "to shut the door on the melancholy influence of a hostile nature."

In their first decade of existence, the gin palaces were phenomenally successful. Jessica Warner has worked out that, on a Friday or Saturday night, a well-sited gin palace could take upwards of a guinea a minute, and competition with pubs set off endless rounds of redecoration and one-upmanship. The most famous gin palace—Thompson & Fearon's, on Holborn Hill in London—was redesigned by John Buonarotti Papworth, one of the leading neoclassical architects, at a cost which was rumored to have exceeded ten thousand pounds (around half a million at 2011 prices). Gin palace owners made fortunes by pushing a "fast food" model of drinking, in which patrons were encouraged to knock back their shots of gin and order more, rather than lingering over a long glass of beer, but they also made robust enemies in the brewing trade and in Parliament. Once again, parallels with the eighteenth century are difficult to escape. Gin palaces were accused of destroying the ancient and wholesome tradition of tavern hospitality, and inciting a wave of crime, violence and misery.

For those who believed in the primacy of free trade, gin palaces were simply filling a gap in the market, and doing so with considerable acumen. But for those who were uneasy with the rampant industrialization of the early nineteenth century—a group which included some of the leading politicians and churchmen in the land—the gin palaces stood for everything that was going wrong in British life. Drinking in a gin palace was, they argued, alarmingly similar to working in a factory: a hard, impersonal experience that did terrible damage to the drinker's friendships, family ties and immortal soul. One casualty of the gin palaces was Branwell Brontë, brother of the more famous (and far more talented) Charlotte, Jane and Anne. The swashbuckling heroes of his own early stories are forever breaking off from their adventures to swig vast measures of claret, brandy and gin, and Branwell appears to have emulated this virile indulgence in his own life. After failing as a portrait painter and poet, he began to frequent gin palaces in Bradford and London, and when he died from tuberculosis at the age of thirty-two, the last piece of writing in his own hand was a letter imploring his family and friends to bring him more gin.

Parliament's response to this new gin craze was swift and—unlike many of its Hanoverian predecessors—effective. The 1830 Beer Act removed duty on British beer and made beer licenses much easier to acquire, and the 1834 Select Committee on Drunkenness censured gin palace owners for disregarding the wellbeing of their clientele. Within a decade or two, public houses offering beer and comfortable seating were once again within the reach of working-class drinkers, and the brief reign of the gin palace was over. But they have not been forgotten, and a few survive in something like their original condition: the Princess Louise in Holborn, the Prince Alfred in Maida Vale, the Café Royal in Edinburgh, the Crown in Belfast. More than this, the look of the gin palace—cut glass, polished brass, mahogany, elaborate plasterwork—came to define the classic High Victorian city pub. When HMS Agincourt was launched in 1919, its luxurious state-rooms led wags to call it "HMS Gin-Palace," and the nickname was transferred to a later generation of motor-cruisers and luxury yachts. But for our purposes, the true legacy of the gin palace lay in giving an aspiring London journalist the subject for one of his greatest essays.

Readers of London's *Monthly Magazine* and *Morning Chronicle* were used to finding articles and squibs signed only with the mysterious tag "Boz." In February 1836 their enthusiastic patronage made *Sketches by Boz,* a collection of stories and reportage, into a minor publishing sensation. "Boz" was, of course, Charles Dickens, and in 1836 he was a young man in a hurry. After working in the notorious boot-blacking factory and as a junior legal clerk, Dickens wanted to make a splash as a journalist and writer—partly for the sake of his reputation, and partly so that he could make enough money to marry Catherine Hogarth, the daughter of a colleague on the *Morning Chronicle.*

*Sketches* gave Dickens an opportunity to demonstrate his already-prodigious aptitude for setting, characterization and dialogue. It included scenes from daily life like "The Half-Pay Captain" and "The Ladies' Society," London set-pieces from "Vauxhall-Gardens by Day" to "The First of May," and short stories like "A Passage in the Life of Mr. Watkins Tottle." And—the icing on the cake—it came with illustrations by George Cruikshank, who possessed a preternatural gift for capturing Dickens' characters from his prose alone. "Boz" presented himself as the cosmopolitan journalist *par excellence,* at home everywhere and with everyone, making friends in the most refined drawing-rooms and the most degraded slums, and tantalizing his respectable readers with the stories he brought back. And his early talents were at their most crystalline in his essay on "Gin-shops," reproduced in full in Appendix 1.

Underlying this piece is one of Dickens' lasting preoccupations: the profound differences between appearances and reality, between the seductive powers of opulent surroundings and the squalid lives that might be lived within them. He begins with an observation which must have struck most Londoners at one moment or another: that the city's trades "run stark staring, raving mad, periodically." A few years back, for instance, haberdashers and linen-drapers had suddenly developed "an inordinate love of plate-glass, and a passion for gas-lights and gilding, stuccoed fronts and gold letters"? This madness is now afflicting the "publicans and keepers of wine-vaults," who in their mania are "knocking down all the old public-houses, and depositing splendid mansions, stone balustrades, rosewood fittings, immense lamps, and illuminated clocks, at the corner of every street":

Ingenuity is exhausted in devising attractive titles for the different descriptions of gin; and the dram-drinking portion of the community as they gaze upon the gigantic black and white announcements, which are only to be equalled in size by the figures beneath them, are left in a state of pleasing hesitation between "The Cream of the Valley," "The Out and Out," "The No Mistake," "The Good for Mixing," "The real Knock-me-down," "The celebrated Butter Gin," "The regular Flare-up," and a dozen other, equally inviting and wholesome liqueurs.

But there is, he notes, an incongruity in the location of these ornate hostelries:

> Although places of this description are to be met with in every second street, they are invariably numerous and splendid in precise proportion to the dirt and poverty of the surrounding neighbourhood. The gin-shops in and near Drury Lane, Holborn, St. Giles's, Covent Garden, and Clare Market, are the handsomest in London. There is more of filth and squalid misery near those great thoroughfares than in any part of this mighty city.

Having whetted his readers' appetites, Dickens now leads them "through the narrow streets and dirty courts which divide [Drury Lane] from Oxford Street" towards his gin palace. It stands at "that classical spot adjoining the brewery at the bottom of Tottenham Court Road, best known to the initiated as the "Rookery," only a few yards from the corner where Hogarth placed "Drunk for a penny . . ." over the doorway of a cellar. The character of the area is still Hogarthian in the extreme, and as he walks towards his assignment Dickens encounters:

> Wretched houses with broken windows patched with rags and paper: every room let out to a different family, and in many instances to two or even three—fruit and "sweet-stuff" manufacturers in the cellars, barbers and red-herring vendors in the front parlours, cobblers in the back; a bird-fancier in the first floor, three families on the second, starvation in the attics, Irishmen in the passage, a "musician" in the front kitchen, and a charwoman and five hungry children in the back one—filth everywhere—a gutter before the houses and a drain behind—clothes drying and slops emptying, from the windows; girls of fourteen or fifteen, with matted hair, walking about barefoot, and in white great-coats, almost their only covering; boys of all ages, in coats of all sizes and no coats at all; men and women, in every variety

of scanty and dirty apparel, lounging, scolding, drinking, smoking, squabbling, fighting, and swearing.

At first glance, the gin palace seems utterly different from its surroundings. "What a change! All is light and brilliancy":

> The gay building with the fantastically ornamented parapet, the illuminated clock, the plate-glass windows surrounded by stucco rosettes, and its profusion of gas-lights in richly-gilt burners, is perfectly dazzling when contrasted with the darkness and dirt we have just left.

Stepping through the door, Dickens finds this pleasing illusion echoed in the interior. A "lofty and spacious saloon'; an elaborately carved and French-polished mahogany bar; a brass rail; chandeliers; two rows of "great casks, painted green and gold," and little plates of cakes and biscuits. The gin palace promises everything a cold, tired drinker might desire with his drink: light, warmth, friendship, food. But the reality is different: it offers gin rather than beer, solitary drinkers rather than friends or workmates, sweet cakes rather than wholesome mutton or potatoes. Even the barmaids give an impression of style over substance:

> [There are] two showily-dressed damsels with large necklaces, dispensing the spirits and "compounds." They are assisted by the ostensible proprietor of the concern, a stout, coarse fellow in a fur cap, put on very much on one side to give him a knowing air, and to display his sandy whiskers to the best advantage.

The "head-dresses and haughty demeanour" of the barmaids contrast starkly with the bearing of the drinkers. A pair of washerwomen, drinking gin and peppermint and nibbling a plate of soft biscuits are a little overawed by the setting, but "the young fellow in a brown coat and bright buttons" feels utterly at home, walking up to the bar "in as careless a manner as if he has been used to green and gold ornaments all his life":

"Gin for you, sir?" says the young lady when she has drawn it: carefully looking every way but the right one, to show that [his] wink had no effect upon her. "For me, Mary, my dear," replies the gentleman in brown. "My name an't Mary as it happens," says the young girl, rather relaxing as she delivers the change. "Well, if it an't, it ought to be," responds the irresistible one; "all the Marys as ever I seen was handsome gals."

But this, again, is mere appearance, an aimless flirtation rather than real affection. And the young man's brash confidence jars with the demeanour of a pair of toothless old men standing next to him at the bar, who came in "just to have a drain," and have quickly made themselves "crying drunk." The illusion of conviviality is finally shattered at closing time, as the passing custom thins out and the occupants of the room dwindle to a straggle of "cold, wretched-looking creatures, in the last stage of emaciation and disease." The very end of the evening is marked with a drunken brawl:

The knot of Irish laborers at the lower end of the place, who have been alternately shaking hands with, and threatening the life of each other, for the last hour, become furious in their disputes, and find-ing it impossible to silence one man, who is particularly anxious to adjust the difference, they resort to the expedient of knocking him down and jumping on him afterwards. The man in the fur cap, and the potboy rush out; a scene of riot and confusion ensues; half the Irishmen get shut out, and the other half get shut in; the potboy is knocked among the tubs in no time; the landlord hits everybody, and everybody hits the landlord; the barmaids scream; the police come in; the rest is a confused mixture of arms, legs, staves, torn coats, shouting, and struggling. Some of the party are borne off to the station-house, and the remainder slink home to beat their wives for complaining, and kick the children for daring to be hungry.

With this disheartening observation, Dickens draws a curtain across the scene, even telling his readers that he has palliated its horrors "because, if it were pursued farther, it would be painful and repulsive." But at the same time, he is not inclined to let them go without heightening their discomfort a little more:

> Well-disposed gentlemen, and charitable ladies, would alike turn with coldness and disgust from a description of the drunken besotted men, and wretched broken-down miserable women, who form no inconsiderable portion of the frequenters of these haunts; forgetting, in the pleasant consciousness of their own rectitude, the poverty of the one, and the temptation of the other.

In other words, his comfortable readers are making a great mistake if they see the gin palaces as nothing more than the refuge of undeserving and despicable scoundrels. Drunkenness is a symptom of a collective failure, for which everyone must be prepared to take some blame:

> Gin-drinking is a great vice in England, but wretchedness and dirt are a greater; and until you improve the homes of the poor, or persuade a half-famished wretch not to seek relief in the temporary oblivion of his own misery, with the pittance which, divided among his family, would furnish a morsel of bread for each, gin-shops will increase in number and splendour. If Temperance Societies would suggest an antidote against hunger, filth, and foul air, or could establish dispensaries for the gratuitous distribution of bottles of Lethe-water, gin-palaces would be numbered among the things that were.

The last story in *Sketches by Boz* makes this point again, in melodramatic style. "The Drunkard's Death" is everything a reader might expect: a tale of poverty, drunkenness, moribund children, and murder, which ends with the main character's suicide by jumping from Waterloo Bridge. Here again, cheap gin is a false comforter, breaking down lives and relationships with the promise of easy, un-earned happiness.

After reading this near-forensic dissection of the evils of the gin palaces, it is something of a surprise to discover that Dickens was a fairly regular drinker of gin. He was fond of the Garrick Club's "Summer Gin Punch," and when he found that a consignment of gin from the distiller Seager Evans had been tampered with, he wrote to suggest that the company change their delivery porters. Gin makes several appearances in his novels (extracts of which are reproduced in Appendix 1) and these appearances are not always so bleak as "Gin-shops" might lead one to expect. Dickens was far too sophisticated a writer to see gin—or, for that matter, money or religion—as simply good or bad. In a famous scene from *A Christmas Carol,* published in 1843, the poor-but-honest Cratchit family toast Christmas with a "hot mixture in a jug with gin and lemons," drunk from "two tumblers and a custard-cup without a handle." But in *Barnaby Rudge,* published in 1841 and set in the violently anti-Catholic Gordon Riots of 1780, the destruction of a gin-distillery on the corner of Fetter Lane and High Holborn becomes a metaphor for the blind violence and monstrous appetites of the London mob:

> The gutters of the street, and every crack and fissure in the stones, ran with scorching spirit, which being dammed up by busy hands, overflowed the road and pavement, and formed a great pool, into which the people dropped down dead by dozens. They lay in heaps all round this fearful pond, husbands and wives, fathers and sons, mothers and daughters, women with children in their arms and babies at their breasts, and drank until they died. While some stooped with their lips to the brink and never raised their heads again, others sprang up from their fiery draught, and danced, half in a mad triumph, and half in the agony of suffocation, until they fell, and steeped their corpses in the liquor that had killed them.

In *Bleak House,* published in 1853, the peculiar death of the alcoholic, illiterate rag-and-bone man Krook draws on older concerns about the physical effects of spirits on the human body, and also symbolizes the way in which strong spirits like gin could burn away the mind and the moral sense:

Here is a small burnt patch of flooring; here is the tinder from a little bundle of burnt paper, but not so light as usual, seeming to be steeped in something; and here is—is it the cinder of a small charred and broken log of wood sprinkled with white ashes, or is it coal? O Horror, he is here! and this, from which we run away, striking out the light and overturning one another into the street, is all that represents him.

Help, help, help! come into this house for Heaven's sake!

Plenty will come in, but none can help. The Lord Chancellor of that Court, true to his title in his last act, has died the death of all Lord Chancellors in all Courts, and of all authorities in all places under all names soever, where false pretences are made, and where injustice is done. Call the death by any name Your Highness will, attribute it to whom you will, or say it might have been prevented how you will, it is the same death eternally—inborn, inbred, engendered in the corrupted humors of the vicious body itself, and that only—Spontaneous Combustion, and none other of all the deaths that can be died.

For an urbane nineteenth-century audience, the notion of spontaneous combustion was something to be scoffed at, and the critic George Henry Lewes attacked Dickens for stretching the credulity of his readers. But Lewes and Dickens were part of a generation that witnessed an equally implausible development. Gin—Carlyle's "infernal principle," Hogarth's "liquid fire"—was becoming, slowly and by degrees, respectable.

In part, this rehabilitation simply reflected the impact of industrialization on so many aspects of Victorian life. One invention—the "continuous still"—revolutionized both the manufacture and the flavor of British gin. This was a truly European innovation: Robert Stein in Scotland, Baglioni in Italy, Cellier Blumenthal in the Netherlands, and Dubrunfaut in France all claimed a hand in its genesis, but it is usually known as the "Coffey still," after the Franco-Irish distiller Aeneas Coffey. Born in Calais, Coffey was educated at Trinity College, Dublin, and on graduating he took a job in the Excise. He rose through the echelons of the service, reaching the dizzy heights of Inspector-General of Excise in Ireland, but in 1824 he resigned. Turning from gamekeeper to poacher, he took over the Dock Distillery in Dublin, and it was here that he carried out the work that made his name.

Up to this point, even the largest pot-stills were no more than scaled-up versions of the alchemists' alembics. Filled with mash and sealed for each "shot," they had to be emptied and cleaned regularly, and the quality of spirit they produced was highly variable. In Coffey's still, patented in 1831, mash and steam could be fed in continuously, with no breaks for replenishment, and the resulting spirit was consistent and clean-tasting. Within a few years British distillers and rectifiers adopted the Coffey still, turning gin manufacture from a medieval craft into a modern industry, and also altering the character of their product. Older pot-still spirits were rough, requiring a heavy mix of botanicals and plenty of sugar to make a palatable drink, along the lines of the eighteenth-century Old Tom. But spirit from a Coffey still required no masking or sweetening, and over a generation or so distillers evolved a new style, lighter and fresher, known as London dry gin.

At the same time, a generation of natural philosophers were unpicking the processes behind fermentation, brewing and distillation. Before his death on the guillotine in 1794 Antoine Lavoisier showed that alcohol was a compound of carbon, hydrogen and oxygen. In 1828 Michael Faraday developed a process for artificially synthesizing alcohol, and in 1858 the Scottish chemist Archibald Scott Couper determined its chemical structure. Theodor Schwann, the pioneer of cell theory, proved that yeast was a micro-organism—*Saccharomyces* or "sugar-mould"—in 1836, and three decades later Louis Pasteur worked out the chemistry underlying the transformation of sugar into alcohol. (Meanwhile, the principles behind Coffey's invention helped to kick-start the chemical industry, making London dry gin a cousin of later plastics, petrol and fertilizers.)

But for drinkers, these technical and intellectual innovations were largely invisible. What they saw was the decline of local distillers and the emergence of new, national brands like Beefeater and Tanqueray. The introduction of a minimum legal still size in the late eighteenth century put many small provincial firms out of business, and at the beginning of the nineteenth century London once again stood at the center of a thriving British gin trade. The West India Docks, opened in 1802, carried botanicals, spices and sugar into the heart of the imperial capital, and canal-boats, carts and coastal vessels brought English grain to the city's markets and exchanges. Gin production required one other ingredient—water—and many of London's distillers took advantage of the (comparatively) sweet natural springs of Clerkenwell and Bloomsbury, outside the bustle of the city's commercial district.

Booth's, Burdett's and Gordon's were all operating in this area by 1800, and in 1830 they were joined by a newcomer—Charles Tanqueray. The fact that Tanqueray was the scion of a deeply pious family of Huguenot clergymen highlights the growing respectability of distilling as a profession and gin as a commodity, and he took full advantage of this to make a fortune. Tanqueray gin was taken up by homesick British colonials around the globe, and also began to find favor in the cocktail shakers of American drinkers—something we'll return to in the next chapter. And gin was on the rise in other, less remote parts of the world, as the Royal Navy's involvement in the Napoleonic Wars gave the Plymouth distillery a new lease of life under the management of Coates & Company. Gin punch became a staple of the officers' mess, particularly when their wives were dining with them, and at a time of national crisis the association of gin with Nelson's fellow naval heroes can have done little to harm its newfound propriety.

Just as London's early modern spirit-makers banded together in the Worshipful Company of Distillers, so their nineteenth-century counterparts formed their own unofficial guild and cartel—the "Rectifiers' Club"—in 1820. Over a monthly lunch at the London Tavern, the city's leading distillers could cement their friendships, impress MPs and ministers, and prevent any disagreeable undercutting by junior competitors. Sir Felix Booth, one of the leading

lights in the Club, backed Sir James Ross's 1829 expedition in search
of the North-West Passage, and for his pains had the icy wastes
of Cape Felix and the Gulf of Boothia named in his honor. The
same 1825 Act of Parliament which had unwittingly paved the way
for the gin palaces also stipulated that distillers could not produce
both "low wines" and rectified gins. For the big-name brands in
the Rectifiers' Club, this meant finding a new and trustworthy
source of base spirit for their products. Some formed partner-
ships with provincial English firms, but most turned to Scottish
whisky distillers, who were enjoying their own renaissance after
the Prince Regent set a fashion for all things Highland. Booth
and the Club lobbied hard for more concessions from the government, and in 1850 they were granted exemption from duty on all
export spirits—a move which turned both established names like
Gordon's and newcomers like Gilbey's and Beefeater, established
in 1857 and 1863 respectively, into some of the first global brands.
With this global identity came a new concern with image and
marketing. Bottles, for example, were no longer just a convenient
way of carrying and storing spirits; they became a symbol of the
company's outlook, its heritage, its quality, and a way for customers
to pick out their favorite brand.

And at home, the growing British taste for whisky over brandy
or gin helped, paradoxically, to reinforce its rising status. No longer
seen as the drink of the urban poor, gin began to appear in the
inventories of reputable grocers like Fortnum & Mason, and on
the sideboards of respectable families (sometimes disguised with
the backslang label "Nig"). Isabella Beeton mentioned gin several
times in her magisterial *Book of Household Management,* published
in 1861, though generally as a solvent rather than an ingredient
in its own right. Mrs. Beeton recommended it as a way of getting
wrinkles out of light-colored silks, as an ingredient in lotions, and
as part of the treatment for "concussion of the brain" and "strong
apoplexy." The first slimming craze, kicked off by the undertaker
William Banting's *Essay on Corpulence, Addressed to the Public,* published in 1863, helped body-conscious Victorians to acquire a taste

for unsweetened London dry gin. And in the third quarter of the nineteenth century the *Phylloxera* aphid—brought from North America to France by over-enthusiastic British botanists—wiped out almost all of the continent's ancient vineyards, and severely dented the production of brandy and other wine spirits. Even entomology, it seemed, was striking a blow for British gin.

But what was the liquid in these new, deep-green, branded bottles actually like? According to John Rack's bestselling *French Wine and Liquor Manufacturer,* published in 1868, a typical London dry gin might be flavored not only with juniper, but also with a selection from more than a dozen botanicals:

> Sweet fennel, orange peel, orange flower water, coriander seed, angel-
> ica root, calamus root, cassia buds, lemon peel, cardamom, oil of cedar,
> sweet almonds, nutmegs, mace, caraway seed, wintergreen [and] honey.

Rack was deeply critical of distillers who thought they could get away with selling "gin" flavored only with turpentine or oil of juniper:

> The liquor at present known by the name of gin in this country, as
> a general thing, is a very different article from that imported from
> Holland, and consists of plain spirit flavored with oil of juniper and
> sometimes oil of turpentine, and small quantities of *certain* aromatics.
> The various recipes, which from time to time have been printed in
> books, produce a flavored spirit, bearing *no resemblance* to Holland
> gin, or the more esteemed samples of London gin. The authors seem
> to have had no practical knowledge on the subject, and appear to
> have imbibed a *juniper-berry mania.* Oil of juniper, in the hands of
> these gentlemen, appears to be a perfect *aqua mirabilis* that readily
> converts whisky into gin, and imparts the rich creamy flavor of
> *Schiedam schnapps* to crude spirit.

But he was not immune to the temptations of adulteration: some of his recipes featured ether, tartaric acid, asafoetida and garlic:

A rich *mellowness* that combines well with gin, turning on the Holland flavor, is given by a very small quantity of garlic, say 4 or 5 cloves to 100 gallons, or about 15 grains of asafoetida, with one grain of ambergris rubbed to a powder with a little white sand or loaf sugar.

And he even proposed a technique for "improving Wine and Spirits by Electricity":

> The process consists in plunging into the vat, two plates of platinum or of silver, having attached to them two wires of the same metal, which are connected with the poles of an electric battery . . . The time necessary to transform a low grade wine or spirit to one of an agreeable and superior quality, is from two to three weeks, with the battery continually working.

Fortunately for nineteenth-century gin-drinkers, Dr. Arthur Hill Hassall was taking a close interest in the matter. Hassall was a physician at the Royal Free Hospital and an enthusiastic amateur microscopist, and he combined these skills with a characteristically Victorian concern for purity and cleanliness. In *A Microscopical Examination of the Water Supplied to the Inhabitants of London and the Suburban Districts,* published in 1850, he provided a pithy and chilling summary of the capital's disgusting plight:

> Under the present system of London Water Supply, a portion of the inhabitants of the metropolis are made to consume, in some form or another, a portion of their own excrement, and moreover, to pay for the privilege.

Hassall's work caught the attention of Thomas Wakley, the crusading editor of *The Lancet,* who engaged him to analyze the purity of every food he could lay his hands on. Hassall's studies, published in *The Lancet* between 1851 and 1854, revealed marzipan carrots colored with red lead, ginger lozenges adulterated with kiln ash, snuff cut with potash, "Havana" cigars filled with apple peel, and coffee mixed with dried horse liver. A collection of these articles—*Food and its Adulterations,* published in 1855—included a section on gin, the contents of which suggest that Hassall had not kept up with changing fashions in this field. He found that gin was still being adulterated in some old-fashioned ways: sweetened with sugar, diluted with water, spiked with turpentine or sulphuric acid. And he noted that unscrupulous refiners were clarifying their spirits with alum, potash and zinc sulphate, sweetening it with lead acetate, and flavoring it with laurel water and spirits of almonds (both of which contained cyanide). But he also expressed deep concern at the high levels of "fixed acrid substances" like grains of paradise, cinnamon and cassia—commonplace botanicals in the new London dry gins.

Hassall's reports helped to provoke government action in the form of the 1860 Food Adulteration Act, and for many of his contemporaries the rising status of gin spoke to a far greater fear—degeneration. Like evolution and capitalism, degeneration was one of the buzzwords of Victorian thought, though unlike them it fell out of use early in the twentieth century. Its impact cut across science, politics and literature from Émile Zola to Sherlock Holmes and H. G. Wells' *The Time Machine.* Different writers took degeneration theory in radically different directions, but they shared a basic concern that the human race was declining, both physically and mentally, individually and collectively. This idea derived much of its intellectual inspiration from Charles Darwin's theory of evolution, but its roots went deep into European culture. In its most fundamental form degeneration theory reflected a growing, almost countercultural unease with the effects of industrialization on the bodies and minds of European populations. Decades of political unrest, culminating in the "Year of Revolutions" in 1848, led governments and their supporters to fear the mob as a degenerate force with a mind of its own. Did the stunted, drunken and amoral working classes in fact represent the future of humanity? And if they did, what were the consequences for the British Empire, that bastion of Christian civilization? Britain might lose a Darwinian struggle for existence with the other European powers, which might in turn be overpowered by the "savages" of Africa and Asia.

With so much at stake, physicians across Europe began to seek out the causes of degeneration, and many agreed that syphilis, city life, and distilled spirits were prime suspects. As we have seen, the idea that over-consumption of gin or brandy might lead to chronic disease was common in the writings of late-eighteenth century physicians like Thomas Trotter and Benjamin Rush. Darwin's grandfather, the poet and freethinker Erasmus Darwin, propounded an early version of alcoholic degeneration in a footnote to his erotically-charged botanical epic "The Loves of the Plants," published in 1791. Darwin senior thought that the myth of Prometheus stealing fire from the gods and concealing it in his bosom, only for his liver to be pecked out by an eagle, was a perfect metaphor for the effect of drinking spirits:

> The swallowing of drams cannot be better represented in hiero-glyphic language than by taking fire into one's bosom; and certain it is, that the general effect of drinking spirituous liquors is an inflamed, schirrous, or paralytic liver, with its various critical or consequential diseases, as leprous eruptions on the face, gout, dropsy, epilepsy, insanity. It is remarkable that all diseases from drinking spirituous liquors are liable to become hereditary, even to the third generation; gradually increasing, if the cause be continued, till the family become extinct.

Bénédict Morel, a French asylum-doctor, took up this idea in his influential *Traité des Dégénérescences,* published in 1857. Morel, a devout Catholic, saw degeneration as a working-out of Christian original sin, and used heavy drinking to demonstrate the way in which a healthy family's heredity could be destroyed in as few as three generations. This disquieting possibility found stark expression in the work of another French physician—Marcel Legrain, author of *Hérédité et Alcoolisme,* published in 1889. According to Legrain, anything more than the most modest consumption of spirits would result in:

> The slow but fatal brutalization of the individual; intellectual and physical sterilization of the race with its social consequences; the lowering of the intellectual level and depopulation, indubitable causes of the decline of civilized nations.

Morel and Legrain's concerns struck a chord with their contemporaries: though most doctors continued to prescribe alcohol, they were also increasingly *au fait* with the idea that heavy drinking might itself be a disease. In 1852 the Swedish physician Magnus Huss coined the term *alcoholismus chronicus* to distinguish the effects of long-term heavy drinking from acute alcohol poisoning. Researchers in other nations followed suit, deploying a veritable thesaurus of terms to describe the condition: dipsomania, habitual drunkenness, *mania a potu, delirium tremens,* alcoholic insanity, alcoholic epilepsy, alcoholic monomania. A survey of British asylum doctors revealed that around fourteen percent of patients in their institutions suffered from chronic alcoholism, and under the 1898 Inebriates Act anyone convicted of drunkenness more than three times within a year could be incarcerated in a state reformatory—proof that the problems of heavy drinking were now as much the province of the medical profession as of the church or the state.

In January 1831 Joseph Livesey, a weaver-turned-cheesemonger from Preston in Lancashire, published issue one of *The Moral Reformer,* priced at sixpence. This was the first national journal dedicated to the principles of a new and radical movement: temperance. Livesey and his fellow temperance advocates made common cause with politicians, physicians and clergymen seeking to end what they saw as the scourge of spirit-drinking. Over the next half-century dozens of journals, hundreds of penny tracts, and innumerable illustrated lectures proclaimed the righteousness and dignity of sobriety. And Preston—"the Jerusalem of temperance," according to one over-awed abstainer—inspired a new coalition of the respectable, bringing the missionary middle class and the self-improving working class together in a typically Victorian crusade against ill-health, apathy and immorality. Temperance meetings, particularly in the industrial north, were soul-stirring affairs, a fusion of the popular theater and the Non-Conformist chapel. Hymns were sung; sermons were preached; and reformed sots made tearful confessions of their misdeeds in front of the assembled congregation. To take the pledge was to gain the admiration and support of one's community; to break it was to shame oneself in the most public way possible.

From the start, the proponents of temperance knew they had a mountain to climb: how could they convert the many Victorian workers who drank startling volumes of alcohol in the course of their daily lives? In the early twentieth century Thomas Okey, Professor of Italian at Cambridge, recalled that his father—a hard-working Spitalfields weaver, and no drunkard—had consumed two large tumblers of gin-and-water and three or four pints of beer per day while seated at his loom. Recognizing this, many early temperance societies demanded abstinence from spirits only, and some were quite opposed to the idea of swearing off beer. In Warrington in 1834 one Richard Mee was preparing to sign a pledge of complete abstinence, but his friend Peter Phillips seized his arm and cried "Thee mustn't, Richard, thee'll die!" Whether he knew it or not, Phillips was employing the same argument Hogarth had used in "Gin Lane" and "Beer Street." Beer was the working-man's nourishment and refreshment; wine had a long Classical and Biblical provenance; but gin was unnatural, fiery and destructive. Even if one took a sympathetic view of Proverbs 31:6—"Give strong drink unto him that is ready to perish"—spirits were difficult to defend, unless one was prepared to take the dubious step of arguing for freedom of pleasure.

Ironically, it was the effects of the 1830 Beer Act that led Livesey and others to rethink their attitudes to beer and gin. The rapid rise of the gin palaces had confirmed their suspicions of distilled spirits, and they initially supported the Beer Act as a blow against gin-drinking. But by making cheap beer available to the industrial working classes, the Act provoked a new wave of drunken disorder in the temperance movement's northern heartland. Livesey was one of the first to call for a move to complete abstinence, and he claimed scientific proof for his argument. Chemists like Lavoisier had proved that the same compound—alcohol—gave beer and spirits their intoxicating powers, making beer little more than gin in disguise. Physiologists had shown that the supporters of beer were wrong to claim it as a super-food: pound for pound, grain was far more nutritious baked into bread than brewed into beer. And the falling prices of tea, coffee and cocoa—often sold by temperance-minded companies like Rowntree, Cadbury and Twinings—meant that beer or gin were not the only options for refreshment after a hard day in the factory.

From August 1832 Livesey's Preston Temperance Society demanded complete abstinence from its members, and a temperance print from the early 1840s illustrates this change of heart. Titled "The English Juggernaut," it riffed on the contemporary English belief that, during his festival, devotees of the Hindu god Lord Jagannath would throw themselves under the wheels of his chariot. A great cart, loaded with barrels and topped with a chimney spouting "Misery, Disease, Death," was crushing hundreds of poor drinkers as they tried to flee. The largest barrel on the cart was marked "Beer," but the cask at the bottom of the pile, on which all the others were stacked, carried the label "Gin." In the background a temple with "Gin" engraved on its portico had fallen into ruin, but a brewery next to it was thriving.

Even if gin had truly been defeated (and what we've seen so far shows that it had not), the temperance movement was far from united in its aims. Chartists—members of the first working class labor movement, based around a "People's Charter" of basic political rights—wanted to free working men from the shackles of alcohol, allowing them to fight more forcefully for their own liberation. But they were deeply uneasy with the idea, implicit in much temperance rhetoric, that the poor were to blame for their own condition because they were lazy and drunken. Ernest Jones, a leading Chartist, accused temperance reformers of confusing cause with consequence:

> Extreme privation breeds extreme indulgence. Had [the working man] not been cast so low yesterday he would not cast *himself* so low today. Had you not denied him *bread* last week, he would have denied *himself gin* in this.

E.P. Thompson famously argued that Methodism played a crucial role in molding Victorian workers to the discipline of factory life, and the historian Brian Harrison has shown that the Chartists saw temperance in much the same light. Why should workers be deprived of beer, their traditional comfort, merely to line the pockets of rich industrialists more efficiently? When advocates of abstinence blamed violent disturbances on the availability of cheap beer, one writer in *The Chartist* commented, acidly, that:

> It is extraordinary that all murders are committed upon beer—gin is quite a tranquilizing, humanity-teaching liquid.

Most Victorian and Edwardian commentators assumed that women drank more spirits than men, particularly after marriage and childbirth. According to an unnamed policeman quoted in Charles Booth's *Life and Labor of the London Poor,* published in 1902, "it is not till they get older that women take to gin and ale and become regular soakers." Female drinking—particularly when it was done in private—was seen to be particularly dangerous. Mainstream Victorian culture insisted that wives and mothers should serve as exemplars of Christian morality for their husbands and children, and the "Angel in the House" was not supposed to be a tippler on the quiet. In the early 1870s temperance groups drew attention to the high consumption of "grocers' gin" in some parts of the country. Coteries of apparently decent housewives were, they claimed, holding tipsy tea parties, with gin served in teacups or sherry glasses. Even some kinds of drug addiction were a little more genteel than gin-drinking, and many patent medicines marketed for women were liberally laced with opium or cocaine.

By the middle of the nineteenth century, temperance organizations began to notice a paradox in their campaigns. As they struggled harder to encourage abstinence, as they gained more members, as they denounced the demon drink in ever-louder tones, so the thirst of Victorian drinkers seemed to be renewed. Working-class pub-goers were sticking to their beer, and the middle classes were increasingly attached to their grocers' gin. What else could possibly be done? Some temperance societies preferred to stick to their established tactic of "moral suasion"—put simply, education and exhortation—but more and more embraced the idea of legislative action. Why not tax alcohol out of existence or, better still, make it illegal?

For any Regency government, this would have been laughed out of the committee room as merely a swift form of political suicide. Every MP had to arrange a generous binge for his electorate on polling day, and brewers and distillers held considerable powers of patronage. But mid-Victorian politics was much more at ease with high seriousness and social reform, and there was moral capital to be gained from supporting the temperance position. In 1853 the United Kingdom Alliance was established as a national political front for temperance advocacy. Four years later it persuaded sympathetic MPs to enter a "Permissive Bill," which would allow local ratepayers to vote on banning the sale of alcohol in their districts.

The Alliance's bill failed, but it caught the attention of a rising star in the Commons: William Ewart Gladstone. As Chancellor of the Exchequer from 1859 to 1866 Gladstone pursued a free trade policy on drink, but when he became leader of the Liberal Party in 1867, and Prime Minister in 1868, he became more sympathetic to the aims of the temperance reformers. In 1872 he led the campaign for a new Licensing Bill, intended to clarify the morass of existing legislation on this subject, and to place new restrictions on spirit sales and pub opening times. For the British temperance movement this was the high-water mark of their political clout, but the Bill was deeply controversial—duties on alcohol represented a third of total government income—and only made it to the statute book on a second attempt. The Liberals went on to lose the 1874 general election: "We have been borne down," Gladstone said, "on a torrent of beer and gin."

Ultimately the British temperance movement lost its struggle for moral authority and political power, but in the U.S. significant lessons were learned from its failure. Benjamin Rush's *Inquiry Into the Effects of Ardent Spirits* had inspired the first American temperance society, established in Saratoga County, New York, in 1808, though its principles were distinctly flexible:

> No member shall drink rum, gin, whiskey, wine, or any distilled spirits, or compositions of the same, or any of them, except by advice of a physician, or in case of actual disease; also, excepting wine at public dinners, under a penalty of 25 cents; provided that this article shall not infringe any religious ordinance.

But the most forceful stimulus for U.S. temperance was the "Second Great Awakening"—a religious revival which began in the 1790s and ran through to the 1840s, and which gave the urban working and middle classes a new sense of moral purpose. Revivalists founded the American Temperance Society in Boston in 1826, and a group of evangelical physicians set up the Pennsylvania Society for Discouraging the Use of Ardent Spirits a few years later. Another Pennsylvanian—Thomas Poage Hunt, the self-styled "Drunkard's Friend"—created a "Cold Water Army" of Sunday school pupils, who gathered to chant excruciating "poetic pledges":

I do not think
I'll ever drink
Whiskey or Gin,
Brandy or Rum,
Or any thing
That will make drunk [sic] come.

or the equally dismal:

Trusting in help from Heaven above,
We pledge ourselves to works of love,
With hearts and hands united stand
To spread a blessing o'er the land.
And now resolve we will not take,
Nor give, nor buy, nor sell, nor make,
Through all the years of mortal life
Those drinks which cause pain, woe and strife—
Rum, Brandy, Whiskey, Cordials fine,
Gin, Cider, Porter, Ale, and Wine.

By 1833 the U.S. had more than five thousand local temperance societies and 23 state organizations, with an estimated (though possibly
exaggerated) million and a quarter members. In May of that year
they came together at a national conference to form the American
Temperance Union, and to deplore the outrageous indulgence of
American drinkers. By the early 1830s city-dwelling American men
were drinking as much as Londoners at the height of the gin craze,
and their tipple of choice was corn whisky. With a unity of purpose
that their British counterparts always lacked, the American
Temperance Union began to call for the Prohibition of alcohol in
all forms, and thanks to the federal structure of the U.S. government
it was able to achieve some notable early successes in state legislatures. Maine passed a "Fifteen-Gallon Law" in 1838, which aimed
at *de facto* Prohibition by banning the sale of spirits in quantities less
than the eponymous fifteen gallons. Though deeply unpopular, and
repealed within eighteen months, the "Fifteen-Gallon Law" gave

temperance campaigners a taste of what they could achieve. Over the next two decades temperance and Prohibition came to rival slavery as the central issues in U.S. politics, a point made by the two runaway bestsellers of the era: Harriet Beecher Stowe's affecting abolitionist masterpiece *Uncle Tom's Cabin,* published in 1852, and Timothy Shay Arthur's juicy Prohibitionist epic *Ten Nights in a Bar-Room and What I Saw There,* published in 1854.

At the outbreak of the American Civil War in April 1861 thirteen states had enacted Prohibition statutes, and over the next generation U.S. drinking habits changed significantly. Gin made a little headway in the North-American market: the first U.S. dry gin distillery, Fleischmann's, opened in Ohio in 1870, and the Meagher brothers began to produce gin in Montreal in 1873. But the total amount of alcohol consumed fell by twenty percent, and American men began to shift their allegiance from whisky to beer. They also began to frequent a distinctively American drinking-place: the saloon, which enjoyed a brief heyday at the end of the nineteenth century. For immigrant workers, set adrift in the great industrial cities, the saloon offered comradeship, a chance to find work and lodgings and to meet others from the old country, and even the possibility of a "free" lunch with a five-cent glass of beer. For the supporters of abstinence, however, saloons were nests of gambling, prostitution and drunken obscenity, and they were subject to increasingly bold attacks by the Women's Christian Temperance Union and the Anti-Saloon League.

These organizations found natural allies in other groups trying to reform American morals, from Anthony Comstock's New York Society for the Suppression of Vice to campaigns against Walt Whitman's *Leaves of Grass* and Mormon polygamy ("Utah's monstrous lust," according to one activist). Spirits burned beneath a cauldron of corruption in which simmered nude paintings, the cinema, music-hall dancers, motor-cars, pornographic novels, and swearing in the presence of women or children. Liquor and lust—the "Devil's Siamese twins"—might corrode the souls of any innocent American youth.

By the end of the nineteenth century this powerful American movement was spoiling for a fight, desperate to finish what the Gin Acts had started a hundred and fifty years before. Drinking and drunkenness was the hottest issue in politics, and after the First World War the U.S. government would carry out a "Great Experiment" to see whether the baleful influence of hard drink could be permanently eradicated. At this turning point in its history, gin occupied a deeply contradictory position. On the one hand, it was more highly regarded than it had been for two centuries; on the other, it was still a literary shorthand for squalor and poverty. And in a twist of fate, it was Prohibition that reconciled these opposing meanings, and made gin into the drink of youth, of style, of modernity—truly the spirit of the age. But before we enter the shadowy world of speakeasies and bathtub gin, we are going to take a trip around the world, one which begins with a malarial fever, and ends with the birth of the cocktail.

# 4

## From Chinchón to Martinez

B E HONEST. HAVE you ever sat down at a bar and ordered a straight gin? Not in preparation for a gin and tonic, not under the guise of a very dry martini—just a single or double measure of gin, served in a shot glass, to be drunk neat. If you are an Anglophone drinker, your answer is fairly easy to predict. Enthusiasts for Dutch genever maintain the tradition of chasing down pints of cold lager with a *kopstoot*—tellingly, "a blow to the head"—but in the early twenty-first century the overwhelming majority of Western consumers prefer their gin with mixers or in cocktails.

Our modern habits may seem unremarkable—modern habits usually do—but they are a direct result of one of the great shifts in the history of gin-drinking. Well into the nineteenth century, most gin was drunk neat, with perhaps an occasional dash of bitters to soften the rough edge of pot-still spirit. This was gin as the merchants of the VOC, William of Orange, William Hogarth, Benjamin Rush, Thomas Rowlandson, and Thomas Carlyle all knew it. But over the course of that remarkable century, first American and then European drinkers began to take their gin in the form of cocktails—classically, a mixture of spirit, bitters, flavoring and syrup—and with a variety of mixers, from quinine-laced tonic water to lime cordial or vermouth.

This changing taste ran in parallel with the shifting character of gin, as the heavy, sweetened Old Toms lost ground to the new London dry gins. Old Tom tended to dominate any mixed drink, but the London dry gins took their place more easily with other flavors. Color, as well as flavor, was an influence. The rich, deep color of neat brandy or whisky was part of the pleasure of drinking, something to be savored; plain, clear gin was perhaps a little too reminiscent of water. But this was not just a matter of taste. Strange as it may seem, cocktails also changed the ethics of gin-drinking. As we have seen, for eighteenth- and nineteenth-century moralists few other vices were so depraved, so unhealthy, and so irretrievably *déclassé*. Cocktails palliated this stigma: to call the drink in your hand a martini was far more stylish, far more appealing, far less loaded with moral and medical and historical baggage, than to call it a glassful of neat or nearly-neat gin. In this sense, the history of respectable gin-drinking is very largely the history of the cocktail.

Cocktail: the word alone evokes the Roaring Twenties and the Bright Young Things, chrome and streamlining, speakeasies and the Charleston—a world we'll explore in the next chapter. But the cocktail was created long before the advent of Prohibition. Almost every notable gin cocktail was originally formulated in the nineteenth century, and three of the most basic cocktail ingredients—bitters, vermouth and soda water—emerged in the eighteenth century, from a ferment of commerce and pleasure which also produced patent medicines and *eau de Cologne*. Indeed, one might even see the cocktail—a small but potent gulp of highly-flavored liquor—as a kind of proto-gin *redux*.

Just as the identity and meaning of gin was forged in the first great age of globalization, so the character of the cocktail owed much to the new European colonies and empires of the Enlightenment. Colonists carried gin with them as they travelled around the world, and their perceptions of the drink were changed irrevocably by this experience. Tonic water, vermouth, bitters, even lime cordial were all responses to the challenges of staying healthy in the hostile milieu of long sea voyages and tropical colonies. When you order a gin and tonic, a martini, a Pink Gin or a Gimlet, you are paying inadvertent tribute to the imperial pretensions of eighteenth- and nineteenth-century Europe. In the course of its travels around the world, the cocktail has been an intensely fruitful subject for modern myth-making, and this chapter is framed with two of the most tantalizing of these myths. We'll conclude with the creation of the martini, but we begin with the feverish delirium of a seventeenth-century Spanish aristocrat.

In the opinion of her physicians, Doña Francisca Henriquez de Ribera, fourth Condesa de Chinchón, was dying. In the summer of 1638 the Condesa had contracted a serious relapsing fever, exacerbated by the humid heat of Lima in Peru, where she lived with her husband, the Conde de Chinchón, a Spanish emissary. She had been bled, blistered and purged, and there was nothing more that could be done; the doctors withdrew, and summoned a priest. At his wits' end, the Conde called on a Jesuit missionary (or possibly a local healer; accounts vary), who offered to treat the Condesa with a native medicine known as *ayac cara* or *quinquina*— "bitter bark" or "bark of barks." The priest (or healer) made an infusion of the bark, and persuaded the Condesa to swallow several mouthfuls of this astringent liquid. Within a few days her fever had settled and she had regained her strength. The Conde and Condesa brought supplies of the bark with them when they returned to their estate at Chinchón in Spain, and introduced it to the Spanish court as "cinchona" or "Jesuits' bark." When botanists came to give a name to the tree whose bark possessed such extraordinary powers, they remembered the Condesa, and called it *Cinchona officinalis*.

So, at least, goes an anecdote told by the Italian physician Sebastiano Bado, writing in his *Anastasis Corticis Peruviae seu Chinae Defensio,* published in 1663. Bado gave no exact date for the events he described, which he had heard about third hand, but claimed that they had taken place around a generation before he was writing. This is just the kind of urban-mythic detail that raises concerns for historians, and Mark Honigsbaum's forensic analysis of Bado's tale shows that a degree of suspicion is not misplaced. The Conde and

Condesa de Chinchón were real historical figures, but the Conde's diary, kept daily over eleven years and detailing his and his wife's health, makes no mention of any miraculous cure. The Condesa, meanwhile, never made it back to Spain: she died in Colombia, of causes that are not recorded, and was buried in Cartagena.

If Bado's story is little more than a charming fiction, what was the truth behind the discovery of this remarkable bark? One place to begin is with malaria, the disease that nearly carried away his Condesa. Malaria is one of the oldest human (and, indeed, animal) diseases: genetic evidence suggests that it has troubled human beings and their ancestors for much of the past million years, accompanying early hominids as they moved out of Africa and across Europe and Asia. Its distinctive symptom is relapsing fever—fits of sweating and shivering which typically recur every three or four days. It is caused by a microscopic parasite with a complicated life cycle both inside and outside of its victims, and spread by the bite of *Anopheles* mosquitoes. At some point in its evolution this parasite diverged into two strains: *Plasmodium falciparum,* prevalent in Africa, which causes a severe and often fatal form of malaria; and *Plasmodium vivax,* prevalent in northern Asia and Europe, which causes a debilitating chronic form known in Britain as ague. Malaria today is almost by definition a tropical disease, but it was for thousands of years an occupational hazard for the inhabitants of low-lying European estuaries and fens—a fact reflected in its Italian name: *mala aria,* "bad air."

But malaria, like cholera, like the Black Death, was and still is a disease of movement, and it has followed migrants and armies across continents and oceans—a process dramatically accelerated by the activities of the VOC, the English East India Company and their peers. Ironically, it seems that malaria reached South America in the blood of Spanish adventurers, and there is little firm evidence to suggest that the indigenous peoples of the continent were aware of cinchona and its properties before their encounters with the conquistadores. The cinchona tree is native to the lower slopes of the Andes, and many different strains are found in a long belt of forest running through Venezuela, Colombia, Ecuador, Peru and Bolivia. Alexander Humboldt, the German explorer and a leading light in Romantic science, gave a typically precise and poetic description:

> This beautiful tree, which is adorned with leaves above five inches long and two broad, growing in dense forests, seems always to aspire to rise above its neighbors. As its upper branches wave to and fro in the wind, their red foliage produces a strange and beautiful effect, recognizable from a great distance.

Modern research has shown that the bark of the cinchona tree contains four alkaloids which act against *Plasmodium*: cinchodine, cinchonidine, quinidine, and, most powerful, quinine. In its purified state, quinine—named after *quina,* the native Peruvian word for bark—is crystalline and white, highly toxic in overdose, and, like many alkaloids, coruscatingly fluorescent under ultra-violet light. The secret of cinchona bark lies in quinine's double effect, not only calming fever and muscle spasms, but also blocking a crucial step in the metabolism of the parasite, incapacitating and eventually killing it.

The exact circumstances of this discovery seem likely to remain a mystery, but by the seventeenth century both Spanish Jesuit missionaries and various native groups appear to have been using it to soothe relapsing fevers. Soon after the conquest of South America, Jesuit priests were sent out to spread the Gospel and the virtues of Spanish civilization amongst the surviving native peoples. In 1631 Agostino Salumbrino, a Jesuit apothecary in the Spanish trading post at Lima, sent samples of cinchona bark back to the order's headquarters in Rome, and by the 1640s it was being used to treat relapsing fevers in the inhabitants of the notoriously sickly Pontine marshes to the south of the city.

But the arrival of cinchona bark in Europe coincided with the climax of the Catholic Counter-Reformation, Rome's great attempt to roll back the gains of Protestantism. Any drug associated with the Jesuits—seen by suspicious Protestant leaders as the Pope's own spies and saboteurs—was unlikely to find favor in England, the Dutch Republic or the German states, and cinchona bark was surprisingly slow to be accepted into the armamentaria of European physicians. When Charles II of England contracted a particularly harsh ague in the early 1670s, his own doctors could not or would not prescribe it, and he was treated in secret by Robert Talbor, who had a personal stash of cinchona bark smuggled out of Spain. Charles recovered, and—to the chagrin of his doctors— offered Talbor, an unlicensed mountebank, membership in the Royal College of Physicians. Talbor clearly had an eye for the main chance, and in 1679 he received three thousand gold crowns for offering the same treatment to Louis XIV, the "Sun King" of France. Physicians quickly realized that the best extracts were made not with water but with wine or spirits: the cinchona alkaloids are insoluble in water, but highly soluble in alcohol. (This had the added bonus of ameliorating the intense bitterness of the bark, which made any decoction difficult to keep down, particularly at the height of a malarial fever.)

By the early eighteenth century, physicians in every Western European nation were using cinchona bark to treat relapsing fevers. The Jesuits had taken it around the world with their missions— even as far as China, where in 1693 they had cured the Qing emperor Kangxi, to the astonishment of his courtiers (who were convinced that these red-haired western-ocean barbarians would fail). And in an age of imperial aspiration, the wider significance of the drug was becoming clear. Cinchona bark was a powerful new medicine, but it also possessed enormous strategic and economic potential. Any army or navy equipped with the drug would stand a much higher chance of surviving and succeeding in a tropical theater of war. Merchants could use it to leverage their influence with Eastern potentates. Slave-owners could increase the efficiency of their chattels, and reduce the expense of replacing slaves who succumbed to malaria. For Protestant nations, the question was no longer whether to trust this enigmatic Jesuitical remedy. Rather, it was how to break the Catholic Spanish monopoly, and obtain a secure and copious supply.

For Spanish traders, however, this monopoly was more of a liability. There were no neatly tended groves of cinchona trees; the bark had to be collected from remote mountainsides by parties of skilled natives. If this task were left to unskilled hands, the trees might be killed. A straggling line of caravans and trading posts, easily intercepted or raided, connected these parties with Spanish-controlled ports, and even when the bark was baled and loaded into Spanish ships it was far from safe. Realizing that there was a profit to be made, canny English buccaneers began to seize cinchona bark along with the more traditional pirate staples of gold, gunpowder and rum. Other nations began, quietly, to investigate the possibility of moving in on the trade. In 1737, during a French-sponsored expedition to Peru—ostensibly to determine the length of a degree of longitude at the equator—the French geographer Charles Marie de la Condamine collected cinchona seeds and data on the conditions in which they grew.

Rumors of these attempts at espionage reached Madrid, and in 1768 the Spanish monarchy did what it could to shore up its monopoly. Troops were sent to guard the caravans, and cinchona bark was exported only in cases sealed with the royal coat of arms. At home, Spanish importers tried to turn their nation into a clearing-house and supply depot for the rest of Europe. They graded cinchona bark into four categories, with the best reserved for official gifts and the royal family, and lower-quality bark given to monastic hospitals or used to make tinctures for export to Britain and France. But this was only a temporary solution: by the early nineteenth century the various South American independence movements had seriously weakened Spanish control over cinchona bark importation, and other European states grew bolder in their efforts to cultivate cinchona trees in their own tropical colonies.

From the late eighteenth century the British army and navy began to exploit the value of cinchona bark in their tropical operations. Under the instructions of the surgeon James Lind—most famous for his work on scurvy, which we'll encounter shortly—the Admiralty issued a wine-based cinchona tonic to the crews of Royal Navy frigates operating off West Africa, and in 1803 Nelson ordered "a dose of Peruvian-bark, in a preparation of good sound wine or spirits," to be taken before sailors made landfall on swampy coasts. But it was the catastrophic Walcheren Expedition of July 1809 which drove home the military necessity of cinchona, even in the least exotic of battlefields. This was an attempt to gain a foothold in Napoleon's Fortress Europe, by landing thousands of British troops on the notoriously sickly Dutch island of Walcheren. Napoleon expected the British to withdraw within a month, and his prediction was not far wrong. In December, after more than four thousand deaths and almost twelve thousand cases of malaria, the expedition was called off.

Walcheren made British commanders realize that they needed their own reliable supply of cinchona bark, one not dependent upon the vagaries of politics and war. By the 1840s British soldiers and colonists in India were consuming seven hundred tons of prophylactic cinchona bark every year, and from 1848 the military and naval rum ration was augmented with regular shots of cinchona tonic. In the 1850s and 1860s British explorers and the Dutch botanist Justus Carl Hasskarl obtained seeds, and experimental plantations were set up in Java, Jamaica and southern India. But the trees did not thrive under their new guardians, and even the enormous Indian plantations—128 million trees by 1883 in Ceylon alone—could supply only a fraction of the British demand. In 1820 two French pharmacists, Pierre-Joseph Pelletier and Joseph Bienaimé Caventou, had discovered that a water-soluble form of quinine could be extracted by boiling cinchona bark in dilute sulphuric acid, and by the late nineteenth century quinine sulphate was the main ingredient in a host of elixirs marketed at Western colonials. Far and away the most successful of these new remedies was a new sparkling "Indian Tonic Water."

Carbonated water was perhaps the most pleasingly serendipitous by-product of late-eighteenth century natural philosophy. In 1772 the theologian and chemist Joseph Priestley, then the minister of the Mill Hill chapel in Leeds, published a short paper on his experiments in a local brewery. After pouring water back and forth between two glasses in the "fixed air" above the fermenting mash, Priestley found he had made a refreshing, sparkling beverage, and he suggested that his readers might produce the same effect by making their own fixed air (in modern terms, carbon dioxide) from oil of vitriol and chalk. This idea was taken up by Jean-Jacob Schweppe, a young German who abandoned his apprenticeship with a watchmaker in Geneva to make his fortune in soft drinks. In 1783 he devised a technique for making Priestley's water on an industrial scale, and seven years later he established a factory in London. Schweppe initially played up the therapeutic potential of his products: a light soda water was perfect for relieving indigestion after a meal, but a strongly-carbonated water would help to ease the agonizing pains of bladder stones.

As with the proto-gins three centuries before, however, the fact that Schweppe's waters were pleasurable to drink quickly overrode their value as medicines, and by the mid-nineteenth century several companies were marketing their own brands of flavored soda waters. Schweppe's were not the first to include quinine—an 1858 patent held by Erasmus Bond, about whom little else is known, described "an improved aerated tonic liquid" flavored with quinine and bitter orange—but in 1870 they began to produce an "INDIAN quinine TONIC," aimed specifically at British colonials who had to begin each day with a dose of bitter quinine sulphate. Adding a little citric acid to the tonic, in the form of lemon juice, helped the quinine to dissolve, and a touch of sugar took the edge off the bitterness. At this crucial moment in the history of the gin and tonic, however, things become frustratingly vague. Cultural historians of drink agree that Schweppe's scored a big success with its new quinine tonic; that British colonials quickly acquired a taste for drinking it with ice and the new London dry gins, particularly as an afternoon chota-peg (from the Hindi word for a small measure); and that they brought this taste with them when they, or their descendents, returned to the mother country. Concrete evidence for this is hard to come by, but it is clear that by the early years of the twentieth century quinine tonics were selling well both in Britain and her colonies, and the gin and tonic was beginning to appear on cocktail menus at some of London's most exclusive hotels.

Quinine has gone on to enjoy a life of its own outside the gin and tonic. Laborers working on the construction of the Panama Canal were given quinine sulphate dissolved in sugary lemonade, and German troops stationed in Tanganyika during the First World War improvised an anti-malarial tonic, albeit a disgustingly bitter one, by steeping cinchona bark in their coffee. Quinine has lent its distinctive character to bitter lemon, the Italian digestif Barolo Chinato, the Scottish favorite Irn-Bru, and the French aperitif *quinquina*—the most famous brand of which, Kina Lillet, plays (as we shall see in the next chapter) a leading role in James Bond's personal martini recipe.


Unlikely as it may seem, one outcome of three centuries of military and medical efforts to overcome malaria, both in Europe and around the world, was a glass of gin and tonic. Another disease—gout, the classic complaint of Enlightenment consumer culture—inspired the creation of a key ingredient in the nineteenth-century gin cocktail. Gout was to the eighteenth century what melancholy was to the high Renaissance, or stomach ulcers were to the Fifties. When they were not examining a Hogarth print or conversing in a coffee-house, male members of the Hanoverian middle classes might well have been consulting a physician about a nasty episode of gout. Typically gout struck a joint in the big toe or thumb, but eighteenth-century physicians understood it as a mutable condition, one that might move around the body and cause headaches or heart palpitations. Like so many diseases, gout had a double face: though it caused agonizing pain, it was also seen to indicate a certain degree of civilization, luxury, ease, even literariness. Just as John Keats rejoiced when he saw spots of tuberculotic blood in his handkerchief, so an eighteenth-century merchant might feel a certain pride when he suffered his first bout of gout; it was a sign that he had made it. Gout was, in the historian Christopher Lawrence's phrase, a patrician malady, and in part this explains why physicians did not expect the gin craze to spark an epidemic of the disease. Gout was for the wealthy and the powerful, the consumers of claret and port. Poor gin-drinkers could not afford the diagnosis, nor hardly even aspire to it.

Most eighteenth-century doctors took their cues on gout from George Cheyne, whose decidedly negative views on gin and other spirits we encountered in the previous chapter. Cheyne saw gout as the result of blood stagnating in the extremities, and in this sense it was a kind of bodily safety valve: the substances which precipitated from the blood in the fingers and toes might have caused more serious mischief if they had been released within the major organs. Cheyne in turn adapted many of his ideas about gout from Thomas Sydenham, the seventeenth-century "English Hippocrates." Sydenham's *Treatise on the Gout,* published in 1683, argued that gout was the result of "ease, voluptuousness, high living, and too free a use of wine and other spirituous liquors." Bleeding and purging could, he thought, be counterproductive, driving "peccant humors" further into the extremities. Instead he recommended a light diet, plenty of fluid, and regular doses of a digestive remedy he called bitters—a kind of proto-gin infused with watercress, horseradish, wormwood, and angelica root.

Sydenham's bitters became a popular remedy for gout—not least because they gave sufferers an excuse to take nips of strong spirit during attacks—and other practitioners sought to emulate their success. In 1712 a recipe for Stoughton's Elixir, devised by the Reverend Richard Stoughton, became one of the first medicines to receive a British royal patent. Stoughton's bitters became one of the most successful British exports to the American colonies, and following the War of Independence distillers in Boston were quick to produce a native version. And in 1783 Nicholas Husson, an officer in the French army, began to sell bitters which included an extract of meadow saffron, *Colchicum autumnale*—one component of which, colchicine, is now known to block the metabolic pathways which cause gout.

Following Stoughton's example, another group of practitioners —quacks—took patent medicines in a more nakedly commercial direction. Travelling from town to town, quacks offered flashy, inexpensive remedies that promised instant results. They were showmen and *bricoleurs,* patching together their credibility from whatever came to hand, and they could work the crowd like a hellfire preacher. Their nostrums were usually based on spirit, colored and flavored with vegetable dyes, spices and substances ranging from malt extract to strychnine. Dr. Radcliffe's Famous Purging Elixir, Bateman's Pectoral Drops, Daffy's Elixir, Godfrey's Cordial, Radcliffe's Royal Tincture—all drew on the fiery potency of alcohol, and all had more in common with Sydenham's bitters than most physicians would have cared to admit.

As the quacks hawked their wares around the marketplaces of Europe, an Italian perfumier, Giovanni Maria Farina, used the basic principles of patent medicines and proto-gins to create one of the most enduring fragrances. Working in Cologne, but homesick for the spring air of his home town, Santa Maria Maggiore, Farina tried to capture its aroma in a perfume. In 1709 he combined bergamot, citron, neroli, orange, rosemary and cardamom, infusing them in neutral spirit to produce a scent which he called *eau de Cologne.* French and Italian aristocrats adored it, and another aspect of this connection between proto-gins and perfume can be found on high streets around the world, where juniper provides woody, masculine notes for many contemporary aftershaves.

Farina's ingenuity shows that, by the middle of the eighteenth century, the idea of spirit-based tonics was being adapted to many new ends. A recipe for bitters from *Adam's Luxury and Eve's Cookery,* published in 1744, contained gentian root, dried orange peel, Virginia snake root, plus:

> . . . half a dram of cochineal and half a dram of loaf sugar. This last will heighten the Bitter to admiration. A few drops of this bitter in a glass of wine or other liquor is good to create an appetite.

Henry Sabine's *Publican's Sure Guide,* published in 1807, offered a recipe for bitters specifically intended to be mixed with gin:

> Three and an half gallons of Spirits (one to five)
> Three penny-weights of Oil of Orange
> Three ditto of Oil of Carraway
> Three ditto of Oil of Wormwood
> One pound of Lump Sugar

> Bruise the Oils well in a mortar with a few knobs of Sugar; steep one ounce of Virginia Snake Root, and one ounce of Coriander in a quart of Spirits for four or five days, and shake them well several times a day, which done, draw it off, and mix the Oils, the Sugar should be dissolved in five quarts of Water, and simmered over the fire, the same as for Gin, and when nearly cold add to your Spirits.— Half an ounce of alum is a sufficient quantity to fine down with.

Peter Jonas and John Sheridan's *Complete Treatise on the Art of Distillation,* published in 1830, gave instructions for making bitters from "common gin" mixed with essential oils of lemon, wormwood and orange:

> This will be a most pleasant cheap bitter, equally wholesome, and as good as many that are much dearer. This is only fit to be taken with gin. The same ingredients, and rectified malt spirits, or molasses spirits, will either of them make a bitter of more general use.

But bitters also took on a new role in the nineteenth century, as Western soldiers, sailors and colonial migrants sought a tonic that would help their bodies adjust to the extremes of tropical climates. The range of botanicals was widened, to include not only cinchona bark but also such novelties as angostura bark, cascarilla, artichoke leaf, blessed thistle leaves, goldenseal rhizome, wormwood leaves, and yarrow flowers. The *Scientific American Cyclopedia of Receipts, Notes and Queries,* published in 1898, advised readers contemplating a long voyage to make up this simple bitters a month or so before they planned to leave:

¾ oz quassia chips
¾ oz powdered catechu
½ oz cardamom
1 oz dried orange peel
1 quart strong whiskey
1 gallon water.

Macerate the quassia chips, powdered catechu, cardamom, and orange peel for ten days in the whiskey. Filter and add the water. Color with mallow or malva flowers.

John Rack's *French Wine and Liquor Manufacturer,* published in 1868, listed eight recipes for medicinal bitters. His "Stomach Bitters" were intended to relieve sea-sickness, and were sweetened with syrup and flavored with cardamom seed, nutmegs, grains of Paradise, cinnamon, cloves, ginger, galangal, orange peel and lemon. And what tropical traveler would dare to embark without a bottle of Rack's "Amazon Bitters (A SPLENDID Recipe)," which included red Peruvian bark, calisaya bark, calamus root, orange peel, cinnamon, cloves, nutmeg, cassia buds, and "red saunders" (sandalwood)?

By the late nineteenth century, however, the most popular bitters were not home-brewed, but made by two companies: Peychaud and Angostura. Antoine Amédée Peychaud—a name to conjure with—was born in 1803, into a wealthy family of coffee-planters. Originally from Bordeaux, the Peychauds owned large and lucrative plantations on what is now the island of Haiti. Their estate was destroyed during the Haitian Revolution of 1804, but they and the infant Antoine fled to New Orleans, and made a new life for themselves in the French Quarter of the city. After training as an apothecary Peychaud opened a pharmacy at 123 Royal Street, where he began to make and sell his own proprietary brand of bitters, flavored with gentian. (One story has Peychaud inventing the cocktail, by dispensing his bitters to customers in a glass known as a *coquetier,* but the cocktail was several decades old by the time Peychaud went into business). By the 1840s Peychaud was marketing his bitters both as a digestive and as a general tonic, and by the time of his death in 1883 they had supplanted Stoughton's as the American bitters of choice.

Peychaud's bitters were sold around the world, but British drinkers tended to prefer the bitters developed by a German doctor, Johann Gottlieb Benjamin Siegert. In the early 1820s Siegert went to South America to serve in Simón Bolívar's revolutionary army, and settled in the Venezuelan river-port of Angostura (now Ciudad Bolívar). Spotting a business opportunity, he devised a new recipe for bitters, and marketed it as a treatment for seasickness amongst the crowds of foreign sailors in the city. By 1830 he had made enough money to set up a factory, and the officers of Royal Navy ships visiting Angostura took up Siegert's tonic with great enthusiasm. At some point in the 1840s—the precise date and circumstances are unknown—they started to drink their favored Plymouth gin with a dash of Angostura bitters. The Pink Gin was originally served at room temperature, though most bars now serve it shaken over ice, and for abstainers a long version, the Campbell, was made with lemonade standing in for the gin. Officials in the Indian Civil Service spiced it up by adding onions pickled with chili—a Gin Piaj—and in colonial Malaya, where stomachs seem to have required more soothing, the Gin Pahit ("bitter gin" in Malay) upped the quantity of bitters from a dash to one part in three. The Pahit makes several passing appearances in the early short stories of W. Somerset Maugham, where it becomes one of the fixtures of colonial life, and Maugham revealed his personal fondness for gin and bitters in his travelogue *The Gentleman In the Parlour,* published in 1930. Burmese officials devised an alternative to this stark combination with the Pegu Club Cocktail, which included lime juice and Cointreau, and from time to time Royal Navy ships still fly the green-and-white "gin pennant"—an invitation to come aboard and take a glass of "Pinkers."

But the early history of the cocktail was not always so cozy. Another late-nineteenth century combination—gin and lime cordial, the Gimlet—owes its existence to a disease that was responsible for tens of thousands of deaths. Over the eighteenth century, scurvy killed more British sailors than the French did. In a notorious four-year circumnavigation beginning in 1740, Commodore George Anson lost almost two-thirds of his crew, thirteen hundred out of two thousand, to the disease. It struck when sailors were forced to live on a monotonous diet of salted meat and hard-tack for more than a month or so at a time. They became lethargic; their gums bled, and their teeth fell out; old wounds reopened; they lost sensation in their limbs; and they died in droves. With no fresh fruit or vegetables in their diet they had, in modern terms, become deficient in vitamin C, and their bodies were unable to maintain or repair vital connective tissues.

Shipboard studies carried out in 1747 convinced the surgeon James Lind that regular doses of lime juice would keep crews healthy, but this discovery created its own problems. Fresh limes did not last long in the fetid holds of ocean-going ships, and boiling or condensing the juice seemed to rob it of its anti-scorbutic powers. Adding rum worked fairly well, but this was never a very satisfactory solution, partly because it gave thirsty sailors an incentive to deplete the lime juice supply. In 1867, just as a new Merchant Shipping Act required civilian vessels to carry lime juice, a Scottish chandler, Lauchlin Rose, came up with a solution. Rose, the descendant of a long line of Edinburgh shipbuilders, realized that lime juice could be preserved by mixing it with small quantities of sulphur dioxide. He established a factory on the dockside in Leith, and began to import tons of limes grown on British plantations in the West Indies. Royal Navy victuallers took up Rose's Lime Juice, and—as with Angostura bitters—at some point an officer seems to have had the bright idea of mixing it with gin. According to some sources, this officer was Sir Thomas Gimlette, Surgeon-General to the Navy at the end of the nineteenth-century, but the name may simply derive from the metal tool used to open barrels of lime juice.

And so we come to the cocktail—a drink, of course, but also a new kind of pleasure, a cultural icon, a global language, and a seemingly inexhaustible vehicle for myth-making and story-telling. Invented in the United States at the end of the eighteenth century, the cocktail in its very earliest incarnations seems to have been consumed as a pick-me-up before the rigors of the day. The name might derive from any one of half-a-dozen ety-mologies, but the current consensus is that it most likely comes from *coquetel,* a traditional wine-cup from Bordeaux, brought to the U.S. by soldiers under the Marquis de Lafayette, who served as a major-general in George Washington's Continental Army between 1777 and 1781. The word began to appear in print in the first decade of the nineteenth century and, according to the mixologist and cocktail historian David Wonderich, the earliest reference came in the *Farmer's Cabinet* for 28th April 1803:

> Drank a glass of coctail [sic]—excellent for the head ... Call'd at the Doct's. found Burnham—he looked very wise—drank another glass of cocktail.

Three years later, on 6th May 1806, an editorial in the *Balance and Colombian Repository,* a New York newspaper, provided a satirical definition of this new beverage:

> A stimulating liquor, composed of spirits of any kind, sugar water, and bitters ... it is supposed to be an excellent electioneering potion inasmuch as it renders the heart stout and bold, at the same time as it fuddles the head.

Patsy McDonough's *Bar-keeper's Guide,* published in 1883, sum-marized the character of the nineteenth-century cocktail:

> The Cocktail is a very popular drink. It is most frequently called for in the morning and just before dinner; it is sometimes taken as an appetizer; it is a welcome companion on fishing excursions and travelers often go provided with it on a railway journey.

These quotations underscore a crucial point, visible in the writings of many early cocktail devotees. For much of the nineteenth century, the cocktail was not the name of a general class of mixed drinks, but a specific drink, containing spirit, bitters, some kind of flavoring or liqueur, and a simple syrup made from sugar and water. When the explorer Richard Burton—the first European to set eyes on Mecca—set out for America in May 1860, he revelled in the sheer variety of drinks he planned to encounter in the Land of the Free:

> I'll drink mint-juleps, brandy-smashes, whiskey-skies, gin-sling, cock-tail, sherry cobblers, rum-salads, streaks of lightning, morning-glory . . . it'll be the most interesting experiment. I want to see whether after a life of 3 or 4 months, I can drink and eat myself to the level of the aborigines.

During the American Civil War the novelist Nathaniel Hawthorne, writing from Willard's Hotel, a renowned watering-hole in the Union capital of Washington, advised his readers to:

> adopt the universal habit of the place, and call for a mint julep, a whiskey skin, a gin cock-tail, a brandy smash, or a glass of pure Old Rye, for the conviviality of Washington sets in at an early hour and, so far as I had an opportunity of observing, never terminates at any hour.

And Dickens, in his *American Notes,* published in 1842, described the drinking habits of Bostonian theater-goers:

There are two theaters in Boston, of good size and construction, but sadly in want of patronage. The few ladies who resort to them, sit, as of right, in the front rows of the boxes. The bar is a large room with a stone floor, and there people stand and smoke, and lounge about, all the evening: dropping in and out as the humor takes them. There too the stranger is initiated into the mysteries of Gin-sling, Cocktail, Sangaree, Mint Julep, Sherry-cobbler, Timber Doodle, and other rare drinks.

Any nineteenth-century American bartender worth his salt would have to know his Cocktail from his Crusta, his Negus from his Cobbler, his Julep from his Timber Doodle. And the prince of nineteenth-century American bartenders, the man who did more than any other to turn the cocktail into a sensation, was "Professor" Jerry Thomas. Born in New York in 1830, Thomas followed the gold rush to California in 1849, but he found better money in bartending than in prospecting, and over the next two decades he made a name for himself as the first celebrity mixologist. He travelled around Europe, showing hundreds of audiences how to prepare drinks from his *Bar-Tender's Guide and Bon Vivant's Companion,* published in 1882. And his example inspired a generation of protégés like Harry Johnson, whose *Bartender's Manual, or, How to Mix Drinks of the Present Style,* published in 1882, is a fascinating repository of mixological lore and early gin cocktails.

On his visits to the U.S. Dickens had noted the popularity of ice in American mixed drinks:

Hark! to the clinking sound of hammers breaking lumps of ice, and to the cool gurgling of the pounded bits, as, in the process of mixing, they are poured from glass to glass!

From 1845 London had its own source of ice, in the form of the Wenham Lake Ice Company on the Strand, and at the Great Exhibition in 1851 Alexis Soyer, legendary chef of the Reform Club, made and sold a range of American iced cocktails. By the 1870s employees of the Bank of England could, if they wished, step out to a cocktail bar on Threadneedle Street, while others frequented new American-style cocktail bars in Claridge's and the Savoy. A bartender in Limmer's Hotel on Conduit Street in the West End was said to have invented the John Collins—gin mixed with lemon juice, sugar and soda water—and other Londoners came up with their own unique contributions to the brave new world of cocktails. James Pimm, a Kentish shellfish-monger, came to London in the early nineteenth century and opened a successful chain of oyster bars catering to City gents in their lunch hours. In 1851 Pimm began to offer his clients a new refreshment to go with their Whitstables and Colchester Natives—a long drink based on a blend of gin, herbs, spices, and fruit, which he called Pimm's No. 1.

Many of "Professor" Jerry Thomas' recipes featured gin, and one in particular made it a central flavor:

3 or 4 dashes of gum syrup
2 do. bitters (Bogart's)
1 wine-glass of gin
1 or 2 dashes of curaçao
1 small piece lemon peel; fill one-third full of fine ice; shake well, strain in a glass.

Towards the end of the nineteenth century, this (capitalized) Gin Cocktail gave birth to the most celebrated (lower case) gin cocktail—the martini. The writer Barnaby Conrad sees the martini as an embodiment of American history at its most magnificently diverse: Dutch and English gin (or, at the height of the Cold War, Russian vodka), mixed with French vermouth, and served with Mediterranean olives, German-Jewish pickled onions, or Caribbean lemons. This most cosmopolitan of cocktails conquered the Western palate with remarkable speed. Originating in the 1870s, it was widely drunk and celebrated in fiction by the end of the nineteenth century. In the first decade of the twentieth century the distinctive, conical glass began to appear, and by the end of the First World War—just in time for Prohibition—the martini had become a staple of cocktail bar menus. And many sonatas have been improvised around this timeless theme. As Lowell Edmunds, the pre-eminent historian of the martini, has noted, over the last century various recipes have called for (amongst other things) sake, rose-water, whisky, olive brine or Chanel No. 5 to be added to the mix, and for garlic, mushrooms, caviar or crystallized violets to be sprinkled into the glass.

Just as gin emerged from an encounter between spirit and juniper in a Dutch still, so the martini was born from a collision between gin and vermouth in an American cocktail shaker. Vermouth is a fortified white wine, in which various spices and botanicals have been steeped. Its name comes from its principal flavoring—wormwood flowers, *wermut* in German—so vermouth is at least a distant relation of absinthe, though it is not usually credited with any significant psychotropic powers. As we saw in Chapter 1, the idea of fortifying and flavoring wines in this way has a long history, and distillers in central Europe were producing their own wormwood cordials, *vinum absinthum,* in the middle of the sixteenth century. The first drink to have been called "vermouth" seems to be the tonic produced in Italy from 1786 by Antonio Benedetto Carpano. Carpano, an apprentice to a wine merchant in Turin, fortified moscato wine with spirit, and infused it with all the botanicals in his master's store-room. There is some evidence that the Cinzano family were making a similar drink in the late fifteenth century, so Carpano may just have been following the local tradition in Turin. But Carpano's vermouth was the first to achieve widespread popularity, and was soon being drunk all over Italy as an aperitif. Italian vermouth, like Carpano's and Cinzano, was comparatively sweet, and by the nineteenth century producers in the south of France—most famously Noilly Prat—were offering a dry version. But it seems to have been in the U.S., in the third quarter of the nineteenth century, that vermouth was introduced to gin.

The origins of the martini must surely rank as one of the great American folk tales, alongside Johnny Appleseed or John Henry, the steel-driving man. In 1862, so the story goes, "Professor" Jerry Thomas was working in a bar in San Francisco. A traveler came in, dusty from the road, and asked for a drink, something new. Thomas asked the man where he was going, and he said he was on his way to Martinez, twenty-six miles north of the city. Thomas made him a mixture of gin, vermouth and bitters, and called it a Martinez, which over time became known as the martini. The power of this tale is that it draws together three strands in the history of the cocktail, making a kind of folkloric syllogism. Thomas was the greatest barman of his age; he once worked within hailing distance of Martinez; later in his career he published a recipe for a cocktail called the Martinez; so he *must* have had a hand in the invention of the martini.

Like the miraculous recovery of the Condesa de Chinchón, the legend of Thomas and the martini is a wonderfully satisfying and tidy anecdote. Sadly, like the Condesa's story, it doesn't stand up to closer inspection. Thomas's recipe for the Martinez appeared more than a quarter of a century after his mythical encounter in Martinez, in the second edition of his *Bar-Tender's Guide,* published in 1887. The Martinez was very different from the dry martini beloved of twentieth-century drinkers, featuring sweet Italian rather than dry French vermouth, plus a dash of curaçao. It has been suggested that the name derives not from the town of Martinez, but from martini vermouth or the martini-Henry rifle (though evidence for either claim is fragmentary at best). And the residents of Martinez have turned the direction of the journey around, arguing that Julio Richelieu, the owner of Julio's Bar on Ferry Street, invented the Martinez in 1849. The un-named traveler is said to have paid for his drink with a gold nugget, and later mentioned the name and the recipe to Thomas in San Francisco.

Edmunds has done a magnificent job in unpicking the tangled history of the Martinez and the martini, and the earliest recipe he has uncovered dates to 1884, in O.H. Byron's *Modern Bartender's*

*Guide.* The recipe is actually for a Manhattan, and the Martinez is mentioned only in passing:

> 2 dashes curaçao
> 2 dashes Angostura bitters
> ½ wine-glass whisky
> ½ wine-glass Italian vermouth.

> Martinez [is the] same as Manhattan, only you substitute gin for whisky.

This suggests that the Martinez was a direct descendent of Thomas' Gin Cocktail, with sweet vermouth standing in for the simple syrup. The first recipe for a cocktail called a martini comes four years later, in Harry Johnson's second edition of his *Bartender's Manual,* published in 1888. American bartenders brought the combination—if not the name—to Britain in 1887, where on Saturday the 5th of March the bar at the American Exposition in London offered adventurous drinkers the opportunity to try gin and sweet vermouth. (This encounter may be the origin of the English upper-crust's taste for gin and It, the "It" standing for Italian vermouth.) And from 1906 British readers could recreate the martini in the comfort of their own drawing-rooms, by following a recipe in the new edition of Mrs. Beeton's *Household Management*:

> Ingredients—½ a wineglassful of good unsweetened gin, ½ a wineglassful of Italian vermouth, 6 drops of rock candy syrup, 12 drops of orange bitters, 1 small piece of lemon peel, crushed ice. Method—Half fill a tumbler with crushed ice, pour over it all the liquids, shake well, then strain into a glass, and serve with a small piece of lemon-peel floating on the surface.

This taste for sweet vermouth may have been a consequence of the movement away from sweetened Old Tom-style gins and towards London dry gins in the mid and late nineteenth century.

By the end of the century, however, as European and American palates were becoming accustomed to the refreshing dryness of the new-style gins, we find two recipes for cocktails which resemble the dry martini. Neither, however, was called a martini. In his *Stuart's Fancy Drinks and How to Mix Them,* published in 1896, the bartender Thomas Stuart described the Marguerite:

1 dash of orange bitters
2 parts Plymouth gin
1 part French vermouth

A similar concoction—the Puritan, possibly so named for its dryness—appeared in Frederic L. Knowles' *The Cocktail Book: A Sideboard Manual for Gentlemen,* published in 1900:

Three dashes orange bitters; one spoonful yellow chartreuse; two-third Plymouth gin; one-third French vermouth. Fill with ice, mix, and strain into a cocktail glass.

As they sipped their Marguerites or Puritans, American drinkers could for the first time read stories in which the martini appeared. It seems that the cocktail's literary debut came in a short story by one Hidley Dhee—almost certainly a pseudonym—in the *Crescent Magazine* on August 1st, 1896:

One of the *jeunesse dorée* in the party tipped his chair back as indication that he had retired from the argument, and as he sipped his martini and inhaled its seductive bouquet, a far-away look came into his baby-blue eyes.

Eight years later John Philip Souza—famous as a composer of military marches, less well-known for his fiction—published *The Fifth String,* a novel set in the steamy world of American classical music. In this extract we encounter Perkins, the manager of the Italian virtuoso violinist Angelo Dotti, on the morning after a hugely successful concert in New York:

Perkins was happy—Perkins was positively joyous, and Perkins was self-satisfied. The violinist had made a great hit. But Perkins, confiding in the white-coated dispenser who concocted his *matin martini,* very dry, an hour before, said he regarded the success due as much to the management as to the artist.

These extracts give a sense of the martini's early status: urban, upmarket, the drink of stylish and successful people, a cocktail to which one might aspire. In O. Henry's *The Gentle Grafter,* published in 1904, two con-men who have abducted the major of a sleepy Georgia town prepare what they think is a high-class lunch:

So at twelve o'clock we had a hot lunch ready that looked like a banquet on a Mississippi River steamboat. We spread it on the tops of two or three big boxes, opened two quarts of the red wine, set the olives and a canned oyster cocktail and a ready-made martini by the Colonel's plate, and called him to grub.

But for all its elegance and modernity, the martini also had a more disturbing face, the lineaments of which we can discern in Elam Harnish, the main character in Jack London's *Burning Daylight,* published in 1910. Before he became a writer London had been a sailor, a hobo and a gold-miner, and he was intimately familiar with the hard-drinking culture of American migrant workers. Harnish acquires the nickname "Burning Daylight" as a prospector in the Yukon gold-fields, where by dint of hard graft and good luck he makes a small fortune. He moves to San Francisco and then New York, accumulating yet more money with a series of successful businesses, and quickly develops a taste for martinis:

Nobody seemed to notice the unusualness of a martini at midnight, though Daylight looked sharply for that very thing; for he had long since learned that martinis had their strictly appointed times and places. But he liked martinis, and, being a natural man, he chose to drink when and how he pleased.

For Harnish, as for so many drinkers who came after him, the martini marks the end of the working day:

> Without reasoning or thinking about it, the strain of the office, which was essentially due to the daring and audacity of his ventures, required check or cessation; and he found, through the weeks and months, that cocktails supplied this very thing. They constituted a stone wall. He never drank during the morning, nor in office hours . . . But the instant the business was finished, his everlasting call went out for a martini, and for a double-martini at that, served in a long glass so as not to excite comment.

Over time Harnish comes to understand his emotional life through the prism of the martini. When he falls in love with Dede Mason, his stenographer, he realizes that "the thought of her was like a cocktail. Or, at any rate, she substituted for a certain percentage of cocktails." But his affair with Dede leads him to reflect on his life of wealth and power:

> What's the good of thirty million when I ain't got room for more than a quart of cocktails a day? . . . Here I am, a thirty times over millionaire, slaving harder than any dozen men that work for me, and all I get is two meals that don't taste good, one bed, a quart of martini.

In the closing pages of the book, Harnish sells his businesses, and goes to live with Dede on a farm in the Midwest. His taste in drinks mirrors his new life: he abandons the martini, and takes only occasional glasses of whisky.

On November 2nd, 1902 the upmarket American magazine *Harper's Weekly* ran an advert for Heublin's Club Cocktails. A rich woman, returning from a taxing day in the boutiques of Fifth Avenue, addresses her butler:

Before you do another thing, *James,* bring me a CLUB COCKTAIL.
I'm so tired shopping[,] make it a MARTINI. I need a little Tonic
and it's so much better than a drug of any kind.

This was the New Woman in all her forward-looking glory, and
she wanted a drink. Women were entering the workforce, the
professions and (within a few decades) the electorate, so why not
the tavern and the bar as well? Cocktails like the martini were
the perfect refreshment and stimulant for these liberated children
of respectable Victorian "drys." At the bar of the Savoy Hotel,
Harry Craddock was mixing gin, Cointreau, Kina Lillet, lemon
juice and a dash of absinthe to make a Corpse Reviver (though
he warned that "four taken in swift succession will unrevive the
corpse again"). In the Holland House Hotel in Manhattan, each
room had an electric "Teleseme"—a dial on which they could
order food and more than three dozen kinds of cocktails from the
hotel's resident mixologist, George Kappeler. And in this innocent
decade the French army's Canon de 75mm Modèle 1897, which
would wreak so much destruction in the fields of Flanders, gave
its name to the "French 75"—a sparkling combination of gin,
lemon juice, simple syrup and champagne.

As these examples suggest, London dry gin made a perfect foil
for the character of the cocktail: aromatic, fresh, its qualities en-
hanced rather than deadened by shaking over ice. And though they
were born in the nineteenth century, gin cocktails became—as
we'll see in the next chapter—one of the defining drinks of the
twentieth century.

A the American taste becomes *more critical* more people insist on GORDON'S GIN

THE 94.4 PROOF OF A GOOD

Permit R-514

# 5

## The Silver Bullet

AT MIDNIGHT ON Friday January 16th, 1920, the people and government of the U.S. began their Great Experiment. Under the Volstead Act, which established the laws and institutions necessary to enforce the Eighteenth Amendment to the Constitution, the commercial production and sale of alcohol for drinking was now prohibited. Some New Yorkers—consciously or unconsciously—aped those who mourned the death of Madame Geneva two centuries before, and held mock-obsequies for John Barleycorn in the city's taverns and saloons. Elsewhere in the city, a more elegant and less rowdy ceremony marked the passing of legal booze. At the Hotel Park Avenue more than two hundred crepe-swathed diners consumed caviar from black china plates, brought to their tables by black waiters. But within an hour of the Volstead Act coming into force, police officers around the country began to hear reports of well-organized heists at bonded warehouses, where beer and spirits were being stored prior to their export or destruction.

If the rise of the cocktail helped to make gin respectable, Prohibition made it fashionable. One of the many ironies of the Eighteenth Amendment was that in trying to stamp out the vices attached to spirit-drinking, it turned the newly-illicit cocktail culture—bootleg hooch, bathtub gin, the speakeasy—into a shorthand for all that was thrilling, fresh and modern. This vision of cocktail culture has (with a short hiatus from the late Sixties to the late Eighties) radically shaped the ways in which twentieth-century drinkers have responded to gin. In the American Century the global reach of U.S.

culture—most influentially through film, but also through literature and lifestyle marketing—has carried the hard-nosed, urban glamor of the Silver Bullet, as martinis were known, around the world.

Yet another irony of Prohibition was the fact that the quality of the gin consumed in speakeasies was in many cases lower than it had been since the gin craze. This marked the beginnings of another shift in the character of gin. As many of the leading nineteenth-century brands became multi-national corporations, so the quality of their products began to stagnate. Many British distillers were hit hard by grain rationing during the Second World War, and though they experienced an Indian summer in the Fifties, they were dealt a double blow by new cultural trends. Sixties youth culture—if one can generalize so sweepingly—tended to see the cocktail as merely another trapping of dull, repressed, suburban life. Baby boomers, or at least their cultural icons, preferred less conventional kinds of stimulant, much to the horror of their martini-guzzling elders (a reaction which seemed, and still seems, fated to repeat the manifold hypocrisies of Prohibition). Over the next two decades new attitudes to health in general, and alcohol in particular, made gin-drinking seem almost as bad a habit as smoking was fast becoming. And like so many episodes in the history of gin, this chapter begins with the ominous spectacle of a moral majority on the march.


By the end of the nineteenth century, as we saw in the previous chapter, the U.S. had a strong and determined temperance movement, one which increasingly had Prohibition on its mind. Many campaigners wanted to make the abolition of alcohol part of the post-Civil War Reconstruction movement, and at a conference in Oswego, New York, in May 1869 a group of temperance activists founded the National Prohibition Party. The Party's candidate received only a nugatory proportion of the popular vote in the 1872 presidential election, but even this was a sign of the growing ambition of the movement. From 1893 the Anti-Saloon League, founded in Ohio, exhorted candidates from all parties to adopt the Prohibitionist line, producing reams of propaganda which claimed that almost all of America's problems, economic, social or moral, could be laid at the door of strong drink.

This sweeping stance came across powerfully in the rhetoric of the League's star orator, Rear-Admiral Richmond Pearson Hobson. Hobson was the Democratic member for Alabama in the House of Representatives, and was feted across the nation as a hero of the 1898 Spanish-American War, during which he tried (and failed) to prevent the Spanish navy from leaving the port of Santiago de Cuba by sinking the collier *Merrimac* in the main channel of the harbor. Hobson's diatribes against the evils of alcohol had much in common with the ideology of degeneration, but they also drew on one of the foundational ideas in U.S. culture—the nation as a city on a hill, an exemplum to the rest of the Christian world:

> In America we are making the last stand of the great white race, and substantially of the human race. If [alcohol] cannot be conquered in Young America, it cannot in any of the old and more degenerate nations. If America fails, the world will be undone and the human race will be doomed to go down from degeneracy to degeneracy till the Almighty in wrath wipes the accursed thing out.

As this extract suggests, race (and racism) was a central theme in the politics of Prohibition—a point also brought out by events in Hobson's neighboring state of Tennessee. In the primaries for the 1908 state governorship election Edward Ward Carmack, a radical Prohibitionist, led a deeply acrimonious campaign against the incumbent, Malcolm Rice Patterson, a temperance moderate. Carmack, a newspaper editor and the recently-retired Democratic state senator, also used his journalistic connections to voice support for lynching and opposition to black voting. When a black farmhand from Louisiana was lynched after being accused of raping and murdering a fourteen-year-old Alabama schoolgirl, Carmack jumped on all of his bandwagons at once. At the time of the attack the alleged murderer was said to have been drunk on Lee Levy gin—a cheap brand produced in Minnesota, which featured on its label a scantily-clad Caucasian woman. One of Carmack's newspapers, the *Tennessean,* published an interview with a Methodist preacher, who claimed that:

> This gin, with its label, has made more black rape fiends, and has procured the outrage of more white women in the South than all other agencies combined. It is sold with the promise that it will bring white virtue into the black brute's power.

Other writers fixed on the name of the brand, arguing that Jewish capitalists were making fortunes by selling gin that spurred poor blacks on to rape:

> The primitive Negro field hand . . . pays his fifty cents for a pint of Mr. Levy's gin [and] absorbs not only its toxic heat, but absorbs also the suggestion subtly conveyed, that it contains aphrodisiacs. He sits in the road or in the alley at the height of his debauch, looking at that obscene picture of a white woman on the label, drinking in the invitation which it carries. And then comes—opportunity.

Patterson somehow managed to traverse this toxic morass of racism and anti-Semitism, and went on to defeat Carmack (who was shot dead that winter on an open street in Nashville, after writing an insulting article about a local military commander). Again, though, it is clear that even the defeats of the nascent Prohibition movement only increased its determination to push its agenda at every possible opportunity and through every conceivable means. One small early triumph came in the form of the 1906 Pure Food and Drug Act. Largely inspired by Upton Sinclair's exposé of the U.S. meat industry's stomach-churning practices in *The Jungle,* published in 1906, the Act also stipulated that any brand of tonic or medicine containing alcohol should be labeled clearly and accurately, so that dry consumers could boycott them if they chose to. And in 1913 the Anti-Saloon League sponsored the first attempt to pass a constitutional amendment banning alcohol—another failure, but one that heralded the shape of things to come.

As support for Prohibition in the U.S. began to gather pace, the British temperance movement was slowly grinding to a halt. Doctors continued to prescribe small doses of brandy for a range of conditions, but fears over urban degeneration fed into a broader set of concerns about the future of the British Empire. If—as new kinds of clinical evidence were suggesting—mothers who drank during their pregnancies gave birth to weaker and sicklier babies, what might this mean for the coming generation of imperial soldiers, civil servants and industrialists? One witness to the 1904 Inter-Departmental Committee on Physical Deterioration, established by the British government to investigate the reality of degeneration, put this point crisply: "If the mother as well as the father is given to drink, the progeny will deteriorate in every way, and the future of the race is imperiled."

Following the well-trodden path of sensationalism, many Edwardian journalists published articles in which they threw up their hands in horror at the irresponsible behavior of the working classes. Some of the most powerful examples came from the typewriter of George Robert Sims—journalist, playwright, dandy, author of "Christmas Day in the Workhouse," and champion bulldog breeder (and, in this capacity, the face of Spratt's Patent Meat Fibrine Vegetable Dog Cakes). In a series of articles published in the spring of 1907 in *Tribune,* a Liberal newspaper with radical leanings, Sims told highly-colored stories of what he had witnessed on his visits to drinking-dens in the East End of London. Poor women were drinking throughout their pregnancies, and, in one particularly Hogarthian scene in a Mile End pub, Sims claimed to have seen a mother using gin to quieten her new-born child:

> Another woman dips a dirty finger in her gin and thrusts it into her baby's mouth, repeating the process several times. Her finger is cleaner when she has finished.

After the outbreak of the First World War a degree of legally-enforced temperance was the order of the day, but this was less a response to the moral and physical menace of degeneration than an attempt to increase industrial productivity and discipline. Under the Defence of the Realm Act, passed in August 1914, less than a fortnight after war was declared, the opening hours of pubs were restricted, and a Central Control Board (Liquor Traffic) created to supervise the sale and availability of alcohol. Duties on beer and spirits were raised, and in some areas—most notoriously around Gretna in Scotland, close to one of the largest munitions factories—"Direct Control" was imposed. Pubs were forced to close on Sundays; on Saturdays no spirits could be sold; the consumption of spirit chasers with pints of beer was banned; and grocers could no longer hold spirit licenses. Whisky and gin producers, too, became part of the war effort: distilled alcohol could be converted into acetone, one key ingredient in the artillery propellant cordite, and distillers came under great pressure to earmark drinkable spirits for supplying front-line troops. British soldiers and sailors usually received a daily rum ration, though the French army banned the consumption of absinthe in 1915, fearing its effects upon already-mutinous regiments, and on the other side of no-man's-land German squaddies took the doling-out of strong drink as a sign that they would be ordered to advance within hours.

On April 6th, 1917, at the request of President Woodrow Wilson, the U.S. Congress voted to declare war on Germany. Wilson had initially resisted U.S. intervention in what was, under the terms of the century-old Monroe Doctrine, the European sphere of influence, even after the sinking of the *Lusitania* in 1915. But now that it was involved, the U.S. was going to show both its allies and enemies in Europe—all members of what Rear-Admiral Hobson had called "the old and more degenerate nations"—how a modern and morally progressive nation fought a war, and one weapon it did not require was alcohol. U.S. troops were not issued with spirit rations, and in the name of physical and spiritual hygiene much effort was devoted to keeping their barracks and troopships dry. And as the first troopships made their way across the Atlantic, the U.S. Senate debated a new bill to amend the Constitution and bring in nationwide Prohibition.

The bill was passed without difficulty—to many senators, it seemed an entirely appropriate course of action in a time of war— but its opponents forced the inclusion of a clause which gave only seven years for ratification by the necessary three-quarters of U.S. state legislatures, after which the bill would lapse. For a while it seemed that this would sink Prohibition, but within a year it had gained the necessary assent, and on January 16th, 1919 the Eighteenth Amendment passed into law. One reason for this sudden burst of enthusiasm may have been a series of reports from war correspondents, pointing out the catastrophic effect of European drinking habits on unprepared doughboys. French and Belgian civilians could not be restrained from pressing bottles of wine and glasses of *aquavit* on their American liberators, and some U.S. regiments—particularly those from already-dry regions—were gaining a reputation for near-constant intoxication.

Though the principle of Prohibition was now enshrined in the Constitution, the practicalities of enforcement required a second piece of legislation. Again, the Anti-Saloon League stepped forward: Wayne Wheeler, the League's attorney and leading lobbyist, drafted a bill which was introduced by Andrew Joseph Volstead, a Republican senator for Minnesota. Passed by the Senate in October 1919—only a few days after Wilson had suffered an incapacitating stroke that effectively ended his political influence, though not his presidency—the Volstead Act put Prohibition into practice, banning the making and selling of alcohol intended for consumption. Enforcement officials were given remarkably wide-ranging and invasive powers to investigate illegal activities, and offenders could be fined, imprisoned and stripped of their property. Comprehensive as the Act was intended to be, its fine print concealed a number of loopholes. Merely owning liquor for private consumption in your home, or indeed brewing your own beer, remained legal. Large-scale distillation could continue, so long as it was strictly for industrial use. And religious communicants, doctors, and veterinarians could legally continue to buy and sell limited quantities of alcohol, albeit under tight regulation.

Volstead himself lost his seat in the Senate in the 1922 elections, but the terms of his eponymous Act continued to shape American culture for more than a decade. For everyday drinkers, its most immediate impact was the closure of all taverns, bars and saloons. But as Bernard de Mandeville might have predicted, a gap in the market on this scale—even one enforced by law—would not go unfilled for long, and within a few months the cellars and backstreet warehouses of many American cities were being turned into new, illicit "speakeasies." As with the martini, various etymologies have been proposed for the name of this Prohibition icon, though the likeliest answer is that it derived simply from the need for clients to keep their voices down, so as not to arouse the suspicions of neighbors or passers-by. The character of speakeasies was as diverse as that of the watering-holes they replaced: many were little more than basement rooms with bottles and barrels on trestle tables, but some—like El Morocco and the Stork Club in New York—were the immediate precursors of the modern nightclub, with bars, dance-floors and dining tables spread over several sumptuous halls.

Speakeasies may have been very different in their atmosphere, but most of them shared two things. First, and for reasons we'll come to in a moment, they sold mainly spirits, and these mainly in cocktails. Second, they were (like eighteenth-century gin shops and nineteenth-century gin palaces) places where men and women could meet, talk and drink on the same terms. Under the Nineteenth Amendment to the Constitution, ratified in August 1920, U.S. women gained the vote, and when combined with Prohibition this brought new and strange kinds of liberation. The clientele at a speakeasy might find themselves crossing all kinds of social and sexual boundaries, in ways that would have been unthinkable in a nineteenth-century tavern.

But speakeasies never had a monopoly on the trade in illegal hooch. Within a few years of the Volstead Act, a few quiet and well-chosen words could elicit a bottle of beer or a flask of gin in otherwise perfectly respectable restaurants, grocers, and even banks. As the historian Iain Gateley has pointed out, U.S. society under Prohibition was increasingly amphibious—dry above, wet below—and this comfortable hypocrisy ran right to the top of public life. President Warren G. Harding was an ardent supporter of Prohibition, but in the privacy of the Oval Office he handed round glasses of whisky to his confidantes. And Alice Roosevelt Longworth—daughter of President Theodore Roosevelt, wife of the Speaker of the House of Representatives, and known as "The Other Washington Monument" for her fearsome talents as a hostess and wit—kept a still in the basement of her townhouse in Washington, D.C., where she produced wine, beer and orange-scented gin. Prohibition was, it seemed, nowhere near as despotic as many American drinkers had feared. According to an editorial in *Outlook* magazine in 1924, it satisfied:

> three tremendous popular passions . . . the passion of the Prohibitionists for law, the passion of the drinking classes for drink, and the passion of the largest and best organized smuggling trade that has ever existed for money.

This trade—known as bootlegging, apparently after the long, flat flasks used to carry hooch in tall boots—was inspired by the same commercial logic which had driven the production of early modern proto-gins. As we saw in Chapter 1, spirits offered a way for sixteenth- and seventeenth-century farmers to concentrate and preserve the value of their harvests. In the nineteenth-century industrial cities spirits had lost ground to beer, but under Prohibition they regained their advantage. For smugglers, the attraction of spirits was exactly that they were stronger than beer or wine, lower in volume but higher in value, and so easier to transport and less likely to be discovered. In the early years of Prohibition most bootleg spirit was based on industrial alcohol, and Gateley has estimated that by 1926 around fifty million gallons, a third of the total volume of U.S. industrial production, was being siphoned off and sold as whisky, brandy, or gin. The Volstead Act had anticipated this possibility, by ordering that all industrial alcohol should be stained or given a repellent flavor with additives, but this proved to be no serious obstacle for the bootleggers and their ingenious chemists. Some sense of their *modus operandi* can be gained from the evidence given by an undercover agent to a Senate subcommittee on bootlegging in 1926:

> You sent in an order for gin, and they would open a spigot on this big tank, run out so much alcohol, and so much water, and so much flavoring extract and coloring fluid, and throw that into the gin. If you wanted a case of Scotch, open the same spigot, run the recovered denatured alcohol into a container in whatever quantity they wanted, the addition of water, a few drops of creosote or essence of Scotch, and a little caramel, and it would come to the bench for Scotch.

Towards the end of Prohibition, some companies began to offer drinkers the opportunity to perform this alchemy in their own homes. An advert in the *New Yorker* in October 1932 hailed the virtues of "Peeko":

> RYE-GIN-RUM-SCOTCH, COGNAC, BOURBON, VERMOUTH, COCKTAIL, APRICOT, MIXED FRUITS, CRÈME DE COCOA, CRÈME DE MENTHE, GRENARDA [sic], BENNÉ. *All perfect, true flavours!* What wonders the human mind evolves! Take PEEKO, (take it once and you'll take no substitute)— all the smooth mellowness of years past has been captured in these flavours. A jar of PEEKO makes a gallon (Gin type makes TWO) and only 75c at your nearest Food or Drug Store. The mixing's easy and requires NO AGING!

In this sense, gin was a gift to the bootleggers (and to anyone trying to turn industrial alcohol into something drinkable). The complex flavors and aromas of brandy or whisky were difficult to imitate convincingly, but a mixture of plain alcohol, water, and juniper oil—or even the eighteenth-century standbys of turpentine and sulphuric acid—would make a reasonably passable gin. At the beginning of the twentieth century American consumers were far more interested in whisky than in gin, and one national register of trademarks lists almost sixteen hundred brands of whisky alongside fewer than seventy brands of gin. By the mid-Twenties, bootleg gin was becoming the spirit of choice in speakeasies, but much of it was extremely rough. There is little evidence that gin was ever made in bathtubs (though, as we'll see, later film-makers helped to make this image part of Prohibition folklore) and "bathtub gin" seems to have been an ironic judgement on the searing and sometimes dirty flavor of illicit spirit.

But if Prohibition gin, fabricated from industrial alcohol and crude flavorings, was harsh, its leading competitor might be even worse. The backwoodsmen of the Appalachian mountains had a long tradition, possibly inherited from their Scottish forebears, of distilling moonshine—"mooney"—and stump whisky, and after the Volstead Act they turned their craft into an industry. By 1930 almost three hundred thousand small pot-stills had been seized, and many more must surely have gone undetected, concealed in windmills, caves, redwood trees, and grain silos. Typically based on corn sugar, moonshine might be flavored with anything from bark to rotten meat, and one Pittsburgh drinker noted that if he left his "mooney gin" standing too long, a green scum formed on the surface.

All this points towards the very practical importance of the cocktail in Prohibition drinking culture, and particularly in the speakeasy. Much of what was sold under counters or behind locked doors was potent but unpalatable in its raw state, and cocktails—particularly strongly-flavored ones like the Gimlet—performed the vital service of making bathtub gin or moonshine whisky into something that could be consumed with a fair degree of pleasure. Books of cocktail recipes became one of the sensations of Prohibition publishing, ostensibly as reminders of less enlightened times, or—under titles like *Giggle Water*—offering collections of dry cocktails, with notes on how they might be made stronger if the Eighteenth Amendment were ever repealed.

For those prepared to pay the right price, however, a supply of premium European gins, whiskies and brandies could be maintained through the activities of smugglers. Like bootlegging, smuggling began within days of the Volstead Act coming into force, taking advantage of the long (and often un-patrolled) borders of the U.S., particularly through Mexico and the Caribbean. Some smugglers, like the legendary William S. McCoy, simply moored their ships in international waters off the U.S. coast, and waited for the word to spread amongst thirsty locals. The Seattle radio station K-FOX, opened in 1924, was reputed to use coded readings of children's stories—Beatrix Potter and A. A. Milne—to pass on news of smuggled shipments. English gin producers had, at first, feared the impact of Prohibition on their reputation and sales, but they quickly realized that their products had a distinct edge over the other kinds of spirits available to American drinkers. The gin scholar Geraldine Coates has estimated that, over the lifetime of the Eighteenth Amendment, they sold around forty million dollars' worth of gin to smugglers, who then carried it into the U.S. Some distillers found themselves getting more involved with smuggling than they may have wished. One order is reported to have stipulated that a consignment of gin be packaged in shockproof and waterproof containers that would float in salt water.

Whatever their private attitudes to this orgy of imaginative law-breaking, U.S. officials had to be seen to be taking action to defend what was now a Constitutional principle. Under the Volstead Act a new federal agency, the Prohibition Bureau, was given responsibility for enforcing the new laws, but it quickly became a byword for corruption. Its agents—known as "Prohis"—were paid less than municipal garbage-men (and received just as little support or respect from the public), and by 1923 more than thirty had been killed in the line of duty. The 1929 St. Valentine's Day Massacre, in which the Chicago gangster Al Capone ordered the execution of seven members from a rival outfit, was only one of many cases which showed that badly paid, badly-treated Prohis could do little to prevent the activities of well-armed and well-organized gangs of bootleggers. Inequalities in the way that the Volstead Act was enforced also damaged the reputation of the Prohibition Bureau. If you were caught in a city speakeasy with a gin cocktail in your hand, you would most probably be fined. If you were found in the same situation on a rural farmstead, you might be put away for years or even decades. In 1929 Etta May Miller, a farmer's wife in Michigan, was jailed for life when a visiting Prohi found a single bottle of gin in her kitchen.

By the early Thirties it was becoming clear to most U.S. citizens that the Great Experiment had failed. In December 1932 the Senate began to debate a bill for repealing Prohibition, and on December 5th, 1933, the Twenty-First Amendment to the Constitution, which undid all the provisions of the Eighteenth Amendment, passed into law. In New York and Chicago effigies standing for Prohibition were variously electrocuted, shot, hanged and drowned, and—if James Costigan's 1977 television drama *Eleanor and Franklin* is to be believed—in the White House President Franklin D. Roosevelt mixed the very first legal martini. Eighty years later, with the benefit of three generations' hindsight, we might want to ask: what were the lasting effects of Prohibition on American culture?

One legacy of these thirteen remarkable years was a new and alluring body of American folklore. Gangsters like Jack "Legs" Diamond, Owen Victor "Owney the Killer" Madden, "Barefoot" Rafer Dooley, and the dashing society bootlegger Raymond "Razor" Gray; Prohis like Izzie Einstein, "Master of Deceit," and the legendary Eliot Ness; speakeasies like the Napoleon, the Five

O'Clock, and the 50-50; and nightclub singers with names like the Kansas Sunshine Baby, "Texas" Guinan, and the Girl with the Poetic Legs. In cinema, television, literature, and pop culture of all kinds, this countercultural pantheon has become shorthand for the gritty glamor of the Twenties. More than this, however, U.S. society changed dramatically over the lifetime of the Eighteenth Amendment. The growth of radio and cinema brought the excitement and danger of metropolitan life to scores of curious (or delighted, or outraged) rural communities. Prohibition took women drinkers out of the private sphere and into the (admittedly illegal) public sphere of the speakeasy, and when it was repealed many women were not inclined to return to their former habits—a prefiguring of the social and cultural revolutions to come in the American Century. And crucially for our purposes, it put gin in the foreground of American cocktail culture. In the words of an article in *Scientific American,* published in March 1934:

> Prohibition ... lifted gin out from the shady and somewhat disreputable regard in which it was held before the dry era and made it fashionable. Tipplers who once disdained it, save in an occasional cocktail, not only learned to drink it, but actually to make it.

The repeal of Prohibition also allowed a new institution—the cocktail party—to come out of the speakeasy and become part of mainstream life. Ironically, the origins of this quintessentially American innovation may well lie in the boredom of a British artist. Alec Waugh—elder brother of Evelyn—claimed that a friend of his, the English painter Christopher Nevinson, invented the cocktail party in 1924. After training at the Slade School, and a brief fling with the English Futurists (brought to an end by an argument with Percy Wyndham Lewis), Nevinson had served in the Friends' Ambulance Service during the First World War, and his experiences led him to create some of the most haunting visual art to emerge from the conflict. Back in London in the early Twenties, he found the long afternoons of late summer stiflingly dull. His solution was to gather a few friends and pass the time until dinner by serving them cocktails. Other stories replace Nevinson with an American hostess named Madame Alfredo de Peña, and later in his life Waugh claimed that the cocktail party was his own invention.

Whatever the truth behind its creation, the cocktail party rapidly became a social institution both in Britain and (from 1933) the U.S. For middle-class families who had neither the inclination nor enough domestic staff to hold large, expensive, Edwardian-style dinner parties, it was an ideal way to entertain friends in a chic and informal way. By the late Twenties a cocktail set, consisting of glasses, implements and a chrome shaker, was a common gift at American weddings, and even respectable households were increasingly happy to display one on their sideboards. New gin cocktails, too, were being created, many of which reflected the continuing influence of the British Empire on European and American tastes. The Straits Sling seems to have been born in the Long Bar of the Raffles Hotel in Singapore in the years around 1915, and was first mixed by a bartender named Ngiam Tong Boon. A recipe for this mixture of gin, kirschwasser, Benedictine, lemon juice, orange bitters, Angostura bitters and soda water, all shaken over ice, appeared in Robert Vermeire's *Cocktails and How to Mix Them,* published in 1922, and by 1930 Harry Craddock's *Savoy Cocktail Book* also included instructions for making a Singapore Sling with the addition of Cointreau, Grenadine and pineapple juice. An early-twentieth century advert for Gordon's gin promoted the cleaner taste of the Gin Fizz:

Teaspoon sugar—Juice one lemon—Dash of cream—Wine glass Gordon dry gin—Fill glass with fine ice—Shake—Strain and fill glass with aerated water.

And for those who did not trust their own mixological skills, Gordon's also offered pre-mixed cocktails like the Perfect, the Piccadilly, the Manhattan and the San Martin. Other new gin cocktails, however, had less appetizing connections. The Monkey Gland, a blend of dry gin, orange juice, pomegranate grenadine and absinthe, shaken over ice, which appeared in the mid-Twenties, appears to have been inspired by Billy Meyers' vaudeville number "Made A Monkey Out of Me." Meyers' song was in turn a riff on the experiments of the Austrian physiologist Eugen Steinach and the French-Russian surgeon Serge Voronoff. Steinach found that older guinea pigs regained their vigor when the sexual organs of younger animals were transplanted into their bodies, and Voronoff went one step further by offering older men a chance to have implants taken from chimpanzee or baboon testicles.

But the drink of choice at most cocktail parties was the martini. By modern standards, martinis in the Thirties were very wet—often only three or four parts gin to one part vermouth—and often had a yellow tint from the addition of orange bitters or vermouth. More adventurous drinkers came up with personal variations on the established theme. At the Fitzroy Tavern in London, Aleister Crowley claimed to have invented the Kubla Khan No. 2—a compound of gin, vermouth and laudanum. The Fitzroy Tavern opened in 1919, though an earlier pub stood on the site, and Crowley returned to Britain in 1923 after being forced by Mussolini's *fascisti* to leave Cefalu in Sicily, but (as with so many aspects of the Great Beast's life) this anecdote is difficult to verify. As the occult historian Alex Owen has noted, we might best see it as part of Crowley's life-long project to enact the decadent fictions of Oscar Wilde and the polymorphously perverse illustrations of Aubrey Beardsley.

Crowley's efforts notwithstanding, the orthodox dry martini, served in a conical glass, was by this point an established favorite with cocktail drinkers across Europe and the U.S., not least with President Roosevelt. By all accounts Roosevelt loved the ritual of martini-making, and at the end of each day he invited his White House staff to a relaxed cocktail party which he called the "Children's Hour," after a line in a poem by Henry Wadsworth Longfellow. Several Children's Hour guests later complained that Roosevelt ruined his martinis with the addition of anisette. But the cocktail could have other, more terminal hazards. In 1941, on a cruise around the Caribbean, the American novelist Sherwood Anderson swallowed the toothpick in a martini, and shortly afterwards died from a perforated colon.

Cocktail parties and "Children's Hours" were one thing, but a further effect of Prohibition was to drive many Americans into exile in Europe. One consequence of this was a crash course in U.S. mixology for British and European bartenders. Another was the creation of some of the most powerful and persistent evocations of Jazz Age life—a phrase coined by one of the leading members of the "Lost Generation," F. Scott Fitzgerald. In Fitzgerald's second novel, *The Beautiful and the Damned,* published in 1922 and set in the world of moneyed New Yorkers, Anthony Patch waits for his inheritance and passes the time by drinking absinthe martinis—half gin and half vermouth, with just a spot of the green fairy "for a proper stimulant." His masterpiece, *The Great Gatsby,* published in 1925, is both a celebration of and a satire on the brittle, gilded lives of American socialites. The mysterious Jay Gatsby turns out to have made his millions as a bootlegger, and the character of Daisy Buchanan—appealing, effervescent and shallow, just like a Gin Fizz—was inspired by Fitzgerald's brief fling with the heiress Ginevra King (named not after the Dutch national drink but after Leonardo da Vinci's portrait of Ginevra da'Benci, painted in 1474). But by the time of *Tender Is the Night,* published in 1934, Fitzgerald's Jazz Age had turned discordant, and the bleak themes of the book reflect his wife Zelda's struggles with schizophrenia and his own descent into alcoholism.

During his time in Paris Fitzgerald was said to have collaborated with Ernest Hemingway in the invention of the White Lady— a mixture of gin, Cointreau, lemon juice and egg white—and Hemingway also used gin as a device in several of his works. When Frederic Henry, the hero of *A Farewell to Arms,* published in 1929, abandons his Italian comrades and flees to the northern town of Stresa, he marks his return to civilization and peace with a plate of sandwiches and several martinis. Another gin cocktail—the gimlet—plays a more poignant part in "The Short Happy Life of Francis Macomber," a short story published in 1936. Macomber and Margot, his wife, are on safari in the African bush, led by Robert Wilson, a professional big-game hunter. When a wounded lion charges at him Macomber panics—a failure for which Margot mocks him when they return to the lodge that evening. Macomber drinks Gimlets to obliterate his shame, while Margot, Hemingway implies, goes to bed with Wilson. The next morning Macomber atones for his cowardice by shooting two buffaloes. One is killed outright but the other is only wounded, and Margot, waiting a hundred yards away in a car, fears her husband will panic again when it charges. She grabs a rifle and fires at the creature, but misses and kills Macomber. His short happy life comes to an end, but he dies knowing that he has killed the buffalo with his last bullet.

As Fitzgerald and Hemingway spun their tales of decadence and cowardice, the young Cole Porter was taking the martini in a more light-hearted direction. In "Two Little Babes in the Wood," a song written for the 1924 revue *Greenwich Village Follies,* Porter re-imagined the folk tale of the "Babes in the Wood." In fine folk-loric style, the Babes are abandoned by their wicked uncle, and the creatures of the forest take care of them. At this point, events take a rather more contemporary turn. A passing tycoon rescues the Babes, takes them to New York, and sets them up as party girls. He smothers them in jewels and silk dresses; he buys them cars and apartments; they acquire admirers and suitors; and their metropolitan makeover is completed when he gives them their first martinis. But in music, as in literature, gin always had a double face, and in the late Twenties Bessie Smith—the greatest female blues singer of her age, possibly of any age—recorded "Gin House Blues." Oddly, Smith sang two different songs under this title. In the first, written by the big band leader and pianist James Fletcher Hamilton Henderson and recorded in March 1926, Smith took her broken heart to a gin house and drowned it. In the second, written by "Harry Burke" (possibly a pseudonym for the pianist James C. Johnson, also famous for his collaboration with Fats Waller) she sang of being alone in the world, with only her sin and her gin for company. This second piece became the canonical "Gin House Blues," particularly after Nina Simone's wrenching performance on *Forbidden Fruit,* released in 1961.

Neither the literary heroes of the Lost Generation, nor the architects of jazz and blues, possessed a monopoly on the metaphorical possibilities of gin. Along with the martini, Prohibition-era America's other great gift to popular culture was a vibrant and adventurous film industry. It was in the cinema, more than anywhere else, that the culture wars of Prohibition were fought and the public's perception of cocktail culture was created. For some filmmakers, strong drink was an enemy of society and the common good; for others, it was a symbol of pleasure and liberation. Drunks might be tragic heroes brought down by the tragic flaw of alcoholism, or bumbling clowns who lifted the moods of those around them. What a character chose to drink, and where they chose to drink it, could reveal a great deal about their background, their mindset, and their own sense of self. As we shall see, gin was rarely part of the plot in early films, but it was very often part of the furniture.

As the cinema began to reach maturity as a mainstream art form, public, political and medical concern had (with the exception of a handful of fascinating French short films made during the absinthe panics of the early twentieth century) moved away from the specific threats associated with different kinds of strong drink, and towards the general threat posed by alcohol in all its forms. Short of having a bottle marked "GIN" or "BEER" in large and contrasting letters, the directors of silent films had no easy shorthand for making audiences realize what was being consumed, and so in many early films the precise identity of an alcoholic drink was less important than the fact that it was alcoholic—a point which could be made

THE BOOK OF GIN

clear in subtitles and by the character's exaggerated reactions. In the first decade of the twentieth century the pioneering director D.W. Griffith—later notorious for *Birth of A Nation,* released in 1915, with its celebration of antebellum slavery and the Ku Klux Klan—produced a series of short films advocating temperance. In *A Drunkard's Reformation,* released in 1909, the eponymous lush takes his wife and daughter to see a play, which turns out to be a melodramatic portrayal of the effects of heavy drinking. The drunkard falls to his knees, begs his family's forgiveness, and goes on the wagon immediately. Griffith's *What Drink Did,* released in the same year, has no such happy ending. A carpenter, under pressure from his workmates, begins to drink beer. He quickly falls into drunken violence, abusing his family and eventually shooting his daughter when she comes to take him home from a bar.

Under Prohibition alcohol may have been banned from American public life, but—as the critic Howard Good has pointed out—it seeped into film in ever-greater quantities. Griffith continued to make films extolling the virtues of moderation and sobriety, like *The Struggle,* released in 1931, his last film as a director and one of his few talkies. But other, younger filmmakers rebelled against the Eighteenth Amendment, particularly in that most seemingly innocent of formats—the comedy short. In *Blotto,* released in 1930, Stan Laurel and Oliver Hardy raid Mrs. Laurel's secret gin stash, hoping to sneak a bottle or two off to the Rainbow Club. But she is one step ahead of them, and when Laurel and Hardy reach the club and take a glass, they find themselves drinking a nauseating liquid containing mustard, chili sauce and cold tea. *Blotto* is a good-natured, knock-about comedy, but in *Scram!,* released two years later, they turn their slapstick into an incisive satire on Prohibition hypocrisy. Judge Beaumont, ostensibly a paragon of temperance, grows tired of Laurel and Hardy's drunken antics, and forces them to leave town. As they go, they fall in with a drunk, who asks them to spend the night at what he claims to be his house. As he fumbles around in his pockets for the key, they find an open window, but as they enter a woman sees them, screams and faints. Pouring a glass of what appears to be water, they prop her up and give her a drink, but her reaction makes it quite clear that they are actually dosing her with gin. Never ones to pass up an opportunity for intoxication, they join her in a toast. As they do so, the real owner of the house returns: Judge Beaumont, who, it turns out, is the biggest secret drinker in town.

Just as Prohibition was being repealed, a new set of restrictions—the Hays Code—threatened to curb the depiction of alcohol in American cinema. Will H. Hays had been appointed chairman of the Motion Pictures Producers and Distributors Association in 1922, with a remit to restore the reputation of the business after the murder trial of Roscoe "Fatty" Arbuckle. Hays began his crackdown by doing a great injustice to the wholly innocent Arbuckle, banning him from appearing in any film and effectively ending his career. His next move was to work up a code of practice that would turn American cinema into a wholesome and decent form of mass entertainment. Vices might appear on screen, but they could not be depicted graphically, and they could not go unpunished. In particular, drinking and drunkenness could not be shown unless they were strictly necessary to the plot. The MPPDA adopted the Hays Code in 1930 and began to enforce it in 1934, but to many directors its rules on the portrayal of alcohol seemed severe in the aftermath of Prohibition. Cocktails continued to serve as a character note and a comic prop in all kinds of cinematic encounters, and the drinking continued when the cameras stopped rolling. It was in this period that the final take of a film became known as the Martini Shot, and the comic actor W.C. Fields was rumored to have drunk up to four pints of pre-mixed martinis each day when he was on set. This staggering volume of liquid refreshment was kept in a silver flask, and referred to as "Mr. Fields' pineapple juice." When one bright spark swapped this for an identical flask containing a soft drink, Fields was heard to complain that someone had put pineapple juice in his pineapple juice.

Within a few years some of the more daring directors were beginning to tackle the subject of Prohibition, and one film—*The*

*Roaring Twenties,* released in 1939—exerted a powerful influence over later depictions of the era. James Cagney plays Eddie Bartlett, a mechanic and war veteran who returns from the First World War to find that a generation of younger men have taken his place in the workshops and garages of his home town. To make ends meet, Bartlett becomes a part-time cab driver with his friend Danny Green, but falls into crime almost by accident, when he is arrested after being asked to deliver a suspiciously bottle-shaped parcel of "meat" to a local speakeasy. The two friends go into bootlegging together, and in one classic scene they sit in Bartlett's bathroom, making bathtub gin (literally) from industrial alcohol and bottles of chemical flavorings. Green, dressed in an apron, sits on the edge of the bath, and uses one of his wife's saucepans to pour the gin into a bottle held by Bartlett. Both men take great care not to spill any of their product—not just, as Bartlett points out, for the sake of profit, but also because the highly concentrated alcohol might catch fire or eat away at their clothes. *The Roaring Twenties* ends in tragedy: Bartlett muscles in on a rival gang led by another old friend, George Hally, played by Humphrey Bogart, but the stock market crash of 1929 and the end of Prohibition leave him broke. By the end of the film he is back behind the wheel of his cab, but a chance encounter with Hally and an argument over the death of a wartime comrade leads to a double murder. Bartlett kills Hally, and is then shot by one of Hally's gang. His last staggering steps carry him towards the gate of a church, where he falls on his back, dead.

Even early film noir, however, had its lighter side. Six films made between 1934 and 1947 offered the cinema-going public a less grim and more seductive sketch of what life without Prohibition might be like. In a series of adventures adapted from Dashiell Hammett's wildly successful novel *The Thin Man,* published in 1934, William Powell and Myrna Loy play Nick and Nora Charles—a private detective, recently retired but soon drawn into a murder investigation, and his well-heeled wife. Both Nick and Nora like a drink, to put it mildly, and there is scarcely a scene which does not feature a martini in one way or another. Early on, in a New York nightclub,

Nick tries to prove his theory that a martini should be shaken in waltz time, but a manhattan should be mixed to the beat of a foxtrot. Their West Highland terrier, Asta, knows all the bars along the route of her daily walk, and Nick's sleuthing leads him through a string of high-class parties, dances and hotels. And Nick and Nora's martinis are not merely refreshment. Consider the timing of the first film: made in 1934, just after the end of Prohibition, it was set in 1902, well before the Eighteenth Amendment was even conceived. In the world of *The Thin Man* the Great Experiment is elided, and martinis, along with dancing, laughter, parties and fine clothes, are not objects of guilt or shame but simply part of daily life. In this sense, the *Thin Man* films reminded American drinkers that they were allowed to have a good time again, no matter what clouds might be building up on their horizons.

Shortly after dawn on Sunday December 7th, 1941 a combined force of fighter-bombers and midget submarines, under the command of Admiral Isoroku Yamamoto of the Japanese Imperial General Headquarters, attacked the U.S. naval base at Pearl Harbor on the island of Oahu in the Hawaiian archipelago. This pre-emptive strike, which sank twelve ships and killed 2,402 American servicemen and civilians, was intended to eliminate any possibility of American intervention in the expansion of the Japanese empire across south-east Asia. Within four days of the attack—"a date which will live in infamy," in Roosevelt's ringing phrase—the U.S. was once again embroiled in a global war, preparing to fight Nazi forces in Europe and Japanese forces in the Pacific.

Over the next four years hundreds of thousands of GIs found themselves posted to theaters of war around the world, and in addition to the staple comforts of chocolate, chewing gum and cigarettes, many units had regular movie screenings to take their minds off the stress and fatigue of combat. *Casablanca,* released in the icy depths of January 1943, has become an icon of wartime American filmmaking, but it also contains what is probably the most well-known invocation of gin in the history of cinema. One could hardly claim that gin plays a particularly important part in the plot of *Casablanca,* and (as with its earlier cinematic appearances), it is simply one of many small touches which offer flashes of insight into the lives of the leading characters. Rick Blaine—Humphrey Bogart's first romantic role after years of playing gangsters like George Hally—runs Rick's Café Américain, a nightclub and gambling den in the Moroccan port of Casablanca. Blaine's life is turned upside down, pitting his painful memories against his sense of right and wrong, when his old flame Ilsa, played by Ingrid Bergman, walks into his gin joint and back into his life. Blaine's predicament, sharpened by his encounters with Nazi officers and Free French resistance fighters, captures the double face of the gin he serves, reflecting the cynical, hard glamor of the speakeasy, but also the clarity and purity of this no-nonsense, fundamentally adult drink.

Wartime and post-war austerity wrought further changes to the status of gin. Once again distilleries concentrated on supplying alcohol to the munitions industry—a move known as "cocktails for Hitler." In Britain, however, the Government Committee on Brewing and Distilling insisted that production of some premium gins and whiskies be maintained, so that they could be exported to the U.S. in reciprocation for Lend-Lease munitions. Gin became notably scarce in the nation's pubs and bars, and black marketeers stepped in to fill this lacuna with smuggled or stolen supplies, or even rough-tasting homemade substitutes like the notorious "Edgware Road Gin." Even before the outbreak of war a series of poor harvests had led many distillers to use a lower-quality base spirit produced from sugar cane, and the conflict brought one or two of the most venerable distilleries almost to bankruptcy. During the Siege of Malta British commanders tried to keep morale up by promising a bottle of Plymouth Gin to anyone who destroyed a German ship or fighter. But in 1941 the Plymouth distillery was badly damaged in an incendiary raid, and the quality of their product fell so rapidly that the Royal Navy ended its two-century association with the brand.

Anyone who had toasted VE Day in May 1945 with a glass of austerity gin and a "Victory Brand Cigarette"—an object of contempt for British soldiers and civilians alike—might have felt a shudder of familiarity four years later as they thumbed through George Orwell's *Nineteen Eighty-Four,* published in 1949. Orwell's masterpiece, written in a farmhouse on the Isle of Jura in the Inner Hebrides as he tried to master the tuberculosis that was killing him, is a deeply pessimistic vision of a totalitarian future. Sweet, oleaginous, synthetic "Victory Gin" is one of the book's principal metaphors for the drudgery and hopelessness of life for Winston Smith and his comrades in the Oceanian province of Airstrip One. Victory Gin is a deeply hollow name, a reminder that under Big Brother there is no possibility of victory or defeat, merely endless and exhausting struggle. Like the rest of the culture, it has been standardized and industrialized, with any sense of its emotional or historical meaning eroded away—a point reflected in Smith's encounters with the drink:

> [Smith] took down from the shelf a bottle of colorless liquid with a plain white label marked VICTORY GIN. It gave off a sickly, oily smell, as of Chinese rice-spirit. Winston poured out nearly a teacupful, nerved himself for a shock, and gulped it down like a dose of medicine.

> Instantly his face turned scarlet and the water ran out of his eyes. The stuff was like nitric acid, and moreover, in swallowing it one had the sensation of being hit on the back of the head with a rubber club. The next moment, however, the burning in his belly died down and the world began to look more cheerful. He took a cigarette from a crumpled packet marked VICTORY CIGARETTES and incautiously held it upright, whereupon the tobacco fell out on to the floor. With the next he was more successful.

In the closing pages of the novel, after betraying Julia, his lover, in Room 101, Smith sits vacantly in the Chestnut Tree Café, reading the propaganda-sheets and drinking more Victory Gin:

He picked up his glass and drained it at a gulp. As always, it made him shudder and even retch slightly. The stuff was horrible. The cloves and saccharine, themselves disgusting in their sickly way, could not disguise the flat oily smell; and what was worst of all was that the smell of gin, which dwelt with him night and day, was inextricably mixed up in his mind with the smell of those—

*Nineteen Eighty-Four* is a book about memory and the politics of remembering, and Victory Gin acts both as an instrument of forgetfulness and a stimulus of the most painful memories. For Smith, flavors and tastes—like the chocolate that Julia shares with him when they sneak away to the countryside—bring back scanty memories of life before the revolution, as though he were Proust consuming a Victory Madeleine in a Moscow tower-block. In the final sentences, even Smith's tears have taken on the sickly aroma of the spirit. Victory Gin, like Big Brother, has invaded his soul.

By having Winston Smith obliterate his despair with glasses of Victory Gin, Orwell captured something of the exhaustion and scarcity—though not the sense of relief and success—experienced in Britain at the end of the Second World War. On the other side of the Atlantic, however, things were very different. For many American civilians the war had not been a time of material deprivation, and the end of the war ushered in a decade of optimism and consumerism, in which the American Dream seemed more attainable than ever. But the outbreak of the Cold War—a term coined by Orwell in an article in *Tribune* in October 1945—brought paranoia, mistrust and the threat of imminent nuclear annihilation. Both confidence and fear led Americans to drink, in new ways and new places, but they continued to place their trust in the martini.

By the late Thirties many American cities, and particularly New York, were witnessing the appearance of new and distinctively modern cocktail bars, with dark wood, chrome fittings, mirrors, andVenetian blinds. In the late Forties and Fifties these became the venue of choice for a new generation of urban drinkers, and spirit manufacturers were quick to capitalize on this trend. Adverts for gin and whisky sometimes took a traditionally aspirational tack, presenting gin and brandy as the drink of East CoastWASPS, associated with old money, wood-paneled studies, tennis whites and Ivy League drink parties. This strategy even came with its own jokes. What's a WASP's idea of a seven-course banquet? Six martinis and a canapé. Increasingly, however, the marketing gurus of Madison Avenue marketed the martini as the drink of progress, a natural partner for fast cars and skyscrapers, grey flannel suits and tab collars, the business lunch and the cocktail hour (which in practice often meant the husband downing a couple of martinis with his colleagues before stepping on to a commuter train, while his wife sat at home and nursed a gin fizz or a highball).

As the cultural aura of the martini shifted, so the cocktail itself began to change. The Fifties were the apex of what Lowell Edmunds has called the dryness fetish, with drinkers finding ways to reduce the proportion of vermouth to a near-homoeopathic dilution. Some rinsed the glass with vermouth and then poured it away; some poured vermouth over ice-cubes in a sieve, before adding the ice to the cocktail shaker; some merely whispered the word "vermouth" over the bottle as they poured in the gin. This last technique had honorable historical precedents: the leading Surrealist film-maker Luis Buñuel held a bottle of Noilly Prat up to the window, so that a ray of sunlight could shine through it and on to his martini, and in the depths of the Blitz Winston Churchill merely bowed in the direction of France as he sloshed Plymouth gin into his glass. Technologically-minded drinkers could purchase a vermouth atomiser, or a Hammacher Schlemmer vermouth dropper, or a Gorham martini spike, which resembled a hypodermic syringe and came in a velvet-lined case. And for those who felt that all this was going a little too far, Bertram Stanleigh mocked the dryness fetish in his *Safety Code and Requirements for Dry Martinis,* published in 1966. According to Stanleigh's code, anything more than one part vermouth to sixteen parts gin was simply too dangerous to drink.

While the martini—no matter how dry—was the quintessence of American modernity, the gin that went into it might well have been produced by a British distillery of one or two centuries' standing. Beefeater capitalized on the wave of enthusiasm for all things British after the coronation of Elizabeth II in 1953, quickly becoming the largest export gin brand, and Tanqueray found its way into the affections of American celebrities and politicians from Bob Hope to John F. Kennedy. British gin did not find favor everywhere—Chinese Communist Party officials preferred the warm, expensive-looking colors of cognac—but the martini became an international symbol of American power. In the late Forties Bernard DeVoto, a Pulitzer Prize-winning historian of the American West, wrote a series of articles on American cocktails, and concluded that the martini was one of the great American contributions to world culture. Nikita Khrushchev, First Secretary of the Soviet Communist Party between 1953 and 1964, described the martini as "America's most lethal weapon," and on at least one occasion it was used in anger (though in a drawing-room rather than on a battlefield). Ernest Bevin, the British Foreign Secretary from 1945 to 1951, had a famously difficult relationship with Dean Acheson, the American Secretary of State. In May 1950, after one particularly unfriendly meeting, he served Acheson a foul "martini" made from equal parts gin, vermouth and lukewarm water.

Some time in the winter of 1945 Truman Capote—twenty-one years old, and already renowned as a writer of short fiction—was invited to a party given by Carmel Snow, the fearsome senior editor of *Harper's Bazaar*. Taking one look at his soft, youthful face, she asked a passing waiter to fetch a glass of milk. Capote thanked her, but said that he would prefer a martini. In post-war fiction, as in post-war life, the martini could be a powerful marker of maturity and all the privileges that came with it. Probably the most famous instance of this is in J. D. Salinger's *Catcher in the Rye,* published in 1951. As he wanders aimlessly around New York, Holden Caulfield and a friend drink martinis and scotches in a hotel bar, but the adult trappings contrast sharply with the juvenile tone of their conversation. Salinger used this device again a decade later in the short story "Franny," published in *Franny and Zooey* in 1961. Over the course of a martini-heavy lunch before the annual Yale-Princeton football game, Franny Glass and her boyfriend Lane Coutell seem to lose touch with one another; Lane is preoccupied with his latest essay on Flaubert, while Franny is troubled by the contents of the book she has been reading—the work of a Russian mystic who advocates continuous, endless prayer.

martinis have also accompanied more genuinely adult fictional encounters. Charles Ryder and Julia Flyte drink them over a flirtatious lunch on a train in Evelyn Waugh's *Brideshead Revisited,* published in 1945, and in Sara Davidson's *Loose Change,* published in 1977, one character receives a proposal of marriage via a diamond ring in a martini at Sardi's Restaurant in New York. But gin's romantic repercussions have also been the stuff of magnificently low comedy. Julian and Sandy, the camp resting actors in *Round the Horne,* broadcast between 1965 and 1968, had a running joke about the effects of gin on Hugh Paddick's Julian. Sandy, played by Kenneth Williams, hinted that his friend had suffered (or enjoyed) an unspecified experience in Bognor. If allowed anywhere near a glass of gin, Julian would be become unbearably maudlin, and would without doubt disgrace himself again.

Julian and Sandy aside, it is fair to say that post-war literature and pop culture has concentrated on the darker and more stylish aspects of gin-drinking. Travis McGee—the hero of more than twenty novels by the American detective-story writer John D. MacDonald, beginning with *The Deep Blue Good-By* [sic] in 1964—consumes gallons of Plymouth gin as he plies his trade as a "salvage consultant" amongst the lowlifes of Fort Lauderdale and Miami. The title of MacDonald's first novel seems to have been inspired by one of the classics of noir detective fiction: Raymond Chandler's *The Long Goodbye,* published in 1953. Chandler's anti-hero, Philip Marlowe, meets Terry Lennox in a bar, and gets to know him over many, many gimlets. When Lennox flees to Mexico after (apparently) murdering his wife, and (again, apparently) is found dead in a hotel room, having written a full confession before killing himself, Marlowe broods on his death over yet another gimlet.

Two other works of fiction published in 1953 offered very different takes on the meaning of gin for post-war drinkers. One of them introduced the most famous, and surely the most culturally influential, martini drinker of the past century. In an exclusive casino at Royale-les-Eaux—a fictional seaside resort on the northern French coast—a Caribbean tycoon breaks off from the baccarat table for a drink, and invents a new kind of martini for his personal assistant:

"A dry martini," he said. "One. In a deep champagne goblet."
"Oui, monsieur."
"Just a moment. Three measures of Gordon's, one of vodka, half a measure of Kina Lillet. Shake it very well until it's ice-cold, then add a large thin slice of lemon peel. Got it?"

The novel is *Casino Royale;* the tycoon is, of course, James Bond; and his companion is the beautiful spy Vesper Lynd—one of only two women (at least in Ian Fleming's original novels and short stories) that Bond falls in love with. He names the cocktail after her, though by the end of the book she is dead by her own hand, unable to bear the strain of life as a double agent. As a reminder of a loss which Bond does not care to recollect, the Vesper appears only once, but his taste for vodka martinis is now legendary, largely thanks to the twenty-two films in which he has (to date) appeared. In the books, however, Fleming has him drinking almost as many gin martinis, plus a liver-pounding selection of other cocktails, champagnes, brandies, bourbons, whiskies and Turkish raki. What seems to be a vodka martini appears in the first film—*Doctor No,* starring Sean Connery, released in 1962—but Connery's Bond does not get to order one until the third film, *You Only Live Twice,* released in 1964. Most early martini recipes specified that the cocktail should be stirred, as shaking made it cloudy with tiny chips of ice. Judging by the crystal clarity of Bond's on-screen martinis, it seems entirely possible that each bartender he encounters takes the courageous step of disregarding his instructions. His signature drink gives every appearance of being stirred, not shaken.

John Cheever's "The Sorrows of Gin," though published in the same year as *Casino Royale,* could hardly be more different in its portrayal of gin-drinking in the affluent suburbs of Fifties America. For many critics and readers Cheever was the laureate of the post-war martini set. Living with his family in the commuter town of Ossining in Westchester County, New York, he found himself trapped in the world which he anatomized in his fiction, and after a near-fatal bout of pulmonary edema, provoked by his heavy drinking, he entered rehab and eventually became an abstainer. For Cheever as for his contemporaries, gin was shorthand for a certain kind of upmarket elegance. In his ominously strange short story "The Swimmer," included in *The Brigadier and the Golf Widow,* published in 1964, the occupants of the elegant gardens through which Neddie Merrill makes his way home drink gin cocktails over ice. "The Sorrows of Gin," meanwhile, is a detached, almost clinical portrayal of the life of a wealthy suburban couple, Kip and Marcia Lawton. The Lawtons are, it seems, rarely sober, and from the isolating perspective of her private day school their daughter, Amy, sees only a succession of awkward cocktail parties and drunken arguments over empty gin bottles. In a chillingly brilliant piece of imaginative writing—made into a 1979 film by Pulitzer Prize-winning playwright Wendy Wasserstein, starring Edward Hermann and Sigourney Weaver—Cheever unpicks the relationship between two aspects of American drinking culture, setting the convivial but superficial world of the cocktail party against the self-destructive excess of the lonely alcoholic. Gin has dissolved the Lawtons' lives, and perhaps their souls, but at the same time it is the only thing keeping them together.

This sense of ambivalence is also visible in the way that post-war American cinema and theater handled gin and its drinkers. Whisky was typically the drink of the hard-case, of those flagrant topers who were quite happy to be seen downing shots in a bar, or even necking it straight from the bottle. Gin, however, was the drink of the neurotic, the repressed, of those who felt a need to conceal, to others and to themselves, the extent of their drinking. It might be hidden in cocktails or with tonic, or gulped at cock-tail party after cocktail party, or even nipped surreptitiously in an empty apartment. In *The Graduate,* released in 1967, Anne Bancroft's Mrs. Robinson nurses a martini as she waits for Dustin Hoffman's gauche Benjamin Braddock to arrive for their assignation at the Taft Hotel. Federico Fellini implied that the main character in *La Dolce Vita,* released in 1961, catches American-style heavy drinking from the vulgar and greedy tourists he encounters in Rome. And Buñuel satirized suburban martini-drinkers in *The Discreet Charm of the Bourgeoisie,* released in 1972, suggesting that just as vermouth had been ousted from the cocktail shaker, so social intercourse had become a bland substitute for erotic passion.

The gin-drinking in Edward Albee's *Who's Afraid of Virginia Woolf,* first staged in 1962, could never be described as bland. As they toss back their cocktails George, a history professor at a small college, and Martha, his wife and the daughter of the college president, engage in some of the most inventive and sustained bouts of in-vective ever enacted on stage. George mocks Martha's choice of gimlets as a drink for amateurs, and when he finds himself alone with Nick, a younger colleague, he tells how he once played tru-ant from his boarding school and visited a gin joint with another boy, who had accidentally killed both his mother and his father, and shortly afterwards was locked up in an asylum. The sweet-sour flavor of the gimlet also runs through David Mamet's *Glengarry Glen Ross,* first staged in 1982 and set amongst a band of hard-drinking, predatory Chicago real-estate agents, who use flattery, bribery and intimidation to unload worthless plots of land on to unsuspecting victims. And in one of the classic post-war depictions of co-dependent alcoholism—Blake Edwards' *Days of Wine and Roses*, released in 1962—Jack Lemmon and Lee Remick lubricate their long slide into misery with martinis, brandy alexanders and, in one scene, neat gin drunk from plastic cups on a bed in a cheap motel. But not all cinematic drinkers are archetypes of melancholy and misfortune. In *Arthur*, released in 1981, Dudley Moore plays a wealthy young gadabout—one of the last comic drunks in American cinema outside of binge-drinking frat-house comedies—whose family threaten to cut him off without a penny if he refuses to marry a well-bred but dull society girl. In one publicity shot for the film, Moore reclines in a bathtub filled with bubbles, a dreamy smile on his lips and a martini glass in his hand.

By 1981 Dudley Moore's martini would have marked him out as something of an anachronism, and would almost certainly have been composed of vodka rather than gin. From the mid-Sixties both gin and the martini entered a period of decline, as tastes, habits and the economics of production all began to shift. In the Fifties American distillers, concerned about their declining stocks of aged spirits, had begun to market vodka as a fashionable alternative to gin and whisky. The obsessive precision of the dryness fetish gave way to a more casual attitude, embodied in the "martini on the rocks," with gin and vermouth splashed carelessly into a glass with ice. Many established gin brands were bought by large international drinks conglomerates, and their character and individuality proved hard to preserve. Though it was endorsed by celebrities like Sir Francis Chichester—who said that the only truly dark moments on his solo circumnavigation in *Gipsy Moth IV* were the times when he ran out of gin—the quality of Plymouth continued to decline. By the early Nineties its strength had been reduced from 40% to 37.5%, and it was being produced only a couple of times a year.

Most importantly, the third quarter of the twentieth century witnessed another revolution in the medical and moral framing of drinking. In 1939 two reformed alcoholics—Bill Wilson, a stockbroker, and Bob Smith, a physician—had published *Alcoholics Anonymous*. Taking their cues from Benjamin Rush and his contemporaries, who had argued that heavy drinking could be seen as a kind of disease, Wilson and Smith argued that alcoholics should not be stigmatized. They were suffering from an illness which could be treated with a twelve-step program, rooted in the principle that the power to reform could only come from outside the mind of the drinker. Alcoholics Anonymous grew rapidly through the Forties and Fifties—by 1957 it was well-known enough to be parodied in a Warner Brothers cartoon, *Birds Anonymous,* in which Sylvester the Cat tries to give up his addiction to pursuing Tweety-Pie— and its influence began to spread around the world, with both the World Health Organization and the American Medical Association reclassifying alcoholism as a disease.

If the Sixties were a bad time for blithe, *Arthur*-style drinking, the Seventies and Eighties were worse. During the 1976 Presidential campaign Jimmy Carter condemned the "three-martini lunch" as the preserve of arrogant, bloated Wall Street bankers, and the identification of fetal alcohol syndrome in the late Seventies led to new calls for women to avoid drinking throughout pregnancy. The new health movement of the same period abandoned the three-martini lunch in favor of mineral water and salads, and the fashion for fitness led many urban consumers to replace the cocktail hour with a visit to the gym.

By the mid-Eighties gin and gin cocktails were firmly out of fashion, and if our story concluded here it would be a sad end to four centuries of global history. As we've seen, however, gin has recovered from a catastrophic decline in its reputation at least twice before, and over the past twenty years it has enjoyed an astonishing return to form and popularity—a true gin renaissance.

Only a few decades after European physicians and missionaries encountered cinchona, the drug had become caught up in political and intellectual arguments over the fruits of Western imperialism. "Peru offers a branch of cinchona to Science," from a seventeenth-century engraving, reproduced in Rassegna Medica, March–April 1955.

# Epilogue

# Gin Renaissance

S TRANGE AS IT may seem to say it, now is the best time in the last five centuries to be drinking gin. Cocktails and cocktail culture are back in fashion, and a new generation of mixologists are creating fresh twists on established favorites. Older brands like Tanqueray and Plymouth have been revitalized, and newer distillers like Sipsmith's and G'Vine are making original and rewarding contributions to the market. Open-minded drinkers can taste small-batch boutique gins flavored with almost any botanical under the sun; independent thinkers can please their own palates with blending kits; and those with more retro tastes can find recreations of seventeenth-century Dutch genever and Victorian Old Tom. This is a high time for gin and its drinkers, and we'll end our journey with an exploration of the factors which have fired this gin renaissance, and with a tour through the still-rooms and laboratories of some leading contemporary gin distillers.

The roots of the gin renaissance lie in the late Eighties, as the U.S. drinks industry sought to arrest and reverse the decline of spirit-drinking in the face of the health boom. By 1988 distilling conglomerates spent more than eight hundred million dollars per year on advertising, and were diverting similarly large amounts into sports and arts sponsorship. In doing so, they hoped to restore the status of gin and other spirits as aspirational consumables, the accoutrements of a stylish and cosmopolitan lifestyle. 1988 also saw the appearance of Bombay Sapphire—the first new premium gin for decades. Created by Michel Roux of Carrilon Importers, who was also responsible for another triumph of lifestyle marketing with Absolut vodka, Bombay Sapphire provided the model for dozens of subsequent boutique gins. Recognizing that even the leading premium brands had lost much of their individuality, Roux emphasized the quality, character, and heritage of Bombay Sapphire. Made to a 1761 recipe in a nineteenth-century carterhead still, using Welsh mountain spring water, and sold in an elegant blue glass bottle, this was about as far from industrial mass-production as a mainstream distiller could get.

In the same year attentive pop-culture observers might have noticed the first stirrings of a cocktail revival, in the shape of James Bridges' film *Bright Lights, Big City*. Based on the 1984 novel by Jay McInerney—who along with Tama Janowitz and Bret Easton Ellis made up the literary "Brat Pack" of the mid-Eighties—*Bright Lights, Big City* follows the fortunes of Jamie Conway, a Kansas-born writer. Conway moves to Manhattan in search of success, but after losing his girlfriend Amanda he falls into a tailspin of partying, drinking and drugging. In McInerney's novel Conway's main vice is cocaine, but in the film this was downplayed, apparently in an effort to preserve the wholesome image of its star, Michael J. Fox, and the cinematic Conway's decline is largely the consequence of cocktails. *Bright Lights, Big City* was hardly a recommendation of the virtues of gin-drinking, but it introduced many young film-goers to the edgy, atmospheric potential of urban bars and clubs. Building on this, the "Cocktail Nation" movement of the early Nineties was yin to grunge's yang, with bands like Royal Crown Revue, the Squirrel Nut Zippers and the Cherry Poppin' Daddies paying affectionate tribute to cocktail culture, lounge music and swing dancing. Teens and twentysomethings could be seen in Hawaiian shirts, golf caps, and even the occasional zoot suit, and cocktails—especially the martini—were back on the menu.

Cocktail Nation achieved a kind of apotheosis in another film—*Swingers*, released in 1996. Set amongst aspiring actors living on the unfashionable east side of Hollywood, *Swingers* starred John Favreau, Vince Vaughn and Heather Graham, and its soundtrack featured swing classics and new tracks by some of the leading Cocktail Nation bands. Favreau plays Mike, a New York comedian who moves to Los Angeles after breaking up with his long-term girlfriend. His best friend Trent, played by Vaughn, introduces him to the retro joys of cocktail-drinking, and teaches him the rules of seduction. By the end of the film Mike has acquired a new sense of fun, a taste for martinis, and a new girlfriend in the shapely form of Graham. Partly through the influence of Cocktail Nation and films like *Swingers,* the martini moved back into mainstream culture through the Nineties—a shift marked by the appearance of many new-tinis, from the appletini to the tartini and even the espressotini.

This fascination with all things martini was given an appropriately postmodern twist in Peter Moody's "docudramedy" *Olive or Twist,* released in 2004. Paul Arensburg, a Los Angeles barman, plays Nick martini, a cycle courier, who must take on the identity of a film noir detective in order to understand the history and meaning of the martini (and also capture the heart of a beautiful and mysterious woman). His adventures are interspersed with footage of interviews with scholars, bartenders, and martini enthusiasts, who extol the virtues of the drink. And fifteen years after *Swingers,* the trend shows no sign of abating. In the acclaimed TV drama *Mad Men,* which has gone through four series since 2007, Don Draper and his stable of advertising executives lubricate their wheeler-dealing and womanizing with defiantly un-PC cigarettes and martinis.

But as the success of Bombay Sapphire suggests, the gin renaissance has not just been a matter of changing perceptions. Over the last twenty years many distillers have returned to an older, artisanal style of distilling, one which emphasizes quality over quantity, to create a wide and idiosyncratic range of gins. The Coffey still, the Victorian innovation which permitted large-scale continuous distillation, has lost ground, as has the practice of "cold compounding"—mixing neutral spirit with essential oils to side-step the need for expensive rectification. Indeed, for distillers who wish to meet the exacting standards of the European Union's Protected Geographical Indication status, now awarded to London dry gin and Plymouth gin, pot-still rectification is a necessity. Once dismissed as the preserve of pre-industrial amateurs, this technique has become the heart of premium gin production, and many brands are proud to tell consumers that their gins are made in eighteenth- or nineteenth-century stills. The "Old Tom" still at Gordon's has been in use for more than two hundred years, and at Plymouth's Blackfriars distillery a 155-year-old still remains in regular use. A single run usually takes seven hours or so, with the master distiller in constant attendance so that he or she can decide when to take the desirable "middle cut."

As distillers have taken a new interest in older techniques of distillation, so they have begun to pay closer attention to the mix of botanicals. More than a hundred are in use across the industry, though most gins contain no more than seven or eight. Juniper—these days often grown in the Balkan states—still predominates, but a modern premium gin might also contain Russian angelica root, Italian almonds, French orris root, Moroccan coriander, West African grains of paradise, or Javanese cubebs. Gordon's, Tanqueray and Booth's add the botanicals to the spirit in the still, while Beefeater allows them to infuse in cold spirit for twenty-four hours before heating, and in the production of Bombay Sapphire the botanicals are held in copper baskets in the neck of the still. Many distillers also produce specialist or seasonal gins with rare and exotic botanicals. In recent years Gordon's have added a Distiller's Cut with lemongrass and ginger, and at Greenall's Joanne Moore, the industry's first female distiller, supervises the production of Berkeley Square gin, inspired by the plants grown in medieval herb gardens, and BLOOM, a floral gin scented with honeysuckle. Tanqueray, meanwhile, has created a gin flavored with Rangpur limes, and Beefeater makes a limited edition winter gin, infused with warm, spicy botanicals.

Many leading British gin producers have enjoyed a new lease on life as a result of the gin renaissance. In 1996, for example, four investors bought the failing Plymouth distillery, and have since worked to restore its status and regain the patronage of the Royal Navy. But the most vibrant strand in contemporary gin production is the work of small-batch distillers, each making their own distinctive boutique gins. This movement first took off in the U.S., where the number of craft distilleries leapt from five in 1990 to almost a hundred by the end of the century, and in the last decade many have been established in Britain, with a cluster of leading lights in London. In the front room of his house in Highgate, Ian Hart, a former city trader, uses a low-temperature vacuum still to produce twelve single-botanical spirits, which he then blends to create Sacred gin. And close to the River Thames at Hammersmith Sam Galsworthy, Fairfax Hall, and master distiller Jared Brown have established the Sipsmith distillery, based around the first brand-new copper pot still to be installed in a London distillery in more than two hundred years.

Bucking the trend for light London dry gins, Christian Jensen has made a splash with his Bermondsey gin, based on heavier, sweeter Thirties models, and Christopher Hayman—a scion of the Burroughs family, who founded Beefeater—produces a classic London dry gin, an Old Tom, and a sweet, aromatic Gin Liqueur. Further afield, the Blackwoods distillery in Catfirth on the Shetland Islands uses botanicals from local meadows and dunes to create a fresh and distinctive gin. Another Scottish firm, William Grant & Sons, historically more famous for their whiskies, makes Hendrick's—one of the most successful new gins of the last decade, flavored with cucumber and rose and sold in a black, apothecary-style bottle. At the Langley distillery near Birmingham the hotel magnate and publisher Martin Miller has developed a London dry gin which is widely acknowledged to be one of the finest premium spirits in the world, and across the Channel Jean Sébastien Robicquet and Bruno de Reilhac have broken all the rules of gin with G'Vine, a grape spirit flavored with the flowers of the green vine.

RICHARD BARNETT

At the same time, gin's ancestor and cousin—genever—continues
to thrive. It is perhaps not as fashionable as gin, and (like sherry)
it has a reputation as old-fashioned and fogeyish. But it is still the
Dutch national drink, and the various styles offer a fascinating insight into the history of genever and gin. *Oude genever*—not aged,
but "old-style"—is made with at least fifteen percent *moutwijn,*
and contains up to twenty grams of sugar per liter. It has a rich
yellow color, and is sweet and juniperous to the taste—perhaps
a drink Hogarth would have recognized. *Jonge genever,* developed
early in the twentieth century, is lighter, with no more than fifteen
percent *moutwijn,* and less than ten grams of sugar per liter. And
*korenwijn,* cask-aged for more than a year, is potent stuff: at least
fifty-one percent *moutwijn,* it is sweet, rich and fiery, the closest
thing there is to a Dutch malt whisky. Genever production is still
dominated by three companies founded in or just after the Dutch
Golden Age. Bols, De Kuypers and A. van Wees each produce a
range of traditional genevers, as well as a variety of flavored spirits
and liqueurs. A newcomer in the field, Zuidam, was founded by
Fred van Zuidam in 1975, and is still owned and run by him and
his family. Zuidam was the first to apply the techniques of craft
distilling to the making of genever, and unlike many British distillers (who have by law to carry out distillation and rectification at
different sites) Zuidam undertake the entire process of manufacture
in-house, from the grinding of grain to cask-aging and bottling.

Bols, Zuidam and other makers of genever continue to celebrate
the flavors of the past, but a pair of young Londoners have set up
a fingerpost towards a new and inspiring future for gin. School-
friends Sam Bompas and Harry Parr went into business together
in 2007, after discovering a shared passion for the culinary and
architectural possibilities of jelly. Based in Southwark, they have
worked with (amongst many others) the architect Norman Foster,
the chef Heston Blumenthal, the London Festival of Architecture,
and Selfridges to create a series of events which owe as much to

performance and installation art as they do to the speakeasy or the gin palace. These have included luminous alcoholic jellies for the DJ and producer Mark Ronson's thirty-third birthday party; a Mayfair townhouse filled with punch made to a Restoration recipe; and a cocktail with a sting in its tail, in the form of a strawberry soaked in ether. But their greatest moment of gin-related genius came in 2009, when (after taking advice from a food historian, a specialist in extreme physiology, and an authority on industrial explosions) they managed to engineer a room of breathable gin and tonic in the cellar of a club in Soho. Dozens of paper-suit-clad participants were able, for the first time in history, to absorb a cocktail through their eyes and mucus membranes.

The gin renaissance, and the brilliance of Bompas and Parr, will surely come as no surprise. Throughout this book, we've seen that the history of gin has always reflected the tensions between ethics and aesthetics, culture and politics, local tastes and global events. Having survived the gin craze and Prohibition, gin can surely survive anything, and perhaps the only thing of which we can be certain is that its meaning and status will continue to change, no doubt for better and for worse. Just when every possibility seems to have been exhausted, the imagination of drinkers and the currents of history and culture will once again take this remarkable spirit to new and remarkable places.

Rubiaceae.

Cinchona Calisaya Wedd.

Calisaya or yellow-bark cinchona—for four centuries the richest
source of quinine, and a central ingredient in early tonic water.
"Cinchona calisaya," from Franz Eugen Köhler, Köhler's
Medizinal-Pflanzen, 3 vols, Berlin, 1897.

# Appendix One

## Selected Texts

*The English Physitian, Or, An Astrologico-Physical*
*Discourse Of The Vulgar Herbs Of This Nation*

by Thomas Culpeper (1652)

Thomas Culpeper's *English Physitian* is one of the ur-texts in the prehistory of gin. A radical republican and the Cambridge-educated son of a clergyman, Culpeper set up as an apothecary in Spitalfields, where he treated London's East End poor for what they could afford, and offered an alternative to what he saw as the expensive, pompous and obfuscating Fellows of the Royal College of Physicians. Living in the first generation to drink juniper-flavored cordials for pleasure as well as good health, Culpeper fused alchemical learning, classical medicine and folk knowledge with his own democratic leanings. He wrote in English rather than Latin, and offered cures which could be compounded from common "vulgar herbs" like juniper:

*Juniper Bush.* For to give a description of a bush so commonly known is needless.

*Place:* They grow plentifully in divers woods in Kent, Warney Common near Brentwood in Essex, upon Finchley Common without Highgate; hard by the New-found Wells near Dulwich, upon a Common between Mitcham and Croydon, in the Highgate near Amersham in Buckinghamshire, and many other places.

*Time:* The berries are not ripe the first year, but continue green two Summers and one Winter before they are ripe; at which time they are all of a black color, and therefore you shall always find upon the bush green berries; the berries are ripe about the fall of the leaf.

*Government and virtues:* This admirable shrub is scarce to be paralleled for its virtues. The berries are hot in the third degree, and dry but in the first, being a most admirable counter-poison, and as great a resister of the pestilence, as any growing: they are excellent good against the biting of venomous beasts, they provoke urine exceedingly, and therefore are very available to dysuries and stranguaries. It is so powerful a remedy against the dropsy, that the very lye made of the ashes of the herb being drank, cures the disease. It provokes the terms, helps the fits of the mother, strengthens the stomach exceedingly, and expels the wind. Indeed there is scarce a better remedy for wind in any part of the body, or the cholic, than the chymical oil drawn from the berries; such country people as know not how to draw the chymical oil, may content themselves by eating ten or a dozen of the ripe berries every morning fasting. They are admirably good for a cough, shortness of breath, and consumption, pains in the belly, ruptures, cramps, and convulsions. They give safe and speedy delivery to women with child, they strengthen the brain exceedingly, help the memory, and fortify the sight by strengthening the optic nerves; are excellently good in all sorts of agues; help the gout and sciatica, and strengthen the limbs of the body. The ashes of the wood is a speedy remedy to such as have the scurvy, to rub their gums with. The berries stay all fluxes, help the haemorrhoids or piles, and kill worms in children. A lye made of the ashes of the wood, and the body bathed with it, cures the itch, scabs and leprosy. The berries break the stone, procure appetite when it is lost, and are excellently good for all palsies, and falling-sickness.

*The Compleat Distiller: Or, The Whole Art Of*
*Distillation Practically Stated*

by William Y-Worth (1705)

Y-Worth is an enigmatic figure in the history of gin. Born (so far as anyone knows) in Rotterdam, he came to London after the Glorious Revolution, and set himself up as a distiller "at the sign of the *Blew Ball* and *Star* at the corner of *King-street* in upper *Moorfields, London.*" Distilling gin and brandy was Y-Worth's day-job, but his passion seems to have been alchemy. He corresponded with Isaac Newton on the quest for the elixir of life, and published dozens of recipes for Paracelsian spagyric medicines. His "Aqua Stomachica major, or, *Stomach Water the greater,*" includes just about every botanical apart from juniper:

> Take of strong Proof Spirit sixteen gallons; Calamus Aromaticus, nine ounces, five drachms; Guajacum green Bark, Avens Roots dry, Galingal, six ounces and a half; Citron Pills dry, Orange Pills dry, white Cinnamon, four ounces, seven drachms, grains fifteen; Worm-wood common dry, Wormwood Roman dry, Spearmint, Rosemary tops, Costmary, sweet Marjoram, wild Thyme, all dry, thee ounces, one drachm and a half; Nutmegs, Cinnamon, four ounces, three drachms, grains fifteen; sweet Foenil seeds, Coriander seeds, eight ounces; Aniseeds two pound, six ounces, three drachms; bruise all that are to be bruised; and then distil into strong Proof Spirit, and dulcifie with white Sugar, sixteen pound.

But Y-Worth was far from ignorant of juniper and its uses. His recipe for "*Potestates Baccarum Juniperi,* or the Powers of Juniper-Berries" is a striking combination of practicality and spagyric learn-ing, and incidentally reveals a traditional Dutch way of relieving colic in infants:

Take of Juniper-berries twenty or thirty pound, or what quantity you please, pound them small, and putting them into a Tub pour thereon Rain-water, adding thereunto an handful of Bay-salt, and so let them stand ten or twelve days, and then distil in a Copper-still with a Refrigeratory, so that pure Oyl will ascend with Water in good quantity; and when the Liquor and Berries are taken out of the Still, if you press through an hair-bag, filtrate and evaporate, you shall find good quantity of Extract.

These Powers [of juniper berries] are of great Service in the Cholick, Gripes, Oppressions of Wind, and Gravel in the Kidneys, Ureters and Bladder, they not only ease violent pains, but also open the obstruction of parts, they prevalently provoke Urine, comfort the Stomack, Bowels and all the Viscera, the Vital Spirits receive the benefit thereof, it is a general Custom in *Holland,* when the Child is troubled with Oppressions of Wind, for the Mother whilst the Child is sucking, to drink of the Powers or Spirits of Juniper, by which the Child is Relieved . . . The Dose is as of other Powers, from fifteen to forty drops, in a Glass of Beer, Wine or Mead.

## The Gin Craze And Its Aftermath

Only a few decades after Culpeper and Y-Worth, the character of gin had darkened dramatically: no longer a gentle, alchemically-inflected herbal tonic, it had become the aggressively corrosive drink of London's poorest inhabitants. One of the most pungent indictments came from Sir John Gonson, chairman of the Westminster justices, in a 1728 speech (and reprinted in his *Five Charges to Several Grand Juries* (1740)):

> Nothing is more Destructive either to the Health or Industry of the poorer Sort of People, on whose Labor and Strength the Support of the Community so much depends, than the immoderate Drinking of *Geneva*. It is common for a starving Sot, intoxicated with this or the like Liquors, to behold his Rags and Nakedness with a stupid Indolence, and either in senseless Laughter, or in low and insipid Jests, to banter all Prudence and Frugality, drowning his pinching Cares, and losing, with his Reason, all anxious Reflections on a Wife, or Children, perhaps crying for Bread in a horrid empty Home. In hot Tempers, it lets loose the Tongue to all the Indecencies and Rudenesses of the most provoking Language, as well as the most hellish Oaths and Curses, and is frequently followed by Quarrels and Fightings, and sometimes has been the cause of Murder. Besides all this, these Houses and Shops are the Receptacles of Thieves and Robbers, and often the Original of them too: For when a Wretch has spent and wasted that, which should support himself, and his Family, it is here, that they Associate and turn House-breakers, and Street-robbers, and so, by quick Progressions, at last make an exit on the Gallows.

Caught between lurid fears of social breakdown and the torrent of revenue from excise on spirits, the British government made several half-hearted attempts to clamp down on gin. One of the most controversial pieces of legislation was the 1736 Gin Act, which came into force on September 30th of that year. Expecting trouble from Jacobite agitators, the government sent out companies of troops in the days before the Act came into force, but the only protests were symbolic funerals and wakes for "Mother Gin." The *Daily Gazetteer,* a government-sponsored propaganda sheet, described one such demonstration in Bristol:

> The Exit of Mother Gin in Bristol, has been enough bewail'd by the Retailers and Drinkers of it; many of the latter, willing to have their Fill, and to take the last Farewell in a respectful Manner of their beloved Dame, have not scrupled to pawn and sell their very Cloaths, as the last Devoir they can pay to her Memory. It was observ'd, Monday, Tuesday and Wednesday, that several Retailers Shops were well crowded, some tippling on the Spot, while others were carrying it off from a Pint to a Gallon, and one of those Shops had such a good Trade, that it put every Cask they had upon the Stoop; and the Owner with sorrowful Sighs said, *Is this not a barbarous and cruel Thing, that I must not be permitted to sell them again?* And pronounc'd a heavy Woe, on the Instruments of their drooping. Such has been the Lamentation, that on Wednesday Night her funeral Obsequies was perform'd with Formality in several Parishes, and some of the Votaries appeared in ragged Cloaths, some without Gowns, and others with one Stocking; but among them all, we don't hear of any that have carried their Grief so far, as to hang or drown themselves, rather chusing the drinking Part to finish their Sorrow; and accordingly a few old Women are pretty near tipping off the Perch, by sipping too large a Draught.

In *To the Mortal Memory of Madam Geneva,* a print published in 1736 to mark the passing of the Gin Act, one anonymous pamphleteer imagined the funeral monument of "Mother Gin," and composed a florid epitaph:

> To the Mortal Memory of Madam Geneva,
> Who died Sept 29th 1736.
> Her Weeping Servants and Loving Friends consecrate This Tomb.

To thee, kind comfort of the starving poor!
To thee Geneva, that art now no more!
This sad but gratefull monument we raise:
Our Arms we yield, no more our Sun shall blaze.
Lo! where supine her mournful Genius lies,
And hollow barrels echo to her cries:
On casks around her sad Attendants stand;
The Bunter weeps with basket in her hand,
His useless Worm the sad Distiller views,
The Boy with heavy heart for Succour sues:
What gave her birth now helps her Tomb to build,
The Tub a Spire, a Globe the Can unfill'd.
High in the Air the Still its head doth rear,
And on its top a Mournfull Granadeer.
The Clean white Apron as a label shown
The dreadful cause of all our Grief makes known.
Hither repair all thee that for her mourn,
And Drink a Requiem to her Peacefull Urn.

After the passage of a further Gin Act in 1752, the gin craze
quickly passed into history. In *The History of England, From the
Revolution of 1688 to the Death of George II* (published in several
volumes between 1757 and 1762) Tobias Smollett—Scottish poet,
novelist and naval surgeon—set down what would become the
received version. Smollett's history came complete with high
politics, moralistic overtones and the unofficial slogan of the gin
craze—"Drunk for a penny, dead drunk for twopence, clean
straw for nothing":

But the most severe opposition [the ministers of George II] underwent was in their endeavours to support a bill which they had
concerted, and which had passed through the house of commons
with great precipitation: it repealed certain duties on spirituous
liquors, and licenses for retailing these liquors; and imposed others
at an easier rate. When those severe duties, amounting almost to a
Prohibition, were imposed, the populace of London were sank into
the most brutal degeneracy, by drinking to excess the pernicious

spirit called gin, which was sold so cheap that the lowest class of the people could afford to indulge themselves in one continued state of intoxication, to the destruction of all morals, industry, and order.

Such a shameful degree of profligacy prevailed, that the retailers of this poisonous compound set up painted boards in public, inviting people to be drunk for the small expense of one penny; assuring them they might be dead drunk for two-pence, and have straw for nothing. They accordingly provided cellars and places strewed with straw, to which they conveyed those wretches who were overwhelmed with intoxication. In these dismal caverns they lay until they recovered some use of their faculties, and then they had recourse to the same mischievous potion; thus consuming their health, and ruining their families, in hideous receptacles of the most filthy vice, resounding with rot, execration, and blasphemy.

Such beastly practices too plainly denoted a total want of all policy and civil regulations, and would have reflected disgrace upon the most barbarous community. In order to restrain this evil, which was become intolerable, the legislature enacted that law which we have already mentioned. But the populace soon broke through all restraint. Though no license was obtained, and no duty paid, the liquor continued to be sold in all corners of the streets: informers were intimidated by the threats of the people; and the justices of the peace, either from indolence or corruption, neglected to put the law in execution.

The new ministers foresaw that a great revenue would accrue to the crown from a repeal of this act; and this measure they thought they might the more decently take, as the law had proved ineffectual: for it appeared that the consumption of gin had considerably increased every year since those heavy duties were imposed. They, therefore, pretended, that should the price of the liquor be moderately raised, and licenses granted at twenty shillings each to the retailers, the lowest class of people would be debarred the use of it to excess; then morals would of consequence be mended, and a considerable sum of money might be raised for the support of the war, by mortgaging the revenue arising from the duty and the licenses.

Upon these maxims the new bill was founded, and passed through the lower house without opposition: but among the peers it produced the most obstinate dispute which had happened since the beginning of this parliament. The first assault it sustained was from Lord Hervey, who had been divested of his post of privy-seal, which was bestowed on Lord Gower; and these two noblemen exchanged principles from that instant. The first was hardened into a sturdy patriot; the other suppled into an obsequious courtier. Lord Hervey, on this occasion, made a florid harangue upon the pernicious effects of that destructive spirit they were about to let loose upon their fellow-creatures.

Several prelates expatiated on the same topics: but the Earl of Chesterfield attacked the bill with the united powers of reason, wit, and ridicule. Lord Carteret, Lord Bathurst, and the Earl of Bath, were numbered among its advocates; and shrewd arguments were advanced on both sides of the question. After very long, warm, and repeated debates, the bill passed without amendments, though the whole bench of bishops voted against it; and we cannot help owning, that it has not been attended with those dismal consequences which the lords in the opposition foretold. When the question was put for committing this bill, and the Earl of Chesterfield saw the bishops join in his division, "I am in doubt (said he) whether I have not got on the other side of the question, for I have not had the honor to divide with so many lawn sleeves for several years."

## Nineteenth-Century Gin Recipes

Much ink has been spilt about the horrors of the gin craze and the dubious pleasures of the gin palace, but what was eighteenth- or nineteenth-century gin actually like? We can get some sense of what our ancestors consumed under the name of gin from books like Peter Jonas and John Sheridan's *Complete Treatise on the Art of Distillation* (1830). Jonas and Sheridan offered several recipes for British distillers, beginning with "Hollands":

> To every twenty gallons of spirits of the second extraction, about the strength of proof spirit, take three pounds of juniper berries, and two ounces of juniper oil, and distil with a slow fire until the feints begin to rise, then change the receiving can; this produces the best Rotterdam gin. An inferior kind is made with a still less proportion of berries, sweet fennel seeds and Strasburgh turpentine, without a drop of juniper oil. It, and a better sort, but inferior to the Rotterdam gin, are made at Weesoppe. The distillers' wash at Schiedam and Rotterdam are still lighter than at Weesoppe. Strasburgh turpentine is of a yellowish brown color, and very fragrant agreeable smell, its taste is the bitterest yet the least acid of the turpentines. The juniper berries are so very cheap in Holland, that they must have more reasons than mere cheapness for being so much more sparing of their consumption than our distillers. Indeed they are not in the habit of wasting anything.

Their "Royal Geneva," meanwhile, was a straightforward distillation of spirit and juniper berries:

> Take of juniper berries, three pounds; proof spirits, ten gallons; water, four gallons. Draw off by a gentle fire till the feints begin to rise, and make up your goods to the strength required with clean water. The distillers generally call those goods, which are made up proof, by the name of *royal*.

"Common Gin," however, was a less appealing prospect, replacing some of the juniper with turpentine and salt:

> Take of ordinary malt spirits, ten gallons; oil of turpentine, two ounces; juniper berries, one pound; sweet fennel and caraway seeds, of each four handfuls; bay salt, three handfuls. Draw off by a gentle fire till the feints begin to rise, and make up your goods to the strength required. Say, ten gallons of spirit will make about fifteen gallons of common gin.

For those inclined to leave out the turpentine, they also offered some hints on the preservation of juniper berries:

> Various are the kinds of berries used in England, and mostly imported from Germany; but if you make use of English berries, let them be fully ripe before they are gathered; and to preserve them, spread them very thin on a boarded floor, leaving the windows and doors open: turn them once a day until they are dry; after which pack them up in barrels, to exclude the air, and they will keep good all the year. Some persons, when they are dry, throw them altogether in a corner, till wanted for use; but treated in this way, they are apt to get mouldy, and give a bad taste to the goods. Other distillers, as soon as their berries are gathered, put them into casks, and cover them with spirits of wine; this way the berries are well preserved; but unfortunately the spirit will extract a great deal of their essential oil. If this method is adopted, you should put into each cask or jar, only the quantity used for one charge of the still; but upon occasion, both the spirits and berries may be put into the alembic. Thus the berries will be finely preserved without any loss of their essential oil, or the spirits made use of to assist in the operation. Among the various kinds of juniper berries, the Italian, have been denominated *rank;* the German, *sweet;* the Trieste, *middling sweet;* and the French, *rank.*

But not all nineteenth-century gin was quite what it seemed. Henry Sabine's *The Publican's Sure Guide, or, Every Man His Own Cellarman* (1807) suggested that tavern-owners could dispense with distillation altogether, and cook up a passable "British Gin" in their kitchens:

Eight gallons of Spirits, (one to five)
One penny-weight of Oil of Vitriol [sulphuric acid]
One ditto of Oil of Juniper
One ditto of Oil of Almonds
Half-a-pint of Spirits of Wine
Two Pounds of Lump Sugar

Mix the Oils with a few knobs of lump Sugar, beating them well in a mortar, adding, by degrees, the Spirits of Wine, then dissolve the two pounds of lump Sugar in six quarts of soft Water, letting it simmer over the fire for half-an-hour, constantly skimming it, and when nearly cold, add the ingredients, stirring it well with a stick; which done, put it to your spirits, and mix it well. To fine the same, take half-an-ounce of allum, and dissolve it in a pint of Water, let it gently simmer over the fire for a few minutes, and when nearly cold, add half-an-ounce of salts of tartar, pour the whole into your cask, and work it for some minutes with a stick.

N.B. Many do not take the trouble of simmering the Sugar and Water, but by doing so you get all the filth from the Sugar, and your Gin will not only require less fining (which often produces an unpleasant roughness), but leaves very little sediment in your Cask when drawn out.

## London's Nineteenth-Century Gin Palaces

A century after the gin craze, London seemed set for another spirituous crisis, as a new generation of "dram-shops" and gin palaces appeared on the city's streets. In Thomas Rowlandson's "The Dram Shop" (1815) a crowd of drinkers queue for gin, while in the cellar a skeleton mixes "aqua fortis" (nitric acid) and "oil of vitriol" (sulphuric acid) to make gin. Beneath the picture a verse by "Dr. Syntax"—a phrenonym for the journalist William Combe—spells out the horrific consequences of consuming "the liquid ill":

A Preacher, I remember well,
Whose fashion was blunt Truths to tell,
Harangu'd his Audience how to shun
Old Nick, as round the world he run;
And thus the fav'rite haunts defin'd
Of the Great Enemy of Mankind.
Avoid the place where the profane
Their Faithless Mysteries maintain;
Nor let those mansions be explored
Where the Dice rattles on the board.
Nor risk your Labor's fair reward
By shuffling the deceitful Card.
In haste, pass by the tempting street
Where the alluring wantons meet;
For thus, as sure as Evil's evil,
You'll meet that Spirit call'd the Devil.
But above all, as you would shun
In Life and Death to be undone,
Indulge not in the liquid ill
That flows from the empoison'd Still,
Thither the Fiend loves to repair,

And Death, too oft, attends him there;
Who, in his never-ceasing rounds,
The Still-man aids as he compounds
Each mixture that's in daily strife
With Health, with Honor, and with Life.
The Dram-shop is the spot that yields
More various ills than all the fields
Where grow the Vices that disgrace
Th' existence of the human race
The Town with beggars it supplies,
And almost fills th' Infirmaries;
Gives half their inmates to the jails,
And multiplies the Hangman's vails.
—Question the sturdy Lab'rer, why
He wears the rags of Poverty?
Wherefore his well-paid, daily task
Denies the Bread his Children ask? ...

For the journalist George Augustus Sala, London's gin palaces required a more thorough and more sympathetic dissection. In an essay published in *Gaslight and Daylight* (1859) he describes an evening spent in a "ginnery" on High Holborn:

Here, first—blatant, gay, and gaudy—is a GIN PALACE—a "ginnery," in full swing.

The Palladio or the Vitruvius who built this palace, has curiously diversified the orders of architecture in its construction. We have Doric shafts with Corinthian capitols—an Ionic frieze—Renaissance panels—a Gothic screen to the bar-parlour. But French polish and gilding cover a multitude of (architectural) sins; and there is certainly no lack of either the one or the other here. Tier above tier surround the walls, supporting gigantic casks, bearing legends of a fabulous number of gallons contained within. Yet are they not dummies; for we may observe spiral brass pipes, wriggling and twisting in snake-like contortions till they reach the bar, and so to the spirit-taps, where they bring the costly hogshead of the distiller home to the lips of the humblest costermonger, for a penny a glass. Beer is sold, and in considerable quantities—a halfpenny a pint cheaper, too, than at other hostelries; but it is curious beer—beer of a half-sweet, half-acrid taste, black to the sight, unpleasant to the taste, brown in the froth, muddy in consistence. Has it been in delicate health, and can that shabby old man, in close confab with the landlord at the door, at the steps of the cellar, be the "Doctor?" Or has it been adulterated, "fined," doctored, patched, and cobbled up, for the amusement and instruction of amateurs in beer—like steam-frigates, for instance, or Acts of Parliament?

The area before the bar, you will observe, is very spacious. At this present second hour of the afternoon, there are, perhaps, fifty people in it; and it would hold, I dare say, full twenty more, and allow space, into the bargain, for a neat stand-up fight. One seems very likely to take place now between the costermonger, who has brought rather an inconvenient number of "kea-rots" and "turmuts" into the bar with him, and a peripatetic vendor of fish—the quality of whose wares he has (with some show of justice, perhaps) impugned. So imminent does the danger appear, that the blind matchseller—who was anon importuning the belligerents—hastily scuttles off; and an imp of a boy, in a man's fustian jacket, and with a dirty red silk kerchief twisted round his bull neck, has mounted the big tub, on which he eats astride, pipe in hand—a very St. Giles's Bacchus—declaring that he will see "fair play." Let us edge away a little to-wards the bar—for the crowd towards the door is somewhat too promiscuous to be agreeable; and it is not improbable that in the *mêlée,* some red-kerchiefed citizen, of larger growth, whose extensor and flexor muscles are somewhat more powerfully developed, may make a savage assault on you, for his own private gratification, and the mere pleasure of hitting somebody.

This ginnery has not only a bar public, but divers minor cabinets, bibulous loose boxes, which are partitioned off from the general area; and the entrances to which are described in flowery, but somewhat ambiguous language. There is the "Jug and Bottle Entrance," and the entrance "For Bottles only." There is the "Wholesale Bar," and the "Retail Bar"; but, wholesale or retail, jug or bottle, the different bars all mean Gin! The long pewter counter is common to all. A counter perforated in elaborately-pricked patterns, like a convivial shroud, apparently for ornament, but really for the purpose of allowing the drainings, overflowings, and outspillings of the gin-glasses to drop through, which, being collected with sundry washings, and a dash, perhaps, of fresh material, is, by the thrifty landlord, dispensed to his customers under the title of "all sorts." Your dram-drinker, look you, is not unfrequently paralytic, woefully shaky in the hand; and the liquor he wastes, combined with that accidentally spilt, tells up wonderfully at the close of the year. There are cake-baskets on the counter, patronised mostly by the lady votaries of the rosy (or livid?) god; but their tops are hermetically sealed, and their dulcet contents protected by a wire dome, or cupola, of convex form. Besides what I have described, if you will add some of my old friends the gold-blazoned boards, bearing the eulogies of various brewers, together with sundry little placards, framed and glazed, and printed in colors, telling, in seductive language, of "Choice Compounds," "Old Tom," "Cream of the Valley," "Superior Cream Gin," "The Right Sort," "Kinahan's L.L.," "The Dew off Ben Nevis," the "Celebrated Balmoral Mixture," "patronised by his Royal Highness Prince Albert" (the illustrious personage, clad in full Highland costume, with an extensive herd of red deer in the distance, is represented taking a glass of the "Mixture" with great apparent gusto); besides these, I repeat, you will need nothing to "complete the costume," as the romancers have it, of a Gin Palace.

Except the landlord, perhaps, who is bald and corpulent, who has a massive watch-chain, and a multiplicity of keys, and whose hands seem to leave the pockets of his trousers as seldom as his keen eye does the gin-drawing gymnastics of his barmen. Gymnastics they are, *tours de force,* feats of calisthenics as agile as any performed by the agile professor whom I have just seen pass, all dirt, flesh-colored drawers, and spangles. A quick, sharp, jerking twist for the spirit tap, allowing to run till the liquor is within a hair's breadth of the top of the measure, and no longer; a dexterous tilt of the "two," or "three out" glasses required; an agile shoving forward of the pewter noggin with one hand, while the other inevitable palm is presented for the requisite halfpence; and oh! such a studious carefulness that one hand is not emptied before the other is filled. It is not everybody can serve in the bar of a Gin Palace. The barman wears a fur cap—generally—sometimes a wide-awake. He is addicted to carrying a piece of straw, a pipe-light, or the stalk of a flower in his mouth, diversifying it occasionally by biting half-crowns viciously. When he gives you change, he slaps it down on the counter in a provocatory manner; his face is flushed; his manner short, concise, sententious. His vocabulary is limited; a short "Now then," and a brief "Here you are," forming the staple phrases thereof. I wonder what his views of human nature—of the world, its manners, habits, and customs—can be like. Or what does the barmaid think of it? I should like to know: the young lady in the coal-black ringlets (like magnified leeches), the very brilliant complexion, and the coral necklace. Mercy on us! what can she, a girl of eighteen, think of the faces, the dress, the language of the miserable creatures among whom she spends sixteen hours of her life every day—every mortal day throughout the year—once in every three weeks (her "day out") excepted?

One word about the customers, and we will rejoin our chariot, which must surely be extricated by this time. Thieves, beggars, costermongers, hoary-headed old men, stunted, ragged, shock-haired children, blowzy, slatternly women, hulking bricklayers, gaunt, sickly hobbledehoys, with long greasy hair. A thrice-told tale. Is it not the same everywhere! The same pipes, dirt, howling, maundering, fighting, staggering gin fever. Like plates multiplied by the electro-process—like the printer's stereo—like the reporter's manifold—you will find duplicates, triplicates of these forlorn beings everywhere. The same woman giving her baby gin; the same haggard, dishevelled woman, trying to coax her drunken husband home; the same mild girl, too timid even to importune her ruffian partner to leave off drinking the week's earnings, who sits meekly in a corner, with two discolored eyes, one freshly blacked, one of a week's standing. The same weary little man, who comes in early, crouches in a corner, and takes standing naps during the day, waking up periodically—for "fresh drops." The same red-nosed, ragged object who disgusts you at one moment by the force and fluency of his Billingsgate, and surprises you the next by bursting out in Greek and Latin quotations. The same thin, spectral man who has no money, and with his hands piteously laid one over the other, stands for hours gazing

with fishy eyes at the beloved liquor—smelling, thinking of, hopelessly desiring it. And lastly, the same miserable girl, sixteen in years,
and a hundred in misery; with foul, matted hair, and death in her
face;—with a tattered plaid shawl, and ragged boots, a gin-and-fog
voice, and a hopeless eye.

Others adopted a more plainly moralistic line. John Cassell, the
founder of the publishing house Cassell & Co, had taken the
pledge before his eighteenth birthday, and throughout his life
he campaigned to improve the lives of London's underclasses. In
1850 he founded *The Working-Man's Friend and Family Instructor*, a
weekly magazine which took the then-radical step of addressing
working-class men, women and children without speaking down
to them. Priced at a penny per issue, the *Working-Man's Friend* was
intended to offer something for all the family: adventure stories,
recipes, travelogues, legal and scientific tutorials, and (in the issue
for October 25th, 1851) an awful and graphically-illustrated warning of the consequences that might befall any "respectable and
virtuous young men" who stumbled into a gin palace:

> We lately directed attention to one of those houses, of which there
> are but too many in the Metropolis, into which respectable and vir-
> tuous young men are frequently allured, to the destruction of their
> health, their property, their morals, and their reputation. We trust
> that the *ad vitam* sketch we furnished of "London Night-Houses"
> will deter many a youth from ever entering such places. We now
> furnish an equally truthful sketch of another class of houses, which,
> as well as the former, abound in the Metropolis, and which are the
> resort of large numbers of our population, though—as our illustra-
> tion shows—of those usually accounted less "polite and respectable"
> than the frequenters of our night-houses and taverns.
>
> Gin-shops present few of the attractions common to taverns and
> public-houses. They are entered, chiefly for the love of the drink,
> by those who have acquired a fatal passion for the fiery compounds
> therein dispensed, or by those who induce others to accompany
> them thither, from mistaken kindness, or with a nefarious design.

Though the doors of these temples of Bacchus stand invitingly ajar, the inmates are not exposed to public gaze. The windows are generally placed high, or else the lower panes are curiously engraved, or have opaque curtains drawn across them, so that passers-by cannot see what is going on within.

In this respect the vendors of ardent spirits differ from all other tradesmen. Bakers, confectioners, ham and beef sellers, butchers, cheesemongers, fruiterers, to say nothing of linen-drapers, hatters, shoemakers, and scores of other useful and necessary trades, are anxious to have their windows as low and as transparent as possible. Each is eager to display his viands or his goods to the best advantage, and large sums are expended expressly for this purpose. But with the proprietors of Gin Palaces it is otherwise. Is it because they are ashamed of their company?—or is it because they know that much of the business transacted there would not bear exposure to the public?

Justly have these haunts of dissipation been compared to "whited sepulchres." The tasteful architecture and costly decorations seem to place in dark and horrid contrast the ill-clad, dirty, miserable wretches, whose hardly-gained pence pay for these expensive exhibitions. Who wishes to look at dead bones, worms, and corruption, so carefully concealed from the eye by the classic skill of the sculptor? And yet the sight of a human body in a state of putrescence would be less painful than the living death and the revolting moral putrefaction which is hourly fed by the proprietors of our gin palaces—aye, even by that smooth-faced, smiling, respectably-clad individual who stands behind the counter and deals out the liquid fire—the distilled and deadly poison—to the maudlin, ghastly beings, who throng around him.

At the left hand of our engraving a sad scene presents itself. There you behold a miserable mother pouring gin into the mouth of her innocent infant; and thus the child is being drenched with death by the very woman who ought to be its guardian angel; and perhaps still, notwithstanding the ravages strong drink have perpetrated upon her own body and soul, yet views with some lingering affection the helpless offspring whom she is madly destroying. Thousands of children are thus annually poisoned by their infatuated parents! It has long ago been shown that these liquors are the source of almost every kind of disease.

We should not exceed the plain intimations of science, if we asserted that no one can use them, even moderately, without shortening his days. None who habitually partake of them die a natural death. The firmest constitution cannot, in the end, resist their baneful influence: what, then, shall be said of the delicate digestive organs, intestines, liver, nerves, and brain of an infant? Here you have the body and the mind poisoned with the same glass; and what is more appalling, all this is done by a mother; at least, if that pitiable-looking woman, with her bonnet half off her head, can deserve such a name; for we cannot help thinking that both language and humanity are outraged when we apply the endearing word mother to a miserable woman who enters a spirit-shop; and especially to one who carries her infant there, and poisons it with gin.

Nearly all the characters portrayed by our artist, have an idiotic, a haggard, or a demoniacal sort of visage; showing that strong drink has committed sad havoc on their physical, mental, and moral constitutions. There is not a natural, or benevolent, or happy countenance among them. It is true that one or two of them are laughing; but, then, their hilarity looks more like the fiendish grin of a tormented spirit than the cheerful mirth of innocence and love. People talk of wine and strong drink "cheering the heart of man," but we have never yet seen the assertion verified. We have heard of multitudes who have become low spirited, melancholy, and deranged, from the use of these beverages; we have visited numbers who have refused to be comforted, because these liquors had paralysed or destroyed every avenue both in mind and body through which any word of consolation could enter. We have known many who were boisterous in their joy so long as these poisons set them on fire, but who sunk into utter wretchedness as soon as the poisonous spirit had evaporated from their frames.

If such liquors could produce real and substantial pleasure, one would suppose that a gin-shop would be a picture of paradise; and yet this is the place, above all others in the world, to see hunger, thirst, rags, nakedness, ill-temper, misery, and crime of every description, written in legible characters on all the frequenters of these abodes of woe. Our artist has been guilty of neither exaggeration nor caricature in the faces he has delineated, and should any doubt our assertion, let them only stand for a short time opposite any gin palace in London, and witness the dress, the features, the language, the gestures, of the men and women who visit these scenes of corruption, and they will no longer accuse our picture or expressions of having gone too far. And yet all these people were made to be happy; and were happy before they became fond of these drinks; yes, and have spent enough in these liquors to make themselves and their families happy; aye, and we may add, that all of them might yet be happy, if they would abandon the glass, and reform their habits.

In contrast with that seemingly well-dressed woman who stands near the bar with the glass in her hand, on which she is casting an eye of so much satisfaction, let our readers look at the outlandish face at her right hand, and, above all, notice that miserable little girl who is dressed in rags, and has no stockings or shoes on, but is exerting every nerve to reach up to the counter and push her mother's gin bottle into the hand of the well-dressed, buxom landlady. Is it any wonder that London is still a disgrace to Christendom; that trade is bad; that seamstresses for want of work submit to the exactions of tyrannical and avaricious employers; when the money that should be spent in clothing is thus wasted in poisons? Is it a marvel that we have ragged schools with pickpockets, or mere infant street-walkers for scholars, when we find the young thus early educated in crime and wretchedness?

We are told on high authority that "woman is the glory of man"; and history elucidates the assertion, for where females are degraded, there men are base, sensual, and depraved. Heaven has ordained that the stronger sex shall not rise, if the weaker is corrupted or depressed. In barbarian, and in some civilized countries, women are slaves, and there the men are indolent, cruel, savage, and vile. Woman makes home, home; woman softens, refines, and ennobles the rougher natures of the "lords of creation." Solomon tells us that the "husband of the good wife is known in the gate," the assembly, or the parliament, "when he sitteth with the elders." We earnestly entreat our friends to bear these facts in mind, and then ask—What hope society can indulge from the future life of that miserable object represented in our engraving, who is so earnest in handing up her gin bottle? What wife or mother will she make? What will her future history be? And yet there are thousands of these young ministering spirits of Bacchus haunting the gin palaces of our country, and thus preparing themselves and others for a life of crime and a hereafter of woe. And sorry are we to add, that with all our philanthropy and professed regard for the poor, yet the drinking habits of our country are chiefly supported by those who boast of their moderation, and wish to be thought the benefactors of their species.

Before we close our observations on the mournful exhibition we have depicted, we would call attention to that decently clad wife, whose face is the picture of grief, and who is trying to drag away from this living hell, that idiot-looking, drunken monster who calls himself her husband. His little daughter is aiding in the work, and grasps his right arm, while a guilty companion is attempting to make him stay; the pot-boy is looking on and apparently mocking, and the very dog is disgusted at the scene. Here is national education with a vengeance! What sort of a man will that pot-boy make? How that decent wife must have every delicate feeling outraged, and what corruption will infect that innocent daughter from the contaminations of the gin-shop! Who in this world can predict the end of that wretched, filthy drunkard who has thus attracted his wife and female child to this haunt of depravity? The thoughts that crowd upon us as we gaze on these various characters, might fill volumes with weeping and lamentation.

The most composed, or rather the most pleased and gratified persons in the scene, are the master and mistress of the establishment. Squalor, filth, and misery are constantly before them, and are nourished and brought to frightful maturity by the strange compounds they supply so readily; but what of that? "By this craft they have their wealth." The "fool's pence" enable "mine host" of the "Queen's Arms," his wife, and their children to flaunt in silks and broad cloth, and to "fare sumptuously everyday," and what have they to do to care for diseased bodies or broken hearts—for deserted wives or neglected children? But the reckoning day will come; a heavy responsibility rests somewhere, and heavy will be the condemnation. In the mean time let every individual take care of himself, and avoid the gin-shop and the use of the mysterious compounds manufactured and sold there, as he would avoid "plague, pestilence, and famine"!

With its engraved glass partitions and dark woodwork, the Princess Louise on High Holborn preserves something of the atmosphere of London's Victorian gin palaces. Photograph copyright the author.

## Charles Dickens And Gin

Gin flows like the Thames through Dickens' writings. No mean tippler himself, Dickens found gin an object of horror and fascination, both a lubricant of conviviality and a fuel for melodrama, never shying away from the reality of life for London's poor gin-drinkers. In *The Life and Adventures of Nicholas Nickleby* (1839) Ninetta Crummles performs with her family's theater troupe as "The Infant Phenomenon," but her small stature is no accident:

> ... for the infant phenomenon, though of short stature, had a comparatively aged countenance, and had moreover been precisely the same age—not perhaps to the full extent of the memory of the oldest inhabitant, but certainly for five good years. But she had been kept up late every night, and put upon an unlimited allowance of gin and water from infancy, to prevent her growing tall, and perhaps this system of training had produced in the infant phenomenon these additional phenomena.

In *Barnaby Rudge: A Tale of the Riots of 'Eighty* (1841) Dickens described the burning of a gin distillery, on the corner of Fetter Lane and High Holborn, during the anti-Catholic Gordon Riots. Here gin becomes literally destructive, incinerating rioters and looters as surely as it obliterates the lives of those who consume it:

> The gutters of the street, and every crack and fissure in the stones, ran with scorching spirit, which being dammed up by busy hands, overflowed the road and pavement, and formed a great pool, into which the people dropped down dead by dozens. They lay in heaps all round this fearful pond, husbands and wives, fathers and sons, mothers and daughters, women with children in their arms and babies at their breasts, and drank until they died. While some stooped with their lips to the brink and never raised their heads again,

others sprang up from their fiery draught, and danced, half in a mad triumph, and half in the agony of suffocation, until they fell, and steeped their corpses in the liquor that had killed them. Nor was even this the worst or most appalling kind of death that happened on this fatal night. From the burning cellars, where they drank out of hats, pails, buckets, tubs, and shoes, some men were drawn, alive, but all alight from head to foot; who, in their unendurable anguish and suffering, making for anything that had the look of water, rolled, hissing, in this hideous lake, and splashed up liquid fire which lapped in all it met with as it ran along the surface, and neither spared the living nor the dead. On this last night of the great riots—for the last night it was—the wretched victims of a senseless outcry, became themselves the dust and ashes of the flames they had kindled, and strewed the public streets of London.

With all he saw in this last glance fixed indelibly upon his mind, Barnaby hurried from the city which enclosed such horrors; and holding down his head that he might not even see the glare of the fires upon the quiet landscape, was soon in the still country roads.

Gin was not necessarily a "bad thing" for Dickens: everything came down to setting, and even the liquid fire of *Barnaby Rudge* could be part of his fantasia on English hospitality. In *A Christmas Carol* (1843) the Cratchit family, poor but earnest and merry, toast Christmas with a tumbler of hot gin punch:

His active little crutch was heard upon the floor, and back came Tiny Tim before another word was spoken, escorted by his brother and sister to his stool beside the fire; and while Bob, turning up his cuffs—as if, poor fellow, they were capable of being made more shabby—compounded some hot mixture in a jug with gin and lemons, and stirred it round and round and put it on the hob to simmer; Master Peter and the two ubiquitous young Cratchits went to fetch the goose, with which they soon returned in high procession . . .

At last the dinner was all done, the cloth was cleared, the hearth swept, and the fire made up. The compound in the jug being tasted, and considered perfect, apples and oranges were put upon the table, and a shovel full of chestnuts on the fire. Then all the Cratchit family drew round the hearth, in what Bob Cratchit called a circle, meaning half a one; and at Bob Cratchit's elbow stood the family display of glass. Two tumblers and a custard-cup without a handle.

These held the hot stuff from the jug, however, as well as golden goblets would have done; and Bob served it out with beaming looks, while the chestnuts on the fire sputtered and cracked noisily. Then Bob proposed:

"A Merry Christmas to us all, my dears. God bless us!"

Which all the family re-echoed.

"God bless us every one," said Tiny Tim, the last of all.

Dickens' first book—*Sketches by Boz* (1836), a collection of essays "illustrative of every-day life and every-day people"—included one essay which has become a classic of nineteenth-century journalism. But "Gin-shops" is more than a piece of reportage: it is a psycho-geography of London drinking, a rollicking piece of Victorian polemic, and an indication of what Dickens would go on to do with his fine ear for English voices and English places:

It is a remarkable circumstance, that different trades appear to partake of the disease to which elephants and dogs are especially liable, and to run stark, staring, raving mad, periodically. The great distinction between the animals and the trades, is, that the former run mad with a certain degree of propriety—they are very regular in their irregularities. We know the period at which the emergency will arise, and provide against it accordingly. If an elephant runs mad, we are all ready for him—kill or cure—pills or bullets, calomel in conserve of roses, or lead in a musket-barrel. If a dog happens to look unpleasantly warm in the summer months, and to trot about the shady side of the streets with a quarter of a yard of tongue hanging out of his mouth, a thick leather muzzle, which has been previously prepared in compliance with the thoughtful injunctions of the Legislature, is instantly clapped over his head, by way of making him cooler, and he either looks remarkably unhappy for the next six weeks, or becomes legally insane, and goes mad, as it were, by Act of Parliament. But these trades are as eccentric as comets; nay, worse, for no one can calculate on the recurrence of the strange appearances which betoken the disease. Moreover, the contagion is general, and the quickness with which it diffuses itself, almost incredible.

We will cite two or three cases in illustration of our meaning. Six or eight years ago, the epidemic began to display itself among the linen-drapers and haberdashers. The primary symptoms were an inordinate love of plate-glass, and a passion for gas-lights and gilding. The disease gradually progressed, and at last attained a fearful height. Quiet, dusty old shops in different parts of town, were pulled down; spacious premises with stuccoed fronts and gold letters, were erected instead; floors were covered with Turkey carpets; roofs supported by massive pillars; doors knocked into windows; a dozen squares of glass into one; one shopman into a dozen; and there is no knowing what would have been done, if it had not been fortunately discovered, just in time, that the Commissioners of Bankruptcy were as competent to decide such cases as the Commissioners of Lunacy, and that a little confinement and gentle examination did wonders. The disease abated. It died away. A year or two of comparative tranquillity ensued. Suddenly it burst out again amongst the chemists; the symptoms were the same, with the addition of a strong desire to stick the royal arms over the shop-door, and a great rage for mahogany, varnish, and expensive floor-cloth. Then, the hosiers were infected, and began to pull down their shop-fronts with frantic recklessness. The mania again died away, and the public began to congratulate themselves on its entire disappearance, when it burst forth with tenfold violence among the publicans, and keepers of "wine vaults." From that moment it has spread among them with unprecedented rapidity, exhibiting a concatenation of all the previous symptoms; onward it has rushed to every part of town, knocking down all the old public-houses, and depositing splendid mansions, stone balustrades, rosewood fittings, immense lamps, and illuminated clocks, at the corner of every street.

The extensive scale on which these places are established, and the ostentatious manner in which the business of even the smallest among them is divided into branches, is amusing. A handsome plate of ground glass in one door directs you "To the Counting-house;" another to the "Bottle Department;" a third to the "Wholesale Department;" a fourth to "The Wine Promenade;" and so forth, until we are in daily expectation of meeting with a "Brandy Bell," or a "Whiskey Entrance." Then, ingenuity is exhausted in devising attractive titles for the different descriptions of gin; and the dram-drinking portion of the community as they gaze upon the gigantic black and white announcements, which are only to be equalled in size by the figures beneath them, are left in a state of pleasing hesitation between "The Cream of the Valley," "The Out and Out," "The No Mistake," "The Good for Mixing," "The real Knock-me-down," "The celebrated Butter Gin," "The regular Flare-up," and a dozen other, equally inviting and wholesome liqueurs. Although places of this description are to be met with in every second street, they are invariably numerous and splendid in precise proportion to the dirt and poverty of the surrounding neighbourhood. The gin-shops in and near Drury Lane, Holborn, St. Giles's, Covent Garden, and Clare Market, are the handsomest in London. There is more of filth and squalid misery near those great thoroughfares than in any part of this mighty city.

We will endeavour to sketch the bar of a large gin-shop, and its ordinary customers, for the edification of such of our readers as may not have had opportunities of observing such scenes; and on the chance of finding one well suited to our purpose, we will make for Drury Lane, through the narrow streets and dirty courts which divide it from Oxford Street, and that classical spot adjoining the brewery at the bottom of Tottenham Court Road, best known to the initiated as the "Rookery."

The filthy and miserable appearance of this part of London can hardly be imagined by those (and there are many such) who have not witnessed it. Wretched houses with broken windows patched with rags and paper: every room let out to a different family, and in many instances to two or even three—fruit and "sweet-stuff" manufacturers in the cellars, barbers and red-herring vendors in the front parlours, cobblers in the back; a bird-fancier in the first floor, three families on the second, starvation in the attics, Irishmen in the passage, a "musician" in the front kitchen, and a charwoman and five hungry children in the back one—filth everywhere—a gutter before the houses and a drain behind—clothes drying and slops emptying, from the windows; girls of fourteen or fifteen, with matted hair, walking about barefoot, and in white great-coats, almost their only covering; boys of all ages, in coats of all sizes and no coats at all; men and women, in every variety of scanty and dirty apparel, lounging, scolding, drinking, smoking, squabbling, fighting, and swearing.

You turn the corner. What a change! All is light and brilliancy. The hum of many voices issues from that splendid gin-shop which forms the commencement of the two streets opposite; and the gay building with the fantastically ornamented parapet, the illuminated clock, the plate-glass windows surrounded by stucco rosettes, and its profusion of gas-lights in richly-gilt burners, is perfectly dazzling when contrasted with the darkness and dirt we have just left. The interior is even gayer than the exterior. A bar of French-polished mahogany, elegantly carved, extends the whole width of the place; and there are two side-aisles of great casks, painted green and gold, enclosed within a light brass rail, and bearing such inscriptions, as "Old Tom, 549"; "Young Tom, 360"; "Samson, 1421"—the figures agreeing, we presume, with "gallons," understood. Beyond the bar is a lofty and spacious saloon, full of the same enticing vessels, with a gallery running round it, equally well furnished. On the counter, in addition to the usual spirit apparatus, are two or three little baskets of cakes and biscuits, which are carefully secured at the top with wicker-work, to prevent their contents being unlawfully abstracted. Behind it, are two showily-dressed damsels with large necklaces, dispensing the spirits and "compounds." They are assisted by the ostensible proprietor of the concern, a stout, coarse fellow in a fur cap, put on very much on one side to give him a knowing air, and to display his sandy whiskers to the best advantage.

The two old washerwomen, who are seated on the little bench to the left of the bar, are rather overcome by the head-dresses and haughty demeanour of the young ladies who officiate. They receive their half-quartern of gin and peppermint, with considerable deference, prefacing a request for "one of them soft biscuits," with a "Jist be good enough, ma'am." They are quite astonished at the impudent air of the young fellow in a brown coat and bright buttons, who, ushering in his two companions, and walking up to the bar in as careless a manner as if he had been used to green and gold ornaments all his life, winks at one of the young ladies with singular coolness, and calls for a "kervorten and a three-out-glass," just as if the place were his own. "Gin for you, sir?" says the young lady when she has drawn it: carefully looking every way but the right one, to show that the wink had no effect upon her. "For me, Mary, my dear," replies the gentleman in brown. "My name an't Mary as it happens," says the young girl, rather relaxing as she delivers the change. "Well, if it an't, it ought to be," responds the irresistible one; "all the Marys as ever I seen was handsome gals." Here the young lady, not precisely remembering how blushes are managed in such cases, abruptly ends the flirtation by addressing the female in the faded feathers who has just entered, and who, after stating explicitly, to prevent any subsequent misunderstanding, that "this gentleman pays," calls for "a glass of port wine and a bit of sugar."

Those two old men who came in "just to have a drain," finished their third quartern a few seconds ago; they have made themselves crying drunk; and the fat comfortable-looking elderly women, who had "a glass of rum-shrub" each, having chimed in with their complaints on the hardness of the times, one of the women has agreed to stand a glass round, jocularly observing that "grief never mended no broken bones, and as good people's wery scarce, what I says is, make the most on 'em, and that's all about it!" a sentiment which appears to afford unlimited satisfaction to those who have nothing to pay.

It is growing late, and the throng of men, women, and children, who have been constantly going in and out, dwindles down to two or three occasional stragglers—cold, wretched-looking creatures, in the last stage of emaciation and disease. The knot of Irish laborers at the lower end of the place, who have been alternately shaking hands with, and threatening the life of each other, for the last hour, become furious in their disputes, and finding it impossible to silence one man, who is particularly anxious to adjust the difference, they resort to the expedient of knocking him down and jumping on him afterwards. The man in the fur cap, and the potboy rush out; a scene of riot and confusion ensues; half the Irishmen get shut out, and the other half get shut in; the potboy is knocked among the tubs in no time; the landlord hits everybody, and everybody hits the landlord; the barmaids scream; the police come in; the rest is a confused mixture of arms, legs, staves, torn coats, shouting, and struggling. Some of the party are borne off to the station-house, and the remainder slink home to beat their wives for complaining, and kick the children for daring to be hungry.

We have sketched this subject very slightly, not only because our limits compel us to do so, but because, if it were pursued farther, it would be painful and repulsive. Well-disposed gentlemen, and charitable ladies, would alike turn with coldness and disgust from a description of the drunken besotted men, and wretched broken-down miserable women, who form no inconsiderable portion of the frequenters of these haunts; forgetting, in the pleasant consciousness of their own rectitude, the poverty of the one, and the temptation of the other. Gin-drinking is a great vice in England, but wretchedness and dirt are a greater; and until you improve the homes of the poor, or persuade a half-famished wretch not to seek relief in the temporary oblivion of his own misery, with the pittance which, divided among his family, would furnish a morsel of bread for each, gin-shops will increase in number and splendour. If Temperance Societies would suggest an antidote against hunger, filth, and foul air, or could establish dispensaries for the gratuitous distribution of bottles of Lethe-water, gin-palaces would be numbered among the things that were.

# Appendix Two

# The Hogarth Sampler

W HAT FOLLOWS ARE not the definitive pronouncements of a gin connoisseur, but the personal reflections of a writer who has spent a year immersed in the language, lore and history of gin. I make no claim to be comprehensive—around a hundred gins or related spirits are on sale in Britain alone—and this is not intended to be a catalog of the best or the most expensive. Rather, it presents the dry gins, genevers, Old Toms, sloe gins and *korenwijns* I have encountered in the course of researching and writing this book. Over the last few decades the gin scene has been much complicated by the growth of large, multinational conglomerates—in many cases it is difficult to be sure exactly where the chain of ownership ends—so this appendix presents the brands as they appear to consumers rather than stockholders, with some brief notes on their history, character and products.

This is a deeply unscientific survey: some gins were drunk in bars, some in the houses of friends, others from my own fridge. Likewise, some were consumed in dry martinis, others with whatever tonic was to hand, and a few straight and chilled. No bribes, solid or liquid, have been taken (or, for that matter, offered), and all spirits mentioned are fairly widely available from British off-licenses and drink websites. Each is given a Hogarth rating from 1 to 5—not an indication of quality, but of flavor. A high score reflects richness, depth, and sweetness, redolent of the eighteenth century. A low score implies lightness, freshness, and dryness, suggestive of chrome cocktail-shakers. All strengths quoted are ABV rather than proof.

Beefeater 24 London Dry Gin—45%
(www.beefeatergin.com)

Established in 1863 by James Burroughs—a Devonian pharmacist who made his fortune in the U.S.—Beefeater capitalized on the international interest around the coronation of Elizabeth II in 1953 to become the most successful British export gin. The company still works out of premises in Kennington, south London: nine botanicals are steeped in neutral spirit for a day before distillation, and each shot takes around seven hours to complete. The process is overseen by master distiller Desmond Payne, who honed his palate in wine cellars and the Plymouth Gin distillery before coming to Beefeater in 1994.

Bottle & label: The bottle is tall and oblong, heavy in the hand, with a thick base and botanical curlicues molded into the glass. The label is clear and square, with the traditional Beefeater logo and a large "24" in san-serif type. The overall effect is Thirties—something one might expect to see behind the bar in a smart colonial hotel.

Principal botanicals: Japanese Sencha tea, Chinese green tea, Seville orange peel, grapefruit peel, lemon peel, juniper berries, coriander seed, licorice, angelica root, angelica seed, almond and orris root.

Tasting notes: the two teas are present but not overwhelming, and are balanced nicely by the citrus peel. A distinctive gin, but not one that would overwhelm other ingredients in a cocktail.

Perfect with / in: Toast the late Queen Mother with a gin and Dubonnet.

Hogarth rating: 3

## Blackwood's Vintage Dry Gin—40%
### (www.blackwoodsgin.net)

Think of the Shetland Islands, and gin may not be the first spirit that springs to mind. Blackwood's distillery, based in the small settlement of Catfirth, is trying to change that with its Vintage Dry Gin. Flavored with sustainably-harvested, hand-picked local botanicals, the gin is produced in small batches in what seems to be the most northerly distillery in the British Isles. "Vintage" reflects the subtle differences from year to year in the balance and flavor of the botanicals, in turn determined by the vagaries of the Shetlandic climate. Blackwood's also produce a limited edition 60% gin—the strength determined by the 60° N latitude of the Shetland Islands.

Bottle & label: The bottle is tubular clear glass, with round shoulders and a medium length neck—rather like a premium whisky bottle. The label is a handsome, rich green, with a Viking longship logo and silver lettering in a retro typeface.

Principal botanicals: Wild water mint, sea pink, angelica, meadowsweet and juniper berries.

Tasting notes: The first impression is freshness: I have no idea what sea pink or wild water mint might taste like in their natural state, but they contribute an uplifting, refreshing flavor which does bring to mind the coastal *machair* of the Hebrides. Beneath these botanicals, there is an excellent dry gin here, not to be drowned with other heavy flavors.

Perfect with / in: A gin fizz.

Hogarth rating: 1

## Bombay Sapphire Gin—40%
### (www.bombaysapphire.com)

Bombay Sapphire was one of the pioneers of the gin renaissance, bringing much-needed freshness to jaded mainstream palates. Ten botanicals are rectified in a carterhead still, and are not steeped in the spirit but held in a copper basket through which the vapor passes. Water from Lake Vyrnwy in north Wales is used to take the spirit down to 40%. The name was inspired by the Star of Bombay, a sapphire presented to Mary Pickford by Douglas Fairbanks Jr. now in the Smithsonian Museum.

Bottle & label: One of the most distinctive gin bottles, made in sapphire-tinted glass with an oblong profile. The label features the logo—a stylized version of the Star of Bombay—and the lettering is in various Victorian-style typefaces, including an elegant copperplate.

Principal botanicals: Juniper berries, lemon peel, licorice, orris root, almond, coriander, angelica, grains of paradise, cassia and cubeb.

Tasting notes: Clean and smooth, dominated by juniper and citrus, but with an underlying touch of complexity from the licorice and almond. Not much else to say, really: this is a high-quality premium gin, and very good for mixing.

Perfect with / in: A negroni.

Hogarth rating: 2

Bramley & Gage Damson Gin—26%<br>(www.bramleyandgage.co.uk)

Edward Bramley Kain and Penelope Gage—with names like these, what else could this husband and wife team do but grow fruit? Twenty years ago they began to produce strawberry, raspberry and blackcurrant liqueurs, and sloe and damson gins, on their fruit farm in south Devon. Now based in a new, purpose-built facility, they have expanded their range to include a small-batch 40% Six O'Clock Gin with elderflower and citrus, inspired by the drinking habits of Edward's great-grandfather—the engineer Edward Kain.

Bottle & label: Tall, thin, clear glass bottle, in the style of a French fruit liqueur bottle, which shows off the deep color of the contents in fine style. The label matches the contents, with a simple logo in a white typeface.

Principal botanicals: Bramley & Gage Six O'Clock, on which this is based, features juniper berries, orange peel and elderflower.

Tasting notes: This is the damson gin that your parents could never quite get right. Rich, voluptuous fruitiness, cut with the sharpness of the damsons and carried by what seems—so far as the palate can tell—to be a fine dry gin. Neither excessively sweet, nor sharp, nor thin: the Goldilocks of damson gins.

Perfect with / in: A damson gin fizz on a hot summer's day.

Hogarth rating: 4

Foxdenton Blackjack—20%

(www.foxdentonestate.co.uk)

The Foxdenton estate in Lancashire has been in the hands of the Radclyffe family since 1367. In 2001 Nicholas Radclyffe took over the estate company—now based in Buckingham—and began to make fruit gins and liqueurs based on the family recipes he inherited. Charles Maxwell, their distiller, has collaborated in the creation of a new 48% London dry gin, flavored with citrus and lime flower, plus a 47% Platinum London Gin and a 60% Export Strength London Gin—the comparatively high ABVs intended to capture and retain as much of the botanical flavor as possible.

Bottle & label: Styled after a pre-war whisky bottle—think *Whisky Galore* or Captain Haddock—and the label is sober, clear and informative. Overall, it screams "boutique liqueur": just the thing you might expect to see at a well-sourced local deli or farm shop.

Principal botanicals: Foxdenton London Dry Gin, on which this is based, features juniper berries, coriander seeds, lemon peel, lime flower, angelica, and orris root.

Tasting notes: Good heavens. This lightly sugared blackcurrant gin is really quite something: acerbic, yes, and certainly nothing like a sweetened sloe gin, but the fruits and the base gin come together in unexpected ways to turn what could have been a mouth-puckering liqueur into a real treat for the nose and the palate.

Perfect with / in: Neat and chilled as an aperitif.

Hogarth rating: 5

G'vine Floraison Gin—40%
(www.g-vine.com)

Many boutique gins claim to be unique, but G'Vine's claim to originality is unshakable. Developed in 2001 by Jean Sébastien Robicquet and Bruno de Reilhac—founders of EuroWineGate—G'Vine is based on grape spirit distilled from Ugni Blanc grapes grown in the Cognac region. And the major botanical is not juniper, but the berries and flowers of the green vine. Flowers picked around June are used to make Floraison Gin, and vine berries picked in the late summer are used to make Nouaison Gin. These, plus nine other botanicals, are macerated in the spirit for two to five days, before being distilled in a small, single-shot Florentine copper still. EuroWineGate also make Cîroc, a grape vodka.

Bottle & label: At first glance one might be forgiven for mistaking G'Vine for an outsize bottle of expensive perfume. Its elegant, waisted clear glass bottle shades into green at the top, and is printed with the large, looping G'Vine "G" and a picture of the principal botanical—the vine flower.

Principal botanicals: Vine flowers, ginger root, licorice, cardamom, cassia bark, coriander, juniper berries, cubeb, nutmeg, and lime peel.

Tasting notes: Two flavors are at play here: the subtle but pervasive overtones of the vine flower, which works with rather than against the juniper, and the grape spirit, which brings a vinous smoothness not always found in gins based on grain spirits. It's not a world away from traditional dry gins, but it has a distinctive character which is floral, fresh and spicy. I'm almost tempted to dab some on my pulse points.

Perfect with / in: If you can forgive the name, you could mix it with Chambord, simple syrup, lime and lemon juice to make a G'Spot.

Hogarth rating: 2

### Gabriel Boudier Saffron Gin—40%
### (www.boudier.com)

Probably most famous as the makers of a multi-award-winning *crème de cassis de Dijon,* the Burgundy-based distillers Gabriel Boudier also produce some of the most distinctive recreations of historic gins. Their Saffron Gin, made in small batches in a copper pot still, is based on a nineteenth-century British recipe, and they also produce a dry gin, a sloe gin, and various *eaux de vie* and fruit liqueurs.

Bottle & label: Clear glass, heavy bottom, round body, square shoulders, understated label in an old-fashioned typeface: sophisticated is the word, and this would look utterly at home behind the bar in any chic West End hotel.

Principal botanicals: Saffron, juniper berries, coriander, lemon, orange peel, angelica seeds, iris and fennel.

Tasting notes: The first sip is taken with the eye: the inviting yellow tone imparted by the saffron is not what my English mind usually associates with gin. Any doubts are, however, dispelled at an instant by the flavor. It is recognizably a gin, but the saffron brings both color and a spicy warmth which chimes beautifully with the other botanicals and the touch of sweetness.

Perfect with / in: Gabriel Boudier recommend trying it neat and on the rocks.

Hogarth rating: 5

## Greenall's Berkeley Square London Dry Gin—40%
### (www.gjgreenall.co.uk)

Another great British name, Greenall's is one of the few gins still produced on (or at least very close to) the site of its original distillery. The present establishment, in Risley, Warrington, is adjacent to the site of Thomas Dakin's 1761 distillery, and—despite a serious fire in 2005—continues to produce London dry gin to a recipe dating from the mid-eighteenth century.

Bottle & label: A disciplined, slightly military rectangle of clear glass, ridged at the sides and with the word "Gin" molded into the lower part. The plain, elegant label sits in a molded recess around the waist of the bottle. Too cool for school, but not unapproachable.

Principal botanicals: Juniper berries, coriander, angelica, cubeb, basil, sage, lavender, kaffir lime leaves.

Tasting notes: Intended to capture the atmosphere of an English physic garden in summer, and it succeeds admirably. Basil and kaffir lime at the top; sage and lavender in the middle, with juniper providing a subtle base. Perhaps too interesting for a swift G&T, but give it space to breathe and it will pay you back.

Perfect with / in: A not-too-dry martini, preferably to be consumed in a garden.

Hogarth rating: 3

## Hayman's Old Tom Gin—40%
### (www.haymansgin.com)

Christopher Hayman's name conceals a striking lineage: his great-grandfather, James Burroughs, established Beefeater Gin in 1863, and Hayman joined the family firm in 1969. In 1987 Beefeater was sold to Whitbread, but a year later Hayman bought back part of the company, established headquarters in London and production facilities in Essex, and began to produce a classic London dry gin. Hayman's also produces a quintuple-distilled 1820 Gin Liqueur, and a version of Sir Walter Raleigh's "Great Cordial," based on the tonic devised by Raleigh while he was imprisoned in the Tower of London.

Bottle & label: Sober, square-shouldered, with a discreet racing green label featuring a black cat—"Old Tom."

Principal botanicals: Not clear, but certainly including juniper berries, coriander and citrus peel.

Tasting notes: Sweet and oily are not usually words of praise, but this Old Tom has them in exactly the right proportions. Sweet (though not too sweet) up front, with a lip-smacking viscosity and the botanicals coming in close behind. Something like a lemon and ginger cake in a glass. If you're looking for an alternative to the tyranny of dry gin, this is well worth trying.

Perfect with / in: A Tom Collins.

Hogarth rating: 5

Hendrick's Gin—41.4%

(www.hendricksgin.com)

Hendrick's was developed by William Grant & Sons in 1999, and is produced at their Girvan distillery on the Ayrshire coast. Hendrick's is a lighter, more contemporary alternative to juniper-heavy gins, and is produced in a handmade 1860 Bennet copper still and a 1948 carterhead still.

Bottle & label: Dark glass, short and cylindrical, with a cork stopper. Diamond-shaped label, on cream-colored paper, with elegant hand-drawn curlicues and a Hogarthian typeface. Have we stepped into an eighteenth-century apothecary's shop?

Principal botanicals: Oil of cucumber, Damascus rose, juniper berries, citrus, chamomile, meadowsweet, caraway seeds, and elderflower.

Tasting notes: One is hard-pushed to find a review of Hendrick's which doesn't include the words crisp, cool, refreshing and unusual. It was created to appeal to a young palate, with less emphasis on juniper, and the result is deliciously different, with rose and cucumber in the nose and citrus and elderflower on the palate. Perhaps not *quite* as iconoclastic as Hendrick's makes out—it is still recognizably a dry gin, and the flavors are subtle rather than bold—but wonderful nonetheless.

Perfect with / in: A Vesper martini—but don't shake it.

Hogarth rating: 2

### Jensen's London Distilled Dry Bermondsey Gin—43% (www.bermondseygin.com)

Full marks for originality: while many contemporary distillers are reaching for lighter and less intense gins, Christian Jensen—a former IT consultant—has made his name with a Thirties-style spirit. Based in Bermondsey and produced by Thames Distillers in Clapham, the Jensen range also includes a 43% London Distilled Old Tom.

Bottle & label: Hipsterish and faintly medicinal—a tall, plain, clear glass bottle, with a white label in lower case.

Principal botanicals: Juniper berries, coriander, orris root, sweet almond, licorice, and angelica.

Tasting notes: This is Christian Jensen's attempt to recreate the kind of London dry gin drunk in the Thirties and Forties, and he has succeeded admirably. Fewer botanicals in this case make for an interesting and well-rounded flavor—not crisp or clean, but smooth and creamy (thanks to the licorice and angelica) with bold juniper and coriander.

Perfect with / in: An Old Fashioned.

Hogarth rating: 5

## Martin Miller's Westbourne Strength Gin—45.2%
### (www.martinmillersgin.com)

Martin Miller made his fortune as a hotel-owner and as the publisher of *Miller's Antique Guides,* but in 1999 he branched out into gin. Based at the Langley Distillery, near Birmingham, Miller's spirits are produced in a late-nineteenth century John Dore copper still nicknamed "Angela," and both have won many international prizes and commendations. But the final blending is done a thousand miles away, in the Icelandic village of Borgarnes with water from the Selyri spring.

Bottle & label: Bold and distinctive, reminiscent of a brandy bottle, overlaid with what appears to be a map of Iceland—a nod to the place where the final blending of Martin Miller's gin takes place.

Principal botanicals: Juniper berries, orange peel, lemon peel, coriander, licorice, cinnamon, cassia, nutmeg, angelica, and orris root.

Tasting notes: This is one of the highest-rated modern gins, and tasting it, one can see why. It's not that this has any particularly unusual botanicals, but they come together to make an exemplary dry gin, with an enticing combination of citrus and spice uppermost on the palate. Smooth, characterful and deservedly admired.

Perfect with / in: A classic g&t.

Hogarth rating: 3

## Plymouth Dry Gin—40%
### (www.plymouthgin.com)

By 1793, when the Coates family began to make gin in Plymouth, their distillery building had already served as a Dominican monastery, a "Mault-house," and a refuge for the Pilgrim Fathers before their voyage to the New World. Since 1880 the British courts have ruled that Plymouth Gin must be made in Plymouth, and the brand now enjoys an EU geographical designation—the only British gin to receive this privilege, and a reflection of the brand's history and status. Plymouth lost its pre-eminence in the mid-twentieth century, but (with renewed support from the Royal Navy) it is back on form, combining spirit and spring-water from Dartmoor with seven botanicals. Products include a 41.2% Original Gin, a 57% Naval Strength Gin, and a Sloe Gin made to an 1883 recipe, for which berries are steeped in the spirit for four months.

Bottle & label: Probably the classic dry gin bottle—clear glass, tall, square-ish. The dark blue label strikes a slightly old-fashioned note, and features a Royal Navy ship of the line in full sail.

Principal botanicals: Juniper berries, orange peel, lemon peel, coriander seeds, angelica root, orris root, cardamom.

Tasting notes: More full-bodied and fruity than a classic London dry gin, with a long citrus-y finish. To be honest, there's little else to add: this is a classic, one of the world's historic spirits, and everyone should try it for themselves.

Perfect with / in: An authentic Royal Navy Pink Gin.

Hogarth rating: 3

### Sacred Gin—40%
(www.sacredspiritscompany.com)

There are small-batch gins, and then there is Sacred. Ian Hart, a former City financier, has turned a ground floor room in his Highgate house into a modern-day alchemist's workshop, and the result of his experimentation is Sacred Gin. Hart uses twelve botanicals, including nutmeg and frankincense, and distils each separately using a low-temperature vacuum in a glass retort and condenser—a process which helps to preserve the complexity of each flavor, and ensures that they do not get lost in the final process of blending the rectified spirits. Hart's products also include Sacred Vodka, gin blending kits containing six single-botanical gins, also available separately, and a shifting range of "exotica" (which at the time of writing includes a gin flavored with Christmas pudding).

Bottle & label: Tall and narrow, with a maroon-and-gold label featuring the Sacred crown logo.

Principal botanicals: Citrus peel, juniper berries, cardamom, nutmeg and frankincense.

Tasting notes: There's a remarkable clarity and intensity of flavor here, balanced with a fragrant creaminess, and the individual botanicals come across distinctly—a consequence of the single-botanical low-temperature rectification. Frankincense adds an unusual, but not unpleasant, note of spicy warmth. As with some of the other boutique gins, this would be wasted in a hastily-gulped g&t, but this is a gin which can be nosed and sipped like a good wine.

Perfect with / in: Ian Hart suggests trying it chilled and neat first, then making a Sacred martini.

Hogarth rating: 1

Sipsmith's London Dry Gin—41.6%<br>(www.sipsmith.com)

Prudence—the Sipsmith's copper still, holding only 300 liters per shot—is the first to be installed in a London distillery in more than two centuries. Sipsmith's is a craft distillery based in Hammersmith, and the rectified spirit emerging from Prudence is blended with water from Lydwell Spring, one of the sources of the Thames. Purchasers can use the Sipsmith's website to check the date on which their bottle was produced. The range also includes a barley vodka and a sloe gin. Further innovations are promised, including (possibly) a mustard vodka.

Bottle & label: A plain and well-proportioned glass bottle, but the label is something else. Rich green, with a sprig of juniper and a copper still morphing into the head of a swan—a pun on the swan-necked alembics of medieval alchemists?

Principal botanicals: Juniper berries, coriander seed, angelica root, licorice root, orris root, ground almond, cassia bark, cinnamon, orange peel, and lemon peel.

Tasting notes: This is a thoroughly well-balanced dry gin, and the comparatively small number of botanicals have the space to provide their distinctive notes without getting swamped. The juniper is dry, uplifted by the citrus peel, and the licorice and orris root come through in the finish. One might drink this neat and chilled, for a refreshing botanical hit, but it gives the impression that it would play very well in all sorts of cocktails.

Perfect with / in: A gin fizz.

Hogarth rating: 2

Tanqueray No. 10 Gin—47.3%

(www.tanqueray.com)

Edward & Charles Tanqueray & Co., Rectifiers, opened a distillery in what was then the suburb of Bloomsbury in 1838. Now owned by Diageo, and produced in Scotland, Tanqueray's leading product is a 43.1% London dry gin, along with Tanqueray Rangpur, flavored with Rangpur limes and aimed at the U.S. market.

Bottle & label: A sort of stretched version of the Tanqueray "cocktail shaker" bottle, tall and fluted in green glass. The label mimics a wax seal and ribbon, and the overall effect is upmarket and elegant.

Principal botanicals: The recipe is a well-kept secret, but it includes juniper berries, chamomile, grapefruit, orange and lime.

Tasting notes: This is the premium gin in a line of premium gins, and No. 10 achieves the startling feat of being both rich and fresh at the same time. Lots of fruit over the juniper, a smooth and soft mouthfeel, and other botanicals (the identity of which remains a mystery) bringing subtle, aromatic undercurrents.

Perfect with / in: A Satan's Whiskers.

Hogarth rating: 3

Wees Distillery Very Old Geneva—40%
(www.de-ooievaar.nl)

Advertised as "the last authentic distillery left in Amsterdam," A. van Wees was established in 1782, and until 1970 delivered its products to bars and restaurants in casks—many of which can be seen on the regular tours offered at the distillery. It has one of the largest range of genevers—seventeen—including *oude* and *jonge* style, plus *korenwijn,* some matured in wooden casks for up to fifteen years. It also produces Three Corners Dry Gin, flavored with juniper and lemon, a lemon genever, and various liqueurs, including Parrotsoup and Little Hans in the Cellar.

Bottle & label: A traditional genever bottle, tall and round and made in yellow-brown ceramic. The label features the Wees crest, and looks as if it might have changed little in two or three centuries—traditional, but sophisticated.

Principal botanicals: Juniper, plus "various herbs."

Tasting notes: "Oude genever" refers to a style, not an age: it contains more maltwine and more sugar than the lighter "jonge genever." But this "oude genever" is also aged in oak barrels, and this, along with the malt wine, makes for a very aromatic drink. Juniper, which in dry gins provides the background for the other botanicals, here cuts through the rich, malty sweetness. This is probably the closest that gin gets to whisky—smoky, smooth, rounded.

Perfect with / in: The classic Dutch *kopstoot*—a pint of cold lager followed by a shot.

Hogarth rating: 5

## Whitley Neill London Dry Gin—42%
## (www.whitleyneill.com)

Johnny Neill is a scion of the Greenall Whitley distilling family, but his Whitley Neill London Dry Gin—launched in 2005—is a radical departure from distilling orthodoxy. Its keynote botanicals are Cape gooseberry and the fruit of the baobab tree, giving an African tone to Neill's small-batch spirit, produced in a century-old potstill near Birmingham.

Bottle & label: Clear glass, and shaped like an old liqueur or whisky bottle. The label really stands out—gold and silver lettering against a red background—and the brand logo is a baobab tree.

Principal botanicals: Cape gooseberry and the fruit of the baobab tree.

Tasting notes: If you're used to drinking London dry gin, this will come as quite a surprise. This is almost as much a liqueur as a gin, with a softness to the palate and an exotic fruity nose. There are more conventional citrus and spice botanicals behind the Cape gooseberry and the baobab fruit, but these two are what really stand out. This could make a thoroughly refreshing change in cocktails where the gin is a principal flavor, and it also makes a delightful summer aperitif.

Perfect with / in: A fruity version of a gin sour.

Hogarth rating: 4

## Zuidam Korenwijn—38%
## (www.zuidam.eu)

Dutch genever tends to be dominated by a small number of ancient distillers, but Zuidam is a striking exception. Established in 1975, Zuidam brings a small-batch, craft sensibility to the entire process of genever production, from the milling and mashing of grain, via distillation and rectification in one of four new copper stills, to the final bottling. Their range includes a dry gin, a genever and a selection of fruit liqueurs.

Bottle & label: Straight out of the sixteenth century, with a charmingly dumpy shape, a cork stopper, a wax seal and a mock-parchment label in cream and blue.

Principal botanicals: Juniper, licorice root and aniseed.

Tasting notes: If you're curious to know what the first European juniper cordials were like, this is for you. The botanicals come through, but are much less forward than in a typical dry gin, and there is a genever-like element of sweetness. In some ways, this has much more in common with whisky, especially with the vanilla flavor from the barrel-aging and the delicate caramel flavors in the finish.

Perfect with / in: Surprisingly good in hot milk, or in a Dutch Trade Wind.

Hogarth rating: 5

# *Notes*

Prologue—The Murder of Mrs. Atkinson
"by throwing her down a pair of Stairs . . ." and subsequent quotations: *Old Bailey Proceedings Online* (www.oldbaileyonline.org, version 6.0, 05 May 2011), February 1732, trial of Robert Atkinson (t17320223-41)
"The spirit drawn by distillation . . .": Johnson, *Dictionary*, vol 1, p 871

## 1. Living Water
Two ground-breaking accounts of the Dutch Golden Age are Schama, *Embarrassment of Riches,* and Cook, *Matters of Exchange.*
"This name is remarkably suitable . . .": Arnaud de Ville-Neuve, *Liber de Vinis* (1310), quoted in Miller & Brown, *Spirituous Journey,* p 50
"a Compleat Method of Physick . . .": Culpeper, *English Physitian,* title page
"[Juniper berries] are admirably good for a cough . . .": Culpeper, *English Physitian,* entry on juniper
"Folkloric uses of juniper": on this, see two excellent essays by Rowan, "The Juniper Tree," and Kendall, "Mythology and Folklore of the Juniper"
"The Juniper Tree": D.L. Ashliman's widely-praised translation is available online at www.pitt.edu/~dash/grimm047.html
"An emanation of the divinity . . .": Llull, *Secunda Magia Naturalis,* quoted in Gateley, *Drink,* p 91
"8. Separate the earth from the fire . . .": from "The Emerald Tablet," translated by Georgio Beato, in *Azoth, sive Aureliæ occultæ philosophorum* (1613)
"A nature, a force, a virtue . . .": Paracelsus, *Archidoxa,* quoted in A.E. Waite (ed.), *Hermetic and Alchemical Writings of Paracelsus the Great,* Alchemical Press, 1992, part II, p. 22, quoted in Ball, *Paracelsus,* p 176
"[Spirit] eases diseases coming of cold . . .": John French, *The Art of Distillation,* 1651, translation of Hieronymus Braunschweig, *Liber de arte destillandi,* 1500, quoted in Gateley, *Drink,* p 92
"It is a general Custom in Holland . . .": Y-Worth, *Compleat Distiller,* p 184

Juliet's nurse drinking aqua vita: see Shakespeare, *Romeo and Juliet*: act 3 scene 2

"like *aqua vita* with a midwife": Shakespeare, *Twelfth Night*, act 2 scene 5

"went about my stilling": Lady Margaret Hoby, quoted in Gateley, *Drink*, p 115

"Distil with a gentle heat...": Hugh Platt, *Delightes for Ladies*, London, 1609, quoted in Coates, *Classic Gin*, p 14

"Aqua Vitae, Aqua Composita...": quoted in Burnett, *Liquid Pleasures*, p 161

"Rue, sage, lavender...": Sir Theodore de Mayerne, *The Distiller of London*, London, 1652, p 96

"Fill me a thousand pots...": John Fletcher, *The Pilgrim*, act 3 scene 6

"HOLLAND, that scarce deserves..." and "Sure when religion..." Marvell, "The Character of Holland," c. 1653

"As noble a sight as ever I saw...": Pepys, *Diary*, entry for 16 Nov 1665

"Genova": Miller & Brown, *Spirituous Journey*, p 108

"Our drunkenness as a national vice...": Defoe, *A Brief Case of the Distillers*, p 17

"Sir W. Batten did advise me...": Pepys, *Diary*, 10 Oct 1663

"suddenly...began to abound...": Defoe, *A Brief Case of the Distillers*, p 26

"Distillation is a converting of Bodies...": Y-Worth, *Compleat Distiller*, p 2

"Nature makes various Degrees of Concoction...": Y-Worth, *Cerevisiarii Comes*, introductory letter

"the Wild and Unruly *Gass*...": Y-Worth, *Cerevisiarii Comes*, p 19

"Liquor Alkahest of Helmont..." and "An Universal Fire...": Y-Worth, *Trifertes Sagani*, "Epistle to the Reader"

"that *Grand Tincture and Divine Essence*...": Y-Worth, *Cerevisiarii Comes*, p 42

"Indefatigable Search": Isaac Newton, quoted in Field & Frank, *Renaissance and Revolution*, p 181


## 2. Rough Spirits

I have been indebted throughout this chapter to the two best recent histories of the gin craze: Dillon's *Madame Geneva* and Warner's *Craze*.

"What can impart ...": Stephen Buck, *Geneva: A Poem in Blank Verse,* London, 1734, quoted in Dillon, *Madame Geneva,* p 92

Two gin crazes: see Warner, *Craze,* p 15

"Martial WILLIAM drank ...": "Alexander Blunt," *Geneva: a poem. Addressed to the Right Honorable Sir R- W-,* London, 1729

"Mother Gin was of Dutch parentage ...": *The Life of Mother Gin,* London, 1736, quoted in Dillon, p 6

"Act for encouraging the distilling ...": quoted in Dillon, p 9

Exchequer statistics: quoted in Burnett, *Liquid Pleasures,* p 162

"The Making of [spirits] ...": Company of Distillers, "Reasons for promoting the British distillery," in *A collection of political tracts,* London, 1736, p 36

"A Spacious Hive ...": Bernard de Mandeville, "The Grumbling Hive," in *The Fable of the Bees, or, Private Vices, Public Benefits,* London, 1724

"Nothing is more destructive ..." and "The rents that are received ...": Bernard Mandeville, *The Fable of the Bees, or, Private Vices, Public Benefits,* London, 1724, vol 1, pp 57–61, and p 82, "Remark G"

"opened his eyes ...": Samuel Johnson, quoted in James Boswell, *Life of Samuel Johnson,* Weds 15 April 1778

"thirty-three pints of Scotch claret ...": James Boswell, quoted in Gateley, *Drink,* p 185

Estimates of literacy rates in London: quoted in editors' introduction, in Brant & Whyman (eds.), *John Gay's "Trivia,"* p 5

"Whoever shall pass among the Streets ...": Lord Lonsdale, *Gentleman's Magazine,* Nov 1743, p 629, quoted in Warner, *Craze,* p 13

Hanoverian London's pleasure district: see editors' introduction, in Brant & Whyman (eds.), *John Gay's "Trivia,"* p 5

"We used to keep ...": John Hill, *A History of the Materia Medica,* London, 1751, quoted in Johnson, *Dictionary,* vol 1, p 863

"For making 10 gallons ..." and subsequent quotations: Ambrose Cooper, *The Complete Distiller,* London, 1757, pp 249–251

Beaufoy, James & Co gin recipe: quoted in Coates, *Mixellany Gin,* p 51.

"to shew the different Specifick Gravity ...": "Mr. Clarke," quoted in *Philosophical Transactions of the Royal Society,* vol 36, 1729–1730, p 277

"Aqua Vitae, Aqua Mirabilis . . .": Daniel Defoe, *A Brief Case of the Distillers and the Distilling Trade*, London, 1726, p 18, quoted in Dillon, *Madam Geneva*, p 8

"Gin-shops are undoubtedly . . .": Henry Fielding, *A Dissertation on Mr. Hogarth's Six Prints Lately Publish'd, viz. Gin-Lane, Beer-Street, and the Four Stages of Cruelty*, London, 1751, p. 18

"In one place not far from East Smithfield . . .": Thomas Wilson, *Distilled Spirituous Liquors the Bane of the Nation*, revised edition, London, 1736, quoted in Dillon, *Madam Geneva*, p 113

Habermas, the "public sphere" and coffee-houses: see Habermas, *Structural Transformation*

"the very Rubbish of the Creation . . ." and subsequent quotations: *A trip from St. James's to the Royal Exchange*, London, 1744, quoted in Warner, *Craze*, p 48

"Go along the streets . . .": "Saynought Slyboots," *The Tavern Scuffle*, London, 1726, quoted in Dillon, *Madam Geneva*, p 21

"PEACHUM: One may know . . .": John Gay, *The Beggar's Opera*, London, 1728, act 3 scene 6

"a Silver Watch . . ." and subsequent quotations: *Old Bailey Proceedings Online* (www.oldbaileyonline.org, version 6.0, 05 May 2011), 4 December 1724, trial of Eleanor Lock (t17241204–68)

"a vast Wood or Forest . . .": Henry Fielding, *An Inquiry into the Causes of the Late Increase in Robbers*, London, 1751, quoted in Rawlings, "General Introduction," in Rawlings (ed.), *Drunks, Whores and Idle Apprentices*, p 24

"like a Dog to his Vomit" and subsequent quotations: "The History of the Remarkable Life of John Sheppard" (1724), in Rawlings (ed.), *Drunks, Whores and Idle Apprentices*, p 68

"his Majesty's plantations in America . . ." and subsequent quotations: "The Life and Actions of James Dalton, (The noted Street-robber)" (1730), in Rawlings (ed.), *Drunks, Whores and Idle Apprentices*, p 94

"springing from the Dunghill": *The Life of Mother Gin; containing, a True and Faithful Relation of her Conduct and Politicks*, London, 1737, quoted in Warner, *Craze*, p 74

"Journeymen taylors and shoemakers ..." and "She bewail'd her faults ...": *The Whole Tryal, Indictment, Arraignment, Examination and Condemnation of Madam Geneva. Taken in Shorthand by Dorothy Addle-Brains, Fore-woman of the Jury,* London, 1713, quoted in Dillon, *Madam Geneva,* p 14

"so much intoxicated with Geneva ...": quoted in Gateley, *Drink,* p 165

"quite intoxicated with Gin ...": quoted in Gateley, *Drink,* p 166

"not drunk in such large Quantities ...": Thomas Wilson, *Distilled Spirituous Liquors the Bane of the Nation,* London, 1736, p 33, quoted in Warner, *Craze,* p 16

"coagulate and thicken the Blood ..." and "We have too frequent Instances ...": Stephen Hales, *A Friendly Admonition to the Drinkers of Brandy, and Other Distilled Spirituous Liquors,* London, 1734, quoted in Gateley, *Drink,* p 165

"The sucking Brat declines ...": *An Elegy on the Much-Lamented Death of the Most Excellent, the Most Truly-beloved, and Universally-admired Lady, Madame Gineva,* London, 1736, p. 7, quoted in Warner, *Craze,* p 99

"On Sunday night ...": quoted in Gateley, *Drink,* p 165.

"Why, the miserable creatures ...": Sir Joseph Jekyll, *The Trial of the Spirits, or, Some Considerations Upon the Pernicious Consequences of the Gin-trade to Great-Britain,* London, 1736, quoted in Gateley, *Drink,* p 166

"We hear that a strong-water shop ...": *Old Whig,* 26 Feb 1736, p 1

"Puss, give me two penny-worth ..." and subsequent quotations: Dudley Bradstreet, *The Life and Uncommon Adventures of Captain Dudley Bradstreet,* London, 1755, quoted in Dillon, *Madam Geneva,* p 163.

Jessica Warner on Gin Act informers: see Warner, *Craze,* p 177

"carry'd in effigy ...": *London Evening-Post,* 15–18 Jan 1737, p 2, quoted in Warner, *Craze,* p 166

"whipping until bloody": quoted in Gateley, *Drink,* p 167

"We have now mortgaged ...": Lord John Hervey, quoted in Gateley, *Drink,* p 169

"We may not sell any thing ...": John Wesley, *The Use of Money,* London, 1743, quoted in Gateley, *Drink,* p 169

"This Day are publish'd ...": *London Evening-Post,* 14 Feb 1751 "from the melancholy consequences ...": quoted in Gateley, *Drink*, p 172

"This *wicked* GIN ...": *London Evening-Post*, 12–14 March 1751, quoted in Warner, *Craze*, p 193

"destroying in the Course of a few Years ...": Bishop Isaac Maddox, *The London Magazine*, March 1751, pp 112–113, quoted in Warner, *Craze*, p 199

"The Drunkenness I here intend ..." and subsequent quotations: Henry Fielding, *An Inquiry into the Causes of the Late Increase in Robbers*, London, 1751, section II.

"In Gin Lane ...": William Hogarth, *Anecdotes of William Hogarth, Written by himself,* London, 1782, ed. John Bowyer Nichols, Cornmarket Press, 1970, p 64

"Buy my ballads ...": quoted in Haslam, *From Hogarth to Rowlandson*, p 128

"Gin, cursed Fiend ..." and subsequent quotations: James Townley, in William Hogarth, "Gin Lane" and "Beer Street," London, 1751

"I must, I will have Gin! ...": Edward Cave, *The Gentleman's Magazine*, March 1751, quoted in Warner, *Craze*, p 195

"reeled as if drunk ..." and "sublime ...": William Hazlitt and Charles Lamb, quoted in Nicholls, *Politics of Alcohol*, p 74

"If we consider all the consequences ...": W.H. Lecky, *A History of England in the Eighteenth Century*, Cambridge, 1879, vol 1, p 479

## 3. The Infernal Principle

"What's the quickest way ...": there are versions of this featuring almost every strong drink available to nineteenth-century Mancunians, but for the general form see Shiman, *Crusade Against Drink*, p 3

"...too surely they do in verity find ..." and subsequent quotations: Thomas Carlyle, "Chartism," in *Critical and Miscellaneous Essays,* London, 1839, vol 3, p 228

"Hegel remarks somewhere ...": Karl Marx, "The Eighteenth Brumaire of Louis Napoleon," *Die Revolution* 1, 1852, online at www.marxists. org/archive/marx/works/1852/18th-brumaire/

"...all or most of the painful and excruciating Distempers ...": George Cheyne, *Essay on Regimen*, 1740, quoted in Austin, *Alcohol in Western Society*, p 316

"In folly [spirit-drinking] causes [the drinker] ..." and subsequent quotations: Rush, *An Inquiry into the Effects of Ardent Spirits,* New York, 1811, p 4

"WATER; Milk and Water; Small Beer ..." and subsequent quotations: John Coakley Lettsom, *Hints to Beneficence,* London, 1797, p 180

"A few years ago, the crops of grain ..." and subsequent quotations: Trotter, *Essay on Drunkenness,* pp 6, 36, 48

"Drown'd in inebriated sleep ...": Thomas Rowlandson, "Death in the Nursery," 1815–16

"I shall have them all dead drunk presently! ...": George Cruikshank, "The Gin Shop," 1829. This is easily confused with a slightly later Cruikshank engraving, also titled "The Gin Shop," made in 1836 for Dickens' *Sketches by Boz*

"It was converted into the very opposite ...": quoted in Dillon, *Madam Geneva,* p 292

On nineteenth-century gin-palaces, see Jessica Warner's excellent and original essay: Warner, "People's Palaces"

Statistics of gin consumption in 1825–26: see Warner, "People's Palaces," p 40

"to shut the door on the melancholy influence ...": Hippolyte Taine, quoted in Harrison, *Drink and the Victorians,* p 48

On Branwell Brontë's drinking habits, see Terry Eagleton's review of *The Brontës: Tales of Glass Town, Angria and Gondal, London Review of Books,* 4 Nov 2010

"run stark staring, raving mad, periodically" and subsequent quotations: Dickens, "Gin-shops," in *Sketches by Boz,* pp 111–113

"hot mixture in a jug with gin and lemons" and subsequent quotations: Dickens, *A Christmas Carol,* p 91

"The gutters of the street ...": Dickens, *Barnaby Rudge,* p 82

"Here is a small burnt patch of flooring ...": Dickens, *Bleak House,* pp 319–320

"concussion of the brain" and "strong apoplexy": Isabella Beeton, *Mrs. Beeton's Book of Household Management,* London, 1861, pp 1073, 1076

"Sweet fennel, orange peel ..." and subsequent quotations: Rack, *French Wine and Liquor Manufacturer,* pp 93, 84, 103, 266

NOTES

"Under the present system of London Water Supply ...": Arthur Hill Hassall, *A Microscopical Examination of the Water Supplied to the Inhabitants of London and the Suburban Districts,* London, 1850

"fixed acrid substances": Hassall, *Food and Its Adulterations,* p 641

"The swallowing of drams cannot be better represented ...": Erasmus Darwin, "The Loves of the Plants," 1791, canto 3, footnote to line 371

"The slow but fatal brutalization ..." Marcel Legrain, *Hérédité et alcoolisme,* Paris, 1889, p 59, quoted in Pick, *Faces of Degeneration,* p 51

"the Jerusalem of temperance": quoted in Shiman, *Crusade Against Drink,* p 19

"Thee mustn't, Richard, thee'll die!': quoted in Harrison, *Drink and the Victorians,* p 45

"Extreme privation breeds extreme indulgence ...": Ernest Jones, *People's Paper,* 30 Sept 1854, quoted in Harrison, *Drink and the Victorians,* p 371

"It is extraordinary that all murders ...": *Chartist,* 31 Mar 1839, p 2, quoted in Harrison, *Drink and the Victorians,* p 83

"it is not till they get older ...": Charles Booth, *Life and Labor of the London Poor,* London, 1902, quoted in Burnett, *Liquid Pleasures,* p 169

"No member shall drink rum, gin, whiskey ...": quoted in Gateley, *Drink,* p 235

"I do not think ..." and "Trusting in help from Heaven above ...": quoted in Kobler, *Ardent Spirits,* p 69

"Utah's monstrous lust": quoted in Kobler, *Ardent Spirits,* p 144

"Devil's Siamese twins": quoted in Woodiwiss, *Crime, Crusades and Corruption,* p 3

4. From Chinchón To Martinez

In this chapter I have been particularly indebted to two fascinating and rewarding texts: Mark Honigsbaum on the history of quinine, and Lowell Edmunds on the history of the martini. See Honigsbaum, *Fever Trail,* and Edmunds, *Martini, Straight Up*

"This beautiful tree ...": Alexander von Humboldt, quoted in Honigsbaum, *Fever Trail,* p 27 "a dose of Peruvian-bark . . .": quoted in Honigsbaum, *Fever Trail,* p 52

"an improved aerated tonic liquid": quoted in Coates, *Classic Gin,* p 146

"INDIAN quinine TONIC": quoted in Gateley, *Drink,* p 330

"ease, voluptuousness, high living . . ." and "peccant humors': Thomas Sydenham, *Treatise on the Gout,* London, 1683, quoted in Porter & Rousseau, *Gout,* p 43

". . . half a dram of cochineal . . ." *Adam's Luxury and Eve's Cookery,* London, 1744, p 200, quoted in Wilson, *Water of Life,* p 232

"Gin Bitters: For Five Gallons . . .": Sabine, *Publican's Sure Guide* (1807), p 12:

"This will be a most pleasant cheap bitter . . .": Jonas & Sheridan, *Complete Treatise,* p 205

"Amazon Bitters (A SPLENDID Recipe)" and "red saunders": John Rack, *French Wine and Liquor Manufacturer* (1868), p 210

"¾ oz quassia chips . . .": *The Scientific American Cyclopedia of Receipts, Notes and Queries,* 1898, quoted in Haigh, *Vintage Spirits,* p 327

"Drank a glass of coctail [sic] . . .": *Farmer's Cabinet,* 28 April 1803, quoted in Miller & Brown, *Spirituous Journey,* p 190

"A stimulating liquor, composed of spirits . . .": *The Balance and Columbian Repository,* on May 6 1806, quoted in Gateley, *Drink,* p 231

"The Cocktail is a very popular drink . . .": Patsy McDonough, *McDonough's Bar-keeper's Guide* Rochester, New York, 1883, p 5

"I'll drink mint-juleps, brandy-smashes, whiskey-skies . . .": quoted in Gateley, *Drink,* p 278

". . . adopt the universal habit of the place . . .": quoted in Gateley, *Drink,* p 315

"There are two theaters in Boston . . .": Charles Dickens, *American Notes,* London, 1842, quoted in Gateley, *Drink,* p 254

"Hark! to the clinking sound of hammers . . .": quoted in Gateley, *Drink,* p 254

"3 or 4 dashes of gum syrup . . .": Jerry Thomas, *Bar-Tender's Guide and Bon Vivant's Companion,* 1862, quoted in Edmunds, *Martini Straight Up,* p 79

Barnaby Conrad's views on the martini are summarized in Edmunds, *Martini Straight Up,* p 36

NOTES

For a useful martini timeline, see Edmunds, *Martini Straight Up,* p xxvii–xxviii *vinum absinthum:* on the origins of vermouth, see Miller & Brown, *Spirituous Journey,* pp 175–177

"2 dashes curaçao . . .": O.H. Byron, *The Modern Bartender's Guide,* 1884, quoted in Edmunds, *Martini Straight Up,* p 79

"Ingredients—½ a wineglassful of good unsweetened gin . . .": Isabella Beeton, *Household Management,* 1906, quoted in Edmunds, *Martini Straight Up,* p 16

"1 dash of orange bitters . . .": Thomas Stuart, *Stuart's Fancy Drinks and How to Mix Them,* 1896, quoted in Edmunds, *Martini Straight Up,* p 83

"Three dashes orange bitters . . .": Frederic L. Knowles, *The Cocktail Book: A Sideboard Manual for Gentlemen,* 1900, quoted in Edmunds, *Martini Straight Up,* p 84

"One of the *jeunesse dorée* in the party . . .": Hidley Dhee, "A Daring Game," *Crescent Magazine,* 1 Aug 1896, p 11, quoted in Edmunds, *Martini Straight Up,* p 16

"Perkins was happy—Perkins was positively joyous . . .": John Philip Souza, *The Fifth String,* 1902, quoted in Edmunds, *Martini Straight Up,* p 15

"So at twelve o'clock we had a hot lunch . . .": O. Henry, *The Gentle Grafter,* 1904, quoted in Edmunds, *Martini Straight Up,* p 16

"Nobody seemed to notice the unusualness . . ." and subsequent quotations: Jack London, *Burning Daylight,* 1910, quoted in Edmunds, *Martini Straight Up,* p 44

"Before you do another thing, James . . .": *Harper's Weekly,* 2 Nov 1902, p 1730, quoted in Murdock, *Domesticating Drink,* p 50

"four taken in swift succession . . .": Harry Craddock, *Drinks of All Kinds,* London, 1895, quoted in Haigh, *Vintage Spirits,* p 94

5. The Silver Bullet

"In America we are making the last stand . . .": Richmond Pearson Hobson, quoted in Gateley, *Drink,* p 355

"This gin, with its label . . .": *Tennessean,* 1908, quoted in Kobler, *Ardent Spirits,* p 193

"The primitive Negro field hand ...": *Collier's Weekly,* 1908, quoted in Woodiwiss, *Crime, crusades and corruption,* p 4

"If the mother as well as the father ...": quoted in Burnett, *Liquid Pleasures,* p 172

"Another woman dips a dirty finger ...": George Robert Sims, "The Cry of the Children," *Tribune,* 4 Feb 1907, quoted in Gutzke, "The Cry of the Children," p 77

On the amphibious nature of U.S. society under Prohibition, see Gateley, *Drink,* p 378

"... three tremendous popular passions ...": *Outlook,* 1924, quoted in Gateley, *Drink,* p 374

On the illegal consumption of industrial alcohol, see Gateley, *Drink,* p 375

"You sent in an order for gin ..." quoted in Gateley, *Drink,* p 376

"RYE–GIN–RUM–SCOTCH ...": *New Yorker,* 15 Oct 1932, p 61, quoted in Murdock, *Domesticating Drink,* p 92

National register of trademarks: Edmunds, *Martini Straight Up,* p 75

"Prohibition ... lifted gin out ...": quoted in Edmunds, *Martini Straight Up,* p 75

"Teaspoon sugar—Juice one lemon ...": quoted in Coates, *Classic Gin,* p 144

"for a proper stimulant": F. Scott Fitzgerald, *The Beautiful and the Damned,* 1922, quoted in Baker, *Absinthe,* p 178

"a date which will live in infamy": the full text of Roosevelt's address, delivered on 8th December 1941, is available at en.wikisource.org/wiki/Pearl_Harbor_speech

"cocktails for Hitler": quoted in Coates, *Mixellany Gin,* p 81

"Edgware Road Gin": quoted in Burnett, *Liquid Pleasures,* p 175

"[Smith] took down from the shelf a bottle ..." and "He picked up his glass and drained it at a gulp ...": Orwell, *Nineteen Eighty-Four,* pp 7 & 301. *Nineteen Eighty-Four* is copyright © George Orwell, 1949.

"'A dry martini,' he said ...": Ian Fleming, "Casino Royale," in *Casino Royale, Live and Let Die, Moonraker,* Penguin Modern Classics, 2003, p 36. "Casino Royale" is copyright © Ian Fleming Publications Ltd 1953, www.ianfleming.com

Jared Brown, master distiller for Sipsmith, nosing the latest batch of gin. Behind him is "Prudence," the first new handmade copper-pot still to be installed in a London distillery since the nineteenth century. Copyright Sipsmith Independent Spirits.

# Bibliography

## Online Sources

Alcohol and Drugs History Society: alcoholanddrugshistorysociety.com

Kendall, Paul "Mythology and Folklore of the Juniper," www.treesforlife. org.uk/forest/mythfolk/juniper.html

London Lives 1690–1800: www.londonlives.org

Marxists Internet Archive: www.marxists.org

Proceedings of the Old Bailey Online: www.oldbaileyonline.org

Rowan, "The Juniper Tree (In Folklore, Healing and Cannibalism)" *White Dragon* Beltane 1996, www.whitedragon.org.uk/articles/juniper.htm

Victorian London: www.victorianlondon.org

## Books, Chapters and Articles

Abel, Ernest L. *Alcohol Wordlore and Folklore* (Prometheus Books, 1987)

Ackroyd, Peter *London: The Biography* (Chatto & Windus, 2000)

Andrews, Corey E. "Drinking and Thinking: Club Life and Convivial Sociability in Mid-Eighteenth-Century Edinburgh" *Social History of Alcohol and Drugs* 22, 2007, pp 65–82

Austin, Gregory A. *Alcohol in Western Society From Antiquity to 1800: A Chronological History* (ABC-Clio Information Services, 1985)

Baker, Phil *The Dedalus Book of Absinthe* (Dedalus Books, 2001)

Ball, Philip *The Devil's Doctor: Paracelsus and the World of Renaissance Magic and Science* (Arrow, 2007)

Barr, Andrew *Drink: A Social History of America* (Carroll & Graf, 1999)

Barton, Patricia "'The Great Quinine Fraud': Legality Issues in the 'Non-Narcotic' Drug Trade in British India" *Social History of Alcohol and Drugs* 22, 2007, pp 6–25

Brant, Clare & Whyman, Susan E. (eds) *Walking the Streets of Eighteenth-Century London: John Gay's "Trivia" (1716)* (Oxford University Press, 2007)

Brennan, Thomas *Public Drinking and Popular Culture in Eighteenth-Century Paris* (Princeton University Press, 1988)

Burnett, John *Liquid Pleasures: A Social History of Drinks in Modern Britain* (Routledge, 1999)

Bynum, William F. "Chronic Alcoholism in the First Half of the Nineteenth Century" *Bulletin of the History of Medicine* 42, 1968, pp 141–143.

Bynum, William F. "Alcoholism and Degeneration in 19th-Century European Medicine and Psychiatry" *British Journal of Addiction* 79, 1984, pp 59–70

Cawood, Clinton "Small is beautiful" *Imbibe* Nov / Dec 2009, pp 114–116

Clark, Peter *The English Alehouse: A Social History, 1200–1830* (Longman, 1983)

Clarke, Paul "History and Character of the Gimlet," in Miller, Anistatia (ed) *Mixologist: The Journal of the American Cocktail* (Mixellany, 2005), pp 57–72

Coates, Geraldine *Classic Gin* (Prion, 2000)

Coates, Geraldine *The Mixellany Guide to Gin* (Mixellany Ltd, 2009)

Cook, Harold J. *Matters of Exchange: Commerce, Medicine and Science in the Dutch Golden Age* (Yale University Press, 2007)

Cornes, Judy *Alcohol in the Movies, 1892–1962* (Macfarland & Company, 2006)

Culpeper, Thomas *The English Physitian, Or, An Astrologico-Physical Discourse of the Vulgar Herbs of This Nation* (London, 1652)

Defoe, Daniel *A Tour Through the Whole Island of Great Britain* [1724–1726] (Penguin Books, 1971)

Defoe, Daniel *A Brief Case of the Distillers and the Distilling Trade* (London, 1726)

Denzin, Norman K. *Hollywood Shot by Shot: Alcoholism in American Cinema* (Aldine de Gruyter, 1991)

Dickens, Charles *Sketches by Boz, Illustrative of Every-Day Life and Every-Day People* [1836] (Chapman & Hall, 1850)

Dickens, Charles *The Life and Adventures of Nicholas Nickleby* (London, 1839)

Dickens, Charles *Barnaby Rudge: A Tale of the Riots of 'Eighty* (London, 1841)

Dickens, Charles *A Christmas Carol* (London, 1843)

Dillon, Patrick *The Much-Lamented Death of Madam Geneva: the Eighteenth-Century Gin Craze* (Review, 2002)

Edmunds, Lowell *martini, Straight Up: The Classic American Cocktail* (Johns Hopkins University Press, 1981)

Field, Judith V. & James, Frank A. J. L. (eds) *Renaissance and Revolution: Humanists, Scholars, Craftsmen and Natural Philosophers in Early Modern Europe* (Cambridge University Press, 1993)

Fielding, Henry *An Enquiry into the Causes of the Late Increase in Robbers* [1751] (Clarendon Press, 1988)

Gately, Iain *Drink: A Cultural History of Alcohol* (Gotham Books, 2008)

George, M. Dorothy *Hogarth to Cruikshank: Social Change in Graphic Satire* (Allen Lane, 1967)

Gonson, Sir John *Five Charges to Several Grand Juries,* fourth edition (London, 1740)

Greene, Phil "Antoine Amédée Peychaud: Pharmacist and New Orleans Cocktail Legend," in Miller, Anistatia (ed) *Mixologist: The Journal of the American Cocktail* (Mixellany, 2005) pp 113–146

Gutzke, David W. " 'The Cry of the Children': The Edwardian Medical Campaign Against Maternal Drinking" *British Journal of Addiction* 79, 1984, pp 71–84

Habermas, Jürgen *The Structural Transformation of the Public Sphere: An Inquiry Into a Category of Bourgeois Society* [1962], trans. Thomas Burger (London, 1989)

Haigh, Ted "The Genealogy and Mythology of the Singapore Sling," in Miller, Anistatia (ed) *Mixologist: The Journal of the American Cocktail* (Mixellany, 2005) pp 73–88

Haigh, Ted *Vintage Spirits and Forgotten Cocktails,* deluxe edition, revised and expanded (Quarry Books, 2009)

Hales, Stephen *A Friendly Admonition to the Drinkers of Brandy, and Other Distilled Spirituous Liquors* (Joseph Downing, 1733)

Harrison, Brian *Drink and the Victorians: The Temperance Question in England 1815–1872,* second edition (Keele University Press, 1994)

Haslam, Fiona *From Hogarth to Rowlandson: Medicine in Art in Eighteenth-Century Britain* (Liverpool University Press, 1996)

Hassall, Arthur Hill *Food and its Adulterations, Comprising the Reports of the Analytical Sanitary Commission of "The Lancet"* (Longman, Brown, Green and Longmans, 1855)

Heron, Craig *Booze: A Distilled History* (Between The Lines, 2003)

Hess, Robert "The Rise and Fall of the martini: Following the Course of the martini Throughout History," in Miller, Anistatia (ed) *Mixologist: The Journal of the American Cocktail* (Mixellany, 2005) pp 37–58.

Holt, Mack P. (ed) *Alcohol: A Social and Cultural History* (Berg, 2006)

Honigsbaum, Mark *The Fever Trail: the Hunt for the Cure for Malaria* (Macmillan, 2001)

Johnson, Samuel *Dictionary of the English Language*, 2 vols (London, 1755)

Jonas, Peter & Sheridan, John *A Complete Treatise on the Art of Distillation; Also the Whole Art of Rectification, In Which is Particularly Treated the Nature of Essential Oils,* fourth edition (Sherwood, Gilbert & Piper, 1830)

Kapoor, Sybil "The Trend: Gin and Tonic? Capital Idea" *Financial Times* Nov 13 2010

Kobler, John *Ardent Spirits: the Rise and Fall of Prohibition* (Michael Joseph, 1974)

Lender, Mark Edward & Martin, James Kirby *Drinking in America: A History* (The Free Press, 1982)

Lettsom, John Coakley *Hints to Promote Beneficence, Temperance and Medical Science* vol 1 (London, 1797)

Levine, Harry Gene "The Alcohol Problem in America: From Temperance to Alcoholism" *British Journal of Addiction* 79, 1984, pp 109–120

"London's Gin 'Palaces,'" in *The Working Man's Friend, and Family Instructor* 1:4, 25 Oct 1851, pp 56–58

Martin, A. Lynn *Alcohol, Sex and Gender in Late Medieval and Early Modern Europe* (Palgrave, 2001)

McCandless, Peter "'Curses of Civilization': Insanity and Drunkenness in Victorian Britain" *British Journal of Addiction* 79, 1984, pp 49–58

McKendrick, Neil, Brewer, John & Plumb, J.H. *The Birth of a Consumer Society: The Commercialization of Eighteenth-Century England* (Europa Press, 1982)

Miller, Anistatia "Down to the Sea in Ships: History of Gin and Plymouth Gin," in Miller, Anistatia (ed) *Mixologist: The Journal of the American Cocktail* (Mixellany, 2005) pp 147–167

Miller, Anistatia & Brown, Jared *Spirituous Journey: A History of Drink. Book One: From the Birth of Spirits to the Birth of the Cocktail* (Mixellany Ltd, 2009)

Mooij, Annet *Doctors of Amsterdam: Patient Care, Medical Training and Research (1650–2000)* (University of Amsterdam Press, 2002)

Murdock, Catherine Gilbert *Domesticating Drink: Women, Men and Alcohol in America, 1870–1940* (Johns Hopkins University Press, 1998)

"Mystagogus, Cleidophorus" [Y-Worth, William], *Trifertes Sagani, or Immortal Dissolvent. Being a Discourse of the Matter and Manner of Preparing the Liquor Alkahest of Helmont* (W. Pearson, 1705)

Nicholls, James "Vinum Britannicum: The 'Drink Question' in Early Modern England" *Social History of Alcohol and Drugs* 22, 2008, pp 190–208.

Nicholls, James *The Politics of Alcohol: A History of the Drink Question in England* (Manchester University Press, 2009)

Owen, Alex *The Place of Enchantment: British Occultism and the Culture of the Modern,* new edition (University of Chicago Press, 2007)

Pennock, Pamela E. *Advertising Sin and Sickness: the Politics of Alcohol and Tobacco Marketing, 1950–1990* (Northern Illinois University Press, 2007)

Pick, Daniel *Faces of Degeneration: A European Disorder, c. 1848–c. 1918* (Cambridge University Press, 1989)

Porter, Roy *Health For Sale: Quackery in England, 1660–1850* (Manchester University Press, 1989)

Porter, Roy & Rousseau, George *Gout: The Patrician Malady* (Yale University Press, 1998)

Rack, John *The French Wine and Liquor Manufacturer: A Practical Guide and Receipt Book for the Liquor Merchant* (Dick & Fitzgerald, 1868)

Rawlings, Philip (ed) *Drunks, Whores and Idle Apprentices: Criminal Biographies of the Eighteenth Century* (Routledge, 1992)

Rocco, Fiammetta *The Miraculous Fever-Tree: Malaria, Medicine and the Cure that Changed the World* (Harper Collins, 2003)

Rorabaugh, W.J. "Drinking in the 'Thin Man' Films, 1934–1947" *Social History of Alcohol and Drugs* 19, 2003, pp 51–68

Rotskoff, Lori *Love on the Rocks: Men, Women and Alcohol in Post-World War II America* (University of North Carolina Press, 2002)

Rumbarger, John J *Profits, Power, and Prohibition: Alcohol Reform and the Industrializing of America, 1800–1930* (State University of New York Press, 1989)

Sabine, H *The Publican's Sure Guide, Or, Every Man his Own Cellarman* (London, 1807)

Sala, George Augustus *Gaslight and Daylight* (London, 1859)

Sanders, Audrey "Twenty-First Century Cocktails," in Miller, Anistatia (ed) *Mixologist: the Journal of the American Cocktail* (Mixellany, 2005) pp 179–191.

Schama, Simon *The Embarrassment of Riches: An Interpretation of Dutch Culture in the Golden Age* (Harper Perennial, 1987)

Seltzer, Michael "Haven An a Heartless Sea: The Sailor's Tavern in History and Anthropology" *Social History of Alcohol and Drugs* 19, 2004, pp 63–93

Shiman, Lilian Lewis *Crusade Against Drink in Victorian England* (Macmillan, 1988)

Smollett, Tobias *The History of England, From the Revolution of 1688 to the Death of George II,* [1757–1765], single volume edition (London, 1875)

Smyth, Adam (ed.) *A Pleasing Sinne: Drink and Conviviality in 17th-Century England* (D.S. Brewer, 2004)

Stewart, Victoria "It's a Gin Thing" *Evening Standard* 9 May 2011, p 27

Thompson, Roger *Unfit For Modest Ears: A Study of Pornographic, Obscene and Bawdy Works Written or Published in England in the Second Half of the 17th Century* (Macmillan, 1979)

Trotter, Thomas *An Essay, Medical, Philosophical, and Chemical, on Drunkenness and its Effects on the Human Body* [1804], edited with an introduction by Roy Porter (Routledge, 1988)

Tyrrel, Ian R *Sobering Up: From Temperance to Prohibition in Antebellum America, 1800–1860* (Greenwood Press, 1979)

Y-Worth, William *Cerevisiarii Comes, Or, The New and True Art of Brewing* (J. Taylor & S. Clement, 1692)

Y-Worth, William *The Compleat Distiller, Or, The Whole Art of Distillation Practically Stated,* second edition (J. Taylor, 1705)

Warner, Jessica *Craze: Gin and Debauchery in an Age of Reason* (Profile, 2003)

Warner, Jessica "The People's Palaces" *History Today* March 2011, pp 19–25

Webb Jr, James L.A. *Humanity's Burden: A Global History of Malaria* (Cambridge University Press, 2009)

Weir, R.B. "Obsessed With Moderation: The Drink Trades and the Drink Question, 1870–1930" *British Journal of Addiction* 79, 1984, pp 93–108

Willis, Justin *Potent Brews: A Social History of Alcohol in East Africa, 1850–1999* (British Institute in Eastern Africa, 2002)

Wilson, C. Anne *Water of Life: A History of Wine-Distilling and Spirits, 500 BC–AD 2000* (Prospect Books, 2006)

Wilson, Thomas *Distilled Spirituous Liquors the Bane of the Nation: Being Some Considerations Humbly Offer'd to the Legislature,* second edition (J. Roberts, 1736)

Winchester, Simon *Krakatoa: The Day the World Exploded* (Penguin, 2004)

Wondrich, David "A Brief History of Punch," in Miller, Anistatia (ed) *Mixologist: The Journal of the American Cocktail* (Mixellany, 2005) pp 15–34

Woodiwiss, Michael *Crime, Crusades and Corruption: Prohibitions in the United States, 1900–1987* (Pinter Publishers, 1988)

# Acknowledgements

For friendship, guidance, expertise, and material which I would otherwise have missed, my heartfelt thanks to Elma Brenner, Rosalind Draper, Geoffrey Elborn, Caroline Essex (especially), David Allan Feller, Alex Hammond, Patricia Hammond, Anne Hardy, Phoebe Harkins, Theresia Hofer, Tom Gillmor, Mike Jay, Allison Ksiazkiewicz, Eric Lane, Marie Lane, Ross MacFarlane, Bill MacLehose, Joanne McKerchar, Anna Morgan, Michael Neve, Mark Pilkington, Kelley Swain, Thea Vidnes, Hannah Westland, Caitlin Wylie, and the staff of the Bishopsgate Library, the library of Pembroke College, Cambridge, and the Wellcome Library. Thanks also to my colleagues and students on the 2011 Pembroke / Kings International Program, Cambridge, for creating a thoroughly congenial atmosphere in which to finish the first draft.

I am indebted to several writers who have mapped aspects of this territory in their work: Phil Baker, Jared Brown, Peter Clark, Geraldine Coates, Patrick Dillon, Lowell Edmunds, Iain Gateley, Ted Haigh, Brian Harrison, Mack P. Holt, Anistatia Miller, and Jessica Warner. It goes without saying that my errors are not their fault.

The photograph of Jared Brown and the Sipsmith's Gin still appears by kind permission of Sipsmith Independent Spirits, and is copyright © Sipsmith Independent Spirits.

The extract from "Casino Royale" by Ian Fleming is reproduced with the permission of Ian Fleming Publications Ltd, London, www.ianfleming.com, and is copyright © Ian Fleming Publications Ltd 1953.

The extracts from *Nineteen Eighty-Four* by George Orwell (Copyright © George Orwell, 1949) are reproduced by permission of

Bill Hamilton as the Literary Executor of the Estate of the Late Sonia Brownell Orwell and Secker & Warburg Ltd.

The images on pages 125, 154, 206, 231 and 249 have been reproduced courtesy of Diageo plc, owners of the GORDON'S® and TANQUERAY® brands.

# Index